Child Psychology

Dedicated to and in memory of René Zazzo,
to whom I owe all my intellectual training
as a researcher in child psychology...
And particularly the 1983 book,
Où en est la psychologie de l'enfant,
for continuing the cycle in the hereafter...

Health and Patients Set

coordinated by
Bruno Salgues

Volume 3

Child Psychology

Developments in Knowledge and Theoretical Models

Jean-Pascal Assailly

iSTE

WILEY

First published 2022 in Great Britain and the United States by ISTE Ltd and John Wiley & Sons, Inc.

ISTE Ltd
27-37 St George's Road
London SW19 4EU
UK

www.iste.co.uk

John Wiley & Sons, Inc.
111 River Street
Hoboken, NJ 07030
USA

www.wiley.com

Library of Congress Control Number: 2021947915

British Library Cataloguing-in-Publication Data
A CIP record for this book is available from the British Library
ISBN 978-1-78630-423-0

MIX
Paper from responsible sources
FSC® C013604

Contents

Preface

Each child must be studied as a lock, unique in its mechanism; and then the special key must be devised to fit that lock, so that the door of opportunity may be pened, as wide as the constitution permits, for each child to develop their individual innate capabilities.

White House Conference, 1932

This book is the first in a two-part series:

1) In this book, we study the evolution of our knowledge in the field of child psychology over the last 40 years.

2) In a future work, we will analyze the impacts of this evolution on practices and policies in the field of childhood (schooling, health, safety, parenthood); for this, we will have to question the practitioners.

In 1983, my teacher, René Zazzo, published one of his last books, *Où en est la psychologie de l'enfant?* and dedicated it to us ("To my students at Nanterre, as a token of my gratitude"). After 40 years, we are picking up the baton.

He particularly pointed out the drifts and aporias in the media conception of psychology ("the psychology of philosophy professors is psychoanalysis, and what psychoanalysis!"); he was disenchanted with the wording and what it covered. The situation has not improved much.

Psychology was for a long time taught in 12th-grade philosophy, tackling various themes such as perception and intelligence, then disappeared from the curriculum in 2003 and was reduced to a few texts by Freud and Lacan. It is amusing to see that National Education adopts the very reductionist view that psychology is the same as psychoanalysis, and vice versa[1].

However, in various countries (United States, Belgium, Switzerland), psychology is still taught in secondary schools.

When the Ministry of Education formed 40 working groups of professionals for curriculum reform, there was not a single psychologist.

In order to provide some balance to adolescents, during what is a risky time in their lives, importance should be placed on reintroducing knowledge of scientific psychology, on how emotions, relationships, self-knowledge, etc. work.

On bookstore shelves, the most noticeable evolution has been the shift from 90% scientific psychology/10% personal development in the 1970s to 90% personal development/10% scientific psychology today. This says much about the popular conception of psychology. Even in "child psychology" sections, there is still a lot of emphasis on personal development.

The divisions that Zazzo analyzed are still there:

– between practice and research;

– between child and genetic psychology;

– between the field and the laboratory;

– between the epistemic subject of Piaget and others and the individual in his totality (do we reduce the child to sectors or development indicators, as neuroscience does now[2], or preserve the psychology of the person?).

Very schematically, the question on which this book is structured (where are we now, 40 years later, and where are we going?) covers two main analyses:

– new developments in child psychology, covering phenomena that did not exist before in a significant way in the real lives of children (e.g. homoparentality, attacks, Covid-19);

– new developments in already long established objects of study (e.g. intelligence, the mother–child relationship), where significant theoretical evolutions have taken place.

1 For other actors, another version is that psychology is only neuroscience today.

2 Neuroscience or the death of the small horse of psychology.

	Less than 15 years old	15–19 years old	20–24 years old
1991	11,808,904	4,353,479	4,392,026
1992	11,846,294	4,186,630	4,399,883
1993	11,841,637	4,050,716	4,427,167
1994	11,809,628	3,934,183	4,428,102
1995	11,756,031	3,894,364	4,362,366
1996	11,676,351	3,949,740	4,242,118
1997	11,601,547	4,024,370	4,084,939
1998	11,532,939	4,067,056	3,956,287
1999	11,521,697	4,073,140	3,848,339
2000	11,558,446	4,068,194	3,809,829
2001	11,613,651	4,037,408	3,867,157
2002	11,645,716	4,033,889	3,945,290
2003	11,669,451	4,040,407	3,996,557
2004	11,680,487	4,103,486	4,014,148
2005	11,696,788	4,152,069	4,037,139
2006	11,715,950	4,171,803	4,044,928
2007	11,778,201	4,146,595	4,029,070
2008	11,827,212	4,121,673	4,003,665
2009	11,917,951	4,059,357	4,030,922
2010	11,998,951	4,011,584	4,030,881
2011	12,060,943	3,977,327	4,014,582
2012	12,123,714	3,923,399	3,985,089
2013	12,186,689	3,909,392	3,955,259
2014	12,221,427	3,944,210	3,877,125
2014	12,318,645	3,966,973	3,890,578
2015	12,349,774	4,009,445	3,819,678
2016	12,320,073	4,075,385	3,765,556

Table A.1. *Historical evolution of the number of French subjects by age group (source: INSEE 2016)*

With regard to historical developments, one question keeps coming up: are the trends in this or that behavior, situation, phenomenon, etc. decreasing, increasing or remaining stable?

This immediately raises the question of the validity of the measurement of the phenomenon: is it actually increasing, or is it just because it is more often detected? Is it actually decreasing, or is it just because we do not pay attention to it anymore?

One of the variables to be controlled in order to know if a phenomenon is stable, increasing or decreasing is, of course, demography: generally, we can say that the number of children and teenagers in France has been stable for 30 years, in a context of strong aging of the population, as the following data shows:

– all ages:
  - 1992: 58 million;
  - 2019: 67 million (increase of 14%);
– between 0 and 19 years old:
  - 1992: 15.5 million;
  - 2019: 15.4 million (increase of 0%, in fact a decrease);
– 65 years and older:
  - 1992: 8.2 million;
  - 2019: 13.1 million (increase of 60%).

The population concerned: how many young people are there?

Schematically, there are 800,000 young French people per age group (12 million children, 4 million adolescents, 4 million young adults). Compared to the birth rate of the 30 years following the end of World War II, there was a certain drop in birth rate in the 1990s, which explains the lower number of 15–24-year-old cohorts today, but we can see how the birth rate has increased since 2000[3].

October 2021

3 A more vigorous parentality policy in France compared with that of our neighbors, is often cited as a factor in this phenomenon.

1

Interdisciplinary Themes

Before addressing the evolution of knowledge in each area of child development, we thought it would be useful to point out the major themes that run through our discipline and guide the work in various fields.

1.1. The question of prediction

Behavioral genetics, like psychoanalysis, looks for causality in the child's past in different ways, but can we predict the child?

The retrospective approach can even prescribe, because by predicting too much, we end up creating "fate neuroses", with prophecies ending up realizing an unfavorable future for the child.

1.1.1. *Prediction before birth*

1.1.1.1. *"To be born or not to be born", "Not to be born at all is best..." (chorus of Oedipus at Colonus)*

Using prenatal diagnoses, doctors and parents can now predict the appearance of diseases and deficiencies (trisomy, cystic fibrosis, etc.); it is even more complex for the birth of a second child when the first child has one of these types of hereditary disease. We can see the risks of eugenics.

Even in the case of normal development, the choice of a child's sex has led to disparities in some countries. Are we going to go as far as selective pairing of parents based on their DNA?

Two strategies are currently available to parents in the case of a proven hereditary risk: to modify the embryo through biotechnology or to medically terminate the pregnancy. Both can pose moral or ethical dilemmas for the parents. This theme will be taken up again in Chapter 2, on the fetus.

1.1.1.2. *Predicting adult problems from childhood*

The links between behavioral problems in children and problems in adulthood are well known and affect almost all areas of life. Various mechanisms may be at work:

– the continuity of a trait from childhood to adult life (the anxious child becomes an anxious adult);

– childhood problems and adult problems may be linked because they share the same risk factors (such as poverty and violence).

1.2. Development concepts

Two major development models have always been in conflict: development in stages and continuum development.

In the stage model (Piaget, Freud), the development of the child's intelligence or sexuality proceeds in chronological stages, from an initial state to a final state, each stage building on the previous one.

In the *continuum* model (Wallon, Zazzo), the stages exist only in the mind of the observer, but the development for the subject himself proceeds progressively, from birth to death.

Does this "*continuum* or stages" debate still make sense? Piaget's stages, or "staircase" model, from the first sensorimotor intelligence step to the final abstract intelligence step, is challenged today, especially in the work on newborns. In this book, we will see that some acquisitions are much earlier than Piaget thought and that the development of intelligence is not linear.

Another more recent model is Siegler's "waves" model: the newborn has various cognitive strategies at his disposal from birth that compete to understand the world; he therefore launches them like overlapping waves to arrive on the shore of understanding. With experience, and depending on the situation, the child will use one strategy or another.

We can also evoke the progressive stabilization of synapses, learning by loss, by inhibition or Bachelard's "philosophy of no"; the child's neurocognitive development takes place through a multiplication and then pruning of the connections between neurons, hence a reduction in the brain's gray matter. This pruning has been described by Changeux (1983) as a selective stabilization of synapses by a "neural Darwinism" mechanism; this maturation takes place in successive waves according to the areas of the brain: first, the regions associated with basic sensory and motor functions, then, up to the end of adolescence, the regions associated with higher cognitive control (notably, inhibitory control). The child also learns to inhibit strategies through experience, imitation or instruction from others.

This leads to a nonlinear development model made up of learning curves revealing explosions, collapses and turbulence.

Functional magnetic resonance imaging (fMRI) allows the visualization of brain dynamics corresponding to the activation/inhibition of cognitive strategies at different ages (macrogenesis) or during learning at a particular age (microgenesis).

1.2.1. *How can we study development? The methodology*

The "royal" way to study development is therefore through longitudinal studies; the principle is always to follow the children during their development, studies can start before or after birth, or during the adolescence of the subject.

The following are some recent examples; their contributions will then be presented through the course of the book in relation to the various fields of development.

1.2.1.1. *Studies with a prenatal onset: the EDEN study (study of pre- and postnatal determinants of child development and health)*

This study (Heude and Forhan 2015) aimed to investigate prenatal and postnatal determinants of child health and development in a French population. Pregnant women at <24 weeks of amenorrhea were recruited to the Poitiers and Nancy university hospitals between 2003 and 2006. Exclusion criteria were: being under 18 years of age, no informed consent, functional illiteracy in French, history of diabetes, plan to change address or no social security coverage.

Of the 3,758 women invited to participate, 2,002 (53%) agreed to enroll in the study. Women with multiple pregnancies were also excluded. With deaths, the number fell to 1,899 infants enrolled at birth. Written informed consent was obtained twice from parents: at enrollment and after the child's birth.

All variables included in the analysis were collected by means of paper self-completed questionnaires, with the exception of anthropometric measurements, which were assessed by clinical examination, and birth term, which was removed from medical records. The children were then followed up at 4, 8, 12 and 24 months and at five or six years.

1.2.1.2. *Studies from birth*

1.2.1.2.1. The ELFE Study (French longitudinal study since childhood)

The ELFE (*Étude Longitudinale Française depuis l'Enfance*) Study is a nationally representative, multidisciplinary birth cohort of infants born to 18,040 women in 349 maternity hospitals in France in 2011. The protocol, design and recruitment procedures of the ELFE survey have been previously described (Vandentorren and Pirus 2006). Participating mothers and infants were recruited while in the maternity units and subsequently monitored. Exclusion criteria were: stillbirth, birth before 33 weeks gestation, multiple births and plans to leave metropolitan France within three years. Mothers had to be able to give informed consent in one of the study languages (French, English, Arabic and Turkish).

Maternity data was collected using standardized interviews by trained interviewers and self-completed questionnaires. Information on obstetric characteristics was collected from maternal recalls and medical records. Two months after delivery, data was collected via telephone interviews.

Information is collected annually and then every two years up to the age of 20, in the form of questionnaires (at home or by telephone), biological samples (at birth, three and six years), environmental measurements and follow-up logbooks (standardized collections of anthropometric measurements, etc.). The medical data is relayed by the parents from health records and completed by a medical examination at two years and a health check-up at six years.

1.2.1.2.2. The EPIPAGE 2 Study (epidemiological study on low-gestational-age infants)

The EPIPAGE (*Étude épidémiologique sur les petits âges gestationnels*) 2 Study is a national study to better understand the development of premature infants. The study focuses on infants divided into three groups: extremely premature (born before the end of the sixth month of pregnancy), very premature (born before the end of the seventh month of pregnancy) and moderately premature (born at the beginning of the eighth month of pregnancy). These children are followed from birth to age 12.

1.2.1.2.3. The 1958 British National Child Development Study

The 1958 British birth cohort study was based on a sample of 18,558 British subjects, all infants born within one week in March 1958 (n = 17,638) and immigrants recruited at ages 7, 11 and 16 (n = 920). Information was collected from parents, teachers and physicians during childhood (birth, 7, 11 and 16 years) and from cosigners during adulthood (23, 33, 42, 45 and 50 years).

1.2.1.2.4. The "Lifeways Cross-Generation Cohort" Study in the Republic of Ireland

Participants were 943 mothers and their offspring, 890 fathers, 938 maternal grandmothers, 700 maternal grandfathers, 537 paternal grandmothers and 553 paternal grandfathers. Infant birth weights were standardized based on gestational age (1990 UK population) and then categorized as low, high or normal birth weights.

Four birth periods were considered: the country's independence (1916–1938); the Emergency Powers Act (1939–1946); the postwar baby boom (1947–1964) and modern Ireland (1964 onward). This is a three-generation cohort study established *a priori* to examine intergenerational influences on infants recruited during pregnancy in 2001–2003.

1.2.1.3. *Studies from childhood*

1.2.1.3.1. The Millennium Study

The Millennium Study is a longitudinal study of a cohort of 18,818 children born in the United Kingdom between September 2000 and January 2002 (Connelly and Platt 2014). It is a multidisciplinary investigation designed to capture the effects of social, economic and health advantages and disadvantages on child development and other outcomes. There have been six surveys to date. The first was collected at about nine months of age, followed by surveys at ages 3, 5, 7, 11 and 14. At the end of the fifth survey, 13,287 children remained in the study.

1.2.1.3.2. The CABLE (Childhood and Adolescent Behaviors in Long-term Evolution) Study

The CABLE Study is a lifestyle research study in which 18 elementary schools were randomly selected in Taipei and Hsinchu, Taiwan. Data on gender, parent–child relationships and internalized symptoms from four waves of follow-up were analyzed: 2003 (9 year-olds), 2006 (12 year-olds), 2009 (15 year-olds) and 2012 (18 year-olds). A latent growth model was used to examine the impact of parent–child relationships and gender on the trajectory of children's internalized symptoms.

1.2.1.3.3. The Bergen Study

The first wave of the longitudinal Bergen Child Study (BCS) assessed a wide range of mental health problems in a total population of Norwegian schoolchildren aged seven to nine years (n = 9,430), using teacher and parent questionnaires in all schools, including special and private schools. Teacher questionnaires (n = 9,152) covered 97% of the population, whereas parent questionnaires (n = 6,295) covered 67% of the population.

1.2.1.4. *Studies from adolescence: the ABCD (Adolescent Brain Cognitive Development) Study*

The Adolescent Brain Cognitive Development (ABCD) Study is the largest long-term study of this type, relating to the relationship between cognitive development and subject health in the United States. It was launched in 2015, just before participants' adolescence (11,878 subjects aged 9–10 years), at 21 research sites across the country to augment data collection such as neuropsychological assessments, biopsies and structural and functional neuroimaging data. The follow-up is planned to last 10 years. In addition to obtaining a nationally representative sample on adolescent brain development, other themes have been added to the survey: gender influences and, cardiovascular and hematological health.

To conclude this brief methodological presentation, there have, of course, been other longitudinal studies around the world, but the sample presented above is representative of the main types.

1.2.2. *The issue of experimental mortality and retention*

Continued participation is essential for the validity of longitudinal studies, such as ABCD, where families are asked to participate in the study throughout the 10-year period.

This therefore means communicating with families every six months by phone and annually in person, and more closely with youth in person as they transition into adolescence.

Moreover, while it is possible to lose a fraction of the subjects, the risk to ongoing validity is mainly non-random loss, which is sometimes not immediately perceived by the experimenters.

When a socioeconomic or sociocultural subgroup becomes progressively underrepresented, the results of the study are no longer generalizable to those subgroups. Similarly, the most at-risk families may be the ones most easily lost to the study, which will compromise the usefulness of the study for these populations.

1.3. To what extent is a dialog or coming together possible between developmental psychology and psychoanalysis? Between the observable and the repressed

Psychoanalysis and developmental psychology have been the two main avenues for approaching the mental functioning of children.

Psychoanalysis operates by reconstructing clinical data obtained during the treatment of children or adults. Developmental psychology seeks to highlight individual differences through observation or comparisons of groups of children, or by studying their developmental trajectories. The psychoanalytical approach to children, which is often therapeutic, focuses on a small number of cases, while the second approach is more experimental and based on statistics.

Are the two approaches completely irreconcilable, or is a coming together, a dialog, possible?

Some psychoanalysts do not think this dialog is possible, such as André Green, who spoke of the "true child" of psychoanalysis deduced from reconstructions and the "real child" of observation, where it was not possible to reach what was repressed. Nevertheless, other authors, such as Pierre Fédida, desire a "unified science" of development, where the results obtained by either of the approaches can be enlightened by the other.

Attachment is one of the most successful examples of the dialog between psychoanalysis and developmental psychology. This theme has brought together approaches as diverse as Bowlby's theory of attachment (presented later in this book), Lacan's family complexes, Bion's maternal alpha function, Winnicott's good enough mother, Brazelton's competence of the baby in communicating with its environment from birth, Lebovici and Golse's transgenerational mandate, Balint's primary attunement and Stern's interpersonal world of the infant.

Between Bowlby's theory of attachment and Melanie Klein's objectal relations theory, a coming together is possible and was developed by Didier Anzieu with his "*pulsion d'attachement*" and "*Moi-Peau*" concepts.

1.4. Between psychology and epidemiology, developmental psychopathology

Unfortunately, due to lack of time and interest, psychoanalysts do not read articles on behavioral genetics and behavioral geneticists do not read articles on psychoanalysis, not even those about particular behaviors, alcoholism or delinquency. Yet these two bodies will influence generations of pediatricians, specialized journalists and therefore parents. Ideally, we need to take a step back, to look at the "big picture", to consider what connects and what does not mutilate knowledge, as Edgar Morin says. We have evoked (Assailly, 2007) the idea of a "river thought", that is, a thought capable of carrying all the alluvium that is brought to us by the currents of thought on the child.

This "river thought" is one of interaction: from the first cell division, each fact, each biological, psychological or sociological event defines us; some weigh very heavily, such as the early relationship with our mother; others, very little, such as a temporary family stress, but the approach must integrate all these elements

For example, what can epidemiology (the science that studies phenomena at the population level) contribute to psychology (the science that studies phenomena at the individual level), and vice versa? In fact, one needs the other: epidemiology needs the observations of psychology in order to understand, within the broad variability of human behavior, what does or does not emerge from pathology; to launch hypotheses on the relationships between the problems of children and the factors that explain these problems, to understand how what it calls "risk" or "protection" is constructed. Psychology needs epidemiology to ensure that what it has observed in a small selected sample of subjects can be found elsewhere, at another time.

These are complementary, rather than conflicting disciplines, each fulfilling its function at different times in the research process. Between these two disciplines, there is a space to create a median approach: developmental psychopathology, in other words, the developmental approach to psychopathological and maladaptive phenomena.

Although this approach is recent, it is already 40 years old and aims to integrate models from various fields (such as genetics, neuroscience, developmental psychology and systems theory) to inform research on the relevant processes of normal and atypical development. These developmental processes are reciprocal and transactional.

Major questions structure this approach.

1.4.1. *The origins and trajectories of adaptation*

We need to understand the steps and mechanisms that lead to the final state. There is an "arborescence" of paths or trajectories that start from birth and can then schematically intersect with a four-entry table of cases:

– continuity of positive factors leading to adaptation (fulfillment);

– continuity of negative factors leading to problems (chronicity);

– initially positive situation which then deteriorates (trouble);

– initially negative situation which then improves (resilience).

The same point of arrival can thus be reached by two different paths, two different developmental processes, which is expressed as the "equifinality" concept. For example, when two children become delinquent, it may be for completely different reasons and not for the same cause.

Conversely, two different futures (or associated futures, as in comorbidity) can have the same starting point, which we will express as the "multiple purposes" concept. Such mechanisms are not specific to child psychology; they can be seen at work in neurobiology, genetics, etc.

Risk factors are those variables that increase the likelihood of the onset, exacerbation or maintenance of a condition.

There are three types of protective factors, those internal or external resources that modify or mitigate the impact of risk factors: dispositional protective factors (temperament, social orientation, cognitive skills and coping skills); protective factors from the family environment (such as relationships and supervision) and protective factors from the extra-familial environment (such as social support).

Of course, these factors work in combination. Two powerful and classically observed protective factors are: having a good relationship with at least one adult caregiver and having good intellectual abilities.

Risk and protective factors operate either in an "additive" (simple, direct effect of a risk factor) or an "interactive" (protective factors play only in interaction with risk factors: they come into play less when stress is low, much more when stress is high) model.

In an additive model, what is important is the notion of cumulative risk factors. It is often observed that it is the accumulation of several stresses rather than a single family stress that causes serious consequences. There is therefore a threshold effect beyond which the child's resistance gives way.

In an interactive model, certain risk factors only come into play in the presence or absence of another risk factor, as do protective factors: for example, a child's difficult temperament only produces harmful effects if it is combined with a mother's rejection. Another example: poverty and exclusion have a more negative impact on native-born children than on immigrants, because the latter develop more solidarity strategies.

1.4.2. *Mediation and moderation*

These are effects of a characteristic of the family environment. In the case of mediation, two variables interact to affect the child's development. For example, parental discord and the child's tendency to assume guilt each have negative interacting effects; in the case of moderation, two variables are not causally related, but one (the parent's ability to maintain good parenting) moderates the negative effects of the other (parental discord).

1.4.3. *Resilience*

This is a form of environmental transaction that allows the subject to overcome traumas and strongly limit their effects. The resilience of the ego (personality trait) is now a well-studied phenomenon, as well as the variations in resilience according to the sociocultural environment, or according to the field of development (academic, social, psychological), since a child can be resilient on the academic level, but not on the psychological level.

1.4.4. *Confounding factors*

A confounding factor is one that explains the causal relationship that we assume at first glance between two variables. For example, when we take 100 children of divorced parents and 100 children of married parents, we generally find more academic failure in the first group. However, academic failure is closely linked to the child's sociocultural background and divorce is more frequent in disadvantaged environments, so sociocultural background is a confounding factor in the link between divorce and academic failure.

Thus, if we control this confounding factor, if we compare 100 children of divorced parents from privileged backgrounds and 100 children of married parents from privileged backgrounds, say, we no longer observe differences between the two groups with respect to academic failure.

1.4.5. *Genetic factors*

For a long time, the influence of parents was conceived as a cause and the adaptation of their children as an effect. The two main theoretical schools, behaviorism and psychoanalysis, although so traditionally opposed, come together to conclude that the way parents educate the child, and what parents do to the child, is extremely important. The spectacular improvements brought about by adoption, or the effects of educational intervention, have shown the crucial effect of the family environment.

At the end of the 1960s, a complementary hypothesis was put forward: children are not only receptors, but they also influence the behavior of their parents. A child's behavior is partly influenced by genetic factors; it is therefore possible to maintain the idea that the parents' behaviors play a crucial role in the adaptation of their children, but with the addition that these behaviors are caused by characteristics of the child under genetic influence.

Behavioral genetics has had a profound influence on how developmental psychologists view how family influences affect children in different ways.

Today, the influence of the family environment on the child can be defined by three main components:

– the influences of genetic factors: genes that parents pass on to each child;

– shared environmental influences: a family environmental characteristic is so massive that it has effects on all children in the family, for example, abject poverty, religious orientation or strong conflict between parents;

– the influences of the non-shared environment: each child is not subject to the same effects due to various causes. For example, girls are not raised in the same way as boys (even today), the mother has a stronger attachment to a particular child, the socioeconomic situation of the family has changed or a particular characteristic of the child under genetic influence causes different reactions in the parents.

Over the past 20 years, research has highlighted the importance of the non-shared environment. Parents are always surprised by this phenomenon: "how and why are my two children so different when they have had the same education?" Well, no! Also, there are two types of effects of the non-shared environment: "differential positivity" (one child receives significantly more of something than the others) and "differential negativity" (one child receives significantly less of something than the others).

Shared and non-shared environments are also related. For example, a common characteristic of the family context (stress, marital discord, lack of money, too many siblings, composition of the siblings) will exacerbate the difference in treatment between children. This is because parents will have limited resources to devote to each child. When stress occurs, it will diminish the resources available and they will be forced to concentrate them on one child.

We can thus be led to the paradox that differences in the way parents treat each child are attributable to aspects of family life that are shared by all children. Finally, differential parental treatment is not necessarily pathogenic: it all depends on whether it is experienced by the child as fair or unfair. For example, the child accepts it when the differential treatment depends on the age or special needs of his or her siblings.

From this framework, two types of work can be conducted. On the one hand, "child-based" studies: the child's genes are the unit of measure and do not directly influence the way the parents treat them, but indirectly, through the parents' reaction to the child's characteristics; for example, siblings are compared with each other. On the other hand, the rarer "adult-based" work: the parent's genes are the unit of measure and we study the role played by genetic proximity on parental behavior, for example, the behavior of mothers who are twins.

We will therefore define:

– genotype/environment interaction: genetic factors influence sensitivity to an environment. For example, divorce has more negative effects on children with a genetic vulnerability to depression; negative life events are a non-shared environmental factor that explains the differences between monozygotic twins in the occurrence of depression. Overly coercive family discipline is a risk factor for adolescent depression, but only in certain social settings;

– genotype/environment correlation: genetic factors select or cause exposure to different environments. For example, a child's physical attractiveness causes positive reactions in parents, educators or peers.

Three types of correlations between genotype and environment are therefore distinguished. These types correspond to three mechanisms by which the genetically influenced characteristics of an individual affect his or her experiences:

– passive correlation: parents and children share the same genotype and the same environment. For example, parents pass on genes related to a difficult trait and express this difficult trait through irritable and negative parenting behavior, which in turn is related to the child's difficult trait. In a child-based construct, this correlation would be categorized as "shared environment influence", whereas in a parent-based construct, it would be categorized as "genetic factor influence";

– evocative or reactive correlation: this results from a reaction of the environment to a characteristic of the child under the influence of genetic factors. Parents react to the child's difficult character with harsh and negative parenting, a "coercion cycle"; a happy child provokes different reactions from a gloomy child, for example. There is a growing acceptance of the idea that children influence how they are treated by others, including their parents, and that parents react differently depending on the child. Adoption studies are the most relevant in highlighting evocative correlations, as they provide information about the biological parents. For example, if we know the psychopathology or addiction of the biological parents, then we can see how it increases the risk of such problems in the adopted child, problems that will in turn influence the parenting behavior of the adoptive parents;

– active correlation: the child actively selects environments that are correlated with his or her genetic characteristics (this is more often true for peers than for parents) or that his or her perceptions of events are genetically influenced (a suspicious child will generally perceive his or her parents' behavior more negatively than a confident child and will act accordingly; a depressed adolescent will isolate himself or herself and inhibit influences from his or her parents).

We must understand all these processes that build parental behavior and its adaptation to the child if we want to be able to improve dysfunctions and their consequences.

1.5. Childhood and culture, anthropological approaches

The vast majority of research in the field of developmental psychology suffers from a strong sampling bias: 91% of the studies focus on children in wealthy, industrialized, democratic Western societies; moreover, even in these societies, children from the middle and upper classes are overrepresented[1].

Work in anthropology and cross-cultural psychology allows us to overcome these knowledge limitations through two approaches: a depth or precision approach, which often relies on detailed and deeply contextualized ethnographic data, typically from one society, and a breadth or size approach, which relies more on experimental data from standardized tasks deployed in many different societies. These two

1 As we like to joke, it is often said that the populations studied by university psychology teachers are… their students.

approaches are complementary, each with its own strengths and weaknesses (see Amir and McAuliffe (2020)).

1.5.1. *The phylogenesis of childhood*

Like other primates, young humans are dependent on others for long periods after weaning and exhibit a unique life history stage called infancy. Follow-up fossil evidence such as the eruption of the first, second and third molars suggests that the duration of this stage of life history has more than doubled over the past 4 million years.

This lengthening and dependence are at the heart of hominization[2], the concept of "neoteny" describes this immaturity at birth of the human baby compared to other species, but it is precisely this immaturity that will allow the development of specifically human characteristics. For example, the infant chimpanzee dominates the infant human in the first months of life in all types of tasks and tests, then progressively, this ratio will reverse.

The length of childhood will allow the human child to acquire an enormous amount of information, directly through its own observations and actions, as well as indirectly through a complex cultural transmission. Moreover, human populations, having colonized the entire planet, live in very different geographical, climatic and social environments, hence the concept of "adaptive phenotypic plasticity" which describes the capacity of an organism to adapt its development to environmental conditions (Amir and McAuliffe 2020).

Adaptation for the individual will consist of developing phenotypes that are suitable to environmental conditions from the start of life; variations in behaviors will result from the responses to the different socioecological indices.

An empirical and developmental example of this type of prediction is that a child's neighborhood hardship enables his or her prosocial behavior to be predicted in an experimental game: children living in difficult, low-income neighborhoods exhibit less prosocial behavior toward strangers than children in less difficult, higher-income neighborhoods. These patterns mirror those observed among adults living in similar economic conditions (Safra and Tecu 2016).

Development during childhood is a period of heightened sensitivity to environmental indices and developmental research in this area tends to exploit

2 We know the formula: what does a human baby look like? A chimpanzee fetus.

variations in these indices as natural experiments to determine downstream behavioral consequences.

A different, but largely compatible, perspective is that derived from "culture-gene coevolution" theory: like adaptive phenotypic plasticity, this approach also offers a rich perspective on child development, but focuses relatively more on the role of cultural transmission in early childhood (Amir and McAuliffe 2020).

This approach draws on the social learning model and focuses on the variation of cultural norms and their internalization as a driving force for behavioral variation across societies; cultural norms are behavioral heuristics that individuals tend to follow when: (1) a sufficiently large number of community members conform to them – the so-called "empirical expectation" (descriptive norms) – and (2) a sufficiently large number of community members expect the individual to conform, also called "normative expectation" (injunctive norms).

Initial propensities for social learning are likely to be equivalent in all populations, and these shared propensities then interact with varying cultural norms across societies to produce variations in behavior. Cross-cultural work distinguishes the characteristics of our psychology and behavior that are sensitive to cultural input in varying degrees.

In contrast to the concept of universality, which assumes that a phenomenon would be observed everywhere in the world, cross-cultural developmental psychology advances the concept of regularity (Rogoff 2003), to track and measure the regularities of child behaviors and developmental trajectories in various environments.

For example, the rejection of an allowance when they receive more than another person seems to appear with some regularity in children in different societies, which does not irrevocably demonstrate that the aversion to having more than another person is universal, but the regularity of its occurrence may lead to new research questions. For example, can the roots of this form of aversion be traced phylogenetically? Can formal models of cooperative interactions foster inequity aversion? Thus, cross-cultural developmental studies can contribute to broader theoretical and evolutionary debates about human behavior (Amir and McAuliffe 2020).

1.5.2. *Theoretical models on the influence of culture on development*

A great many theoretical models exist to explain the influence of culture on the child: Bronfenbrenner's ecological systems model (1977), Whiting's psychocultural research model (1977), Vygotsky's sociocultural-historical theory (1980), Harkness and Super's developmental niche model (1994), Weisner's ecocultural model (2002), Rogoff's transformation of participation approach (2003), Keller's ecocultural model of child development (2013) and Worthman's bioecocultural model of child development (2010).

A general characteristic of these models is that they all seek, in one way or another, to contextualize child development as a dialog between the individual and the various social, ecological and cultural inputs he or she receives.

Harkness and Super's model, for example, focuses on three elements: the physical and social environments in which the child lives, child education and child care customs and the psychology of caregivers. The authors, and others, have used this framework to assess how parents' ethnic theories of child development help shape practices, such as daily infant routines, and how these practices in turn influence child behaviors, such as patterns of play and social interaction.

Similarly, Bronfenbrenner's (1977) ecological systems model, undoubtedly the best-known theoretical development framework, provides a guide for examining how the immediate, internal and external environments in which children live shape their development, with particular attention paid to individual differences, such as temperament, and the ever-changing nature of these pathways over time.

This framework has been used to examine a wide range of behaviors, for example, bullying and peer victimization among youth in the United States, in order to assess how microsystems such as parent–youth relationships, exosystems such as exposure to media violence and macrosystems such as religion all contribute to child behaviors and beliefs.

However, the concept of "culture" is a confusing one; in Bronfenbrenner's model, the child sits in concentric spheres of cultural influence, with macro- and microsystems influencing his or her development. However, separation of the individual from his or her culture can be problematic, as culture is not separate, but rather a product of human activity (Rogoff 2003).

Indeed, development is a continuous process by which people are transformed by participating in culture, and their participation in turn transforms culture itself; the distinction between biology and culture is also flawed, as they are not alternative influences, but inseparable aspects of the system in which individuals develop. More contemporary conceptualizations thus attempt to position development in both cultural and biological contexts.

1.5.3. *Ethnographic approaches and monocultural analyses*

The ethnographic study of child development has its roots in the field of academic anthropology and has generally focused on furthering our knowledge by positioning child development within the wider sociocultural environment in which it occurs. Anthropologists Margaret Mead (1928) and Bronisław Malinowski (1929) were the first to suggest the importance of cultural environment in development and to question the idea that the behavior of children in the West is necessarily generalizable to other contexts. Thus, the adolescence crisis was challenged by Mead and the Oedipus complex by Malinowski.

These early ethnographies involved months, even years, of fieldwork and resulted in intimate ethnographies that integrated the lives of children into the complex cultures in which they found themselves. The majority of ethnographic work on child development in the early 20th century focused on detailed descriptions of cultural groups, such as the Hopi, Navajos, Tikopians and indigenous communities of New Guinea. A few notable exceptions have examined child behavior across populations, to allow for comparisons. For example, the transition to adulthood in Western societies is more discontinuous than in "traditional" societies, and adults in agricultural societies are more likely to assign tasks to children than those in gathering societies (Amir and McAuliffe 2020).

Then, during the last century, subsequent waves of ethnographic work focused on assessing the usefulness of psychological theories, such as Freudian psychoanalysis and Piagetian cognitive development among children in various societies. The second half of the century saw the advent of a more modern form of ethnography, which often involved the quantification of behavioral observations. These meticulous observational studies have fundamentally reshaped our understanding of developmental variation (Amir and McAuliffe 2020).

For example, while prolonged infant crying was (and still is) common in Western societies, the generalization of this model outside the West was challenged by pioneering work on the behavior of Kung infants. Through intensive observational work, anthropologists demonstrated that Kung babies cried much less than Dutch babies because parents responded quickly and reliably (Amir and McAuliffe 2020).

These close observation methods have also been used to study a wide variety of developmental behaviors, such as the duration of infant vocalizations, the percentage of time spent with different adults and time spent playing, foraging or working, among other variables.

This helps us to better understand child development by providing ecologically valid measures of relevant behaviors in the environments where they occur. In addition, observational data is less likely to be skewed by self-reported biases, such as socially desirable responses.

Despite the growing body of observational work on child development, some researchers have argued that ethnographic literature alone is not sufficient to constitute an anthropology of childhood. In other words, while mono-cultural studies deepen our understanding of child development, more theory and cross-cultural reasoning are needed to create frameworks with greater explanatory power (LeVine 2008).

Researchers have attempted to address this through meta-ethnographic approaches that compare child development in different populations. Anthropologist Mel Konner's "distillation of childhood" in hunter-gatherer populations (2010) has been a particularly important model in this line of research; by comparing the ethnographies of several hunter-gatherer societies such as the Hadza of Tanzania and the Martu of Australia, Konner catalogued 11 aspects of infant and child care, such as frequency of nursing, mixed play groups and self-sufficiency.

This view of child development has allowed us to better understand the similarities and differences between these various societies. For example, in all societies surveyed, infants are breastfed frequently and for long periods of time – 32 months on average. These results, combined with data from other sources, such as geochemical analyses of fossilized hominid teeth, suggest that breastfeeding is a consistent and probably ancient feature of human development. Ethnographic comparisons have also examined other aspects of early development, such as variation in learning strategies and parent–child relationships (Amir and McAuliffe 2020).

This meta-ethnographic approach has also been greatly facilitated by the HRAF (Human Relations Area Files), which maintains an archive of cultural information, a corpus of nearly 800,000 pages of ethnographic work about more than 300 different cultural, ethnic and religious groups from around the world. The technique of using and comparing archived ethnographic surveys has sometimes been called the "holocultural" approach. This approach has yielded a number of new insights into the role of cultural systems in child development.

For example, HRAF data allows us to study how different levels of social and political integration have influenced corporal punishment inflicted on children: societies with higher levels of social hierarchy and those in which non-relatives help to raise children are more likely to practice corporal punishment.

Similarly, subsistence strategy is related to child labor: hunter-gatherer children do relatively less economic work than food producers and agricultural societies assign work to children more often than hunter-gatherers. Learning begins in infancy, with children accompanying their parents on foraging expeditions, continues through early and middle childhood, primarily in the context of mixed groups, and matures in adolescence, when adults begin to teach children complex skills more directly (Amir and McAuliffe 2020).

An exemplary case study of the use of the multisite approach is an investigation by House and Silk (2013) into the "ontogeny" of social behavior. Using a forced-choice task, the authors investigated the emergence of prosocial behavior in 3–14 year-olds in Aka, American, Fijian, Himba, Martu and Shuar societies. They presented children with a choice between a 1–1 offer, which would offer one reward to the child and another to a peer (the "prosocial" choice), and a 1–0 offer, which would offer one reward to the child and none to a peer (the "other consideration" choice).

In a second task, children were offered a choice between the same prosocial offer (1–1) and a more advantageous option (2–0). Compared to the first trials, where the child received a reward regardless of choice, the second trials were costly from the child's perspective: either they would receive two rewards or they had to share with a peer.

The results of this study showed an interesting pattern of cross-cultural variation: when faced with the first choice, children in all societies increasingly chose the prosocial option (1–1) based on their age, and there was relative homogeneity in children's schools across sites. However, when faced with the second, more costly choice, children showed much more variation, suggesting that culture plays a more important role in children's sharing behavior when costs are involved.

Perhaps one of the most interesting results is the finding that in late childhood children's choices begin to converge with those of adults in their respective societies, elucidating the developmental period during which local norms can exert considerable influence on social behavior.

Contrast studies between Western and non-Western populations have been conducted largely to test the generalization of results. For example, merit-based equity judgments were compared among children in Germany, Namibia and Kenya: merit-based allocations roughly corresponded to the Western/non-Western divide, with German children assigning allocations based on merit, while Samburu children were relatively more likely to assign allocations based on equality. This result is related to the types of interactions common in these societies; indeed, frequent or infrequent interactions with outsiders could influence the relative value of merit or equality, respectively, in these societies (Amir and McAuliffe 2020).

In recent years, researchers have made great strides in formulating new methods for measuring cultural distance. In particular, Muthukrishna and Henrich (2019) have developed a new measure to help researchers design, plan and justify comparative psychological projects.

Based on a mathematical method originally intended to calculate the degree of genetic distance between two populations (called the fixation index, or F_{ST}), the team created a new measure, called the cultural F_{ST}, to calculate cultural distance from a large survey of cultural values in various societies. These methods are already gaining popularity in studies of cross-cultural variation in adult behavior.

1.5.4. *The accuracy and/or extent of data*

In practice, the logistics of conducting cross-cultural research can sometimes involve a trade-off between breadth and precision: the collection of detailed ethnographic data across a wide range of communities by a single person, or even a single team, demands a great deal of time and effort, but there is much to be gained by combining and integrating the main points from these two approaches. Beatrice and John Whiting's work on the emergence of social behavior, often referred to as the "Six Cultures" (1977), is a particularly significant and influential example of this successful overlap. This ambitious and unprecedented project had a series of interlocking parts. Working with their field teams, the researchers first produced detailed general ethnographies of the children's host societies – in Kenya, Okinawa, India, the Philippines, Mexico and the United States – that included descriptions of the children's upbringing and lives at the cultural level.

Next, the teams worked with families in each of these communities, conducting structured interviews with mothers. Finally, the field teams collected a large number of standardized observations of children's behavior, resulting in more than 2,000 five-minute observations and nearly 10,000 coded interactions of approximately 134 children between the ages of 3 and 11.

Lamenting the fact that most existing cross-cultural work simply describes differences, rather than systematically exploring them, the authors used their body of data to address some of the most important issues in child development at the time, such as the effects of gender, age, birth order and culture on social behavior.

They also documented consistent gender differences among children, such as girls being more likely to ask for help, while boys were more likely to seek attention and dominance. These early insights into the role of culture in child socialization, and in particular in the development of prosocial behaviors, laid the groundwork for new waves of work to unpack the concept of culture.

An enduring lesson from the Six Cultures study is the effectiveness of the model for studying child development, a research model that focuses on the causes of fundamental societal characteristics, such as ecology and economics, on children's formative practices, which in turn lead to variations in adult behaviors (Konner 2010).

To conclude this chapter, psychologists have begun to pay closer attention to considerations of culture and context when assessing human behavior. These waves of change have also reached developmental psychology, within which cross-cultural work is beginning to gain importance. Through meticulous work, we have learned more than ever about behavioral diversity in the early years of life, in different contexts, as research on children in diverse societies around the world helps us to understand the development, function and evolution of human behavior.

1.6. Childhood and family in history

Has childhood always existed? What a question! We recall that for Philippe Ariès (1973) the child and the family, such as we know them today, only appeared for the first time in the 18th century. Before that, the traditional, large family was guided by the function of economic survival, whereas today, the modern family is guided by the well-being of its members and the affective function.

In the traditional family, the socialization of the child was rigorous and the child's duty was obedience. Education took place within the family framework, and the child entered the world of adults and work very early; adolescence did not exist.

On this point, the descriptions of Norbert Elias (1973) about his process of civilization are very enlightening, and this in all aspects of the child's life: contrary to Rousseau, according to Elias, the child was, in all respects, a "miniature adult", wearing the same clothes as their parents, eating the same food, sleeping in their bed and going to work with them in the morning.

It was only in the 18th century that the "modern child" appeared among the bourgeoisie and was over-invested in, until it became the "king child" of today. Declines in fertility have obviously also played a role in this phenomenon: when we have a single child, we invest more in them than if we have eight.

Children are no longer an asset (as they still are today in developing countries), but a cost that parents accept or refuse. However, when they decide to have children, they then expect them to be perfect. The result is an overestimation of the skills of the babies and then of the children, an overstimulation in all aspects of development, which requires an effort that may exceed the children's capabilities, and a total availability of the parents, which is not without complications (Parrat-Dayan 1997).

Indeed, feminism, the employment of women and the desire for equality between men and women will disrupt the family and maternal and paternal roles and further complicate this problem.

The adult, especially initially the mother, realizes that she may make educational mistakes that will ultimately influence the child's personality. Moreover, as early as the 1940s, psychologists had already begun to speak of these mothers as "bad", "anxious", "hostile", "distressed", "rejecting", "overprotective", "aggressive" and, consequently, responsible for child illnesses (Parrat-Dayan 1997).

Faced with this responsibility and the anxiety of doing the wrong things[3], parents have turned to books on child rearing, which have been enjoying an exponential growth in popularity. These books testify to doctors' conception of the mother–child relationship in each era and of the place that the child should occupy in society.

Thus, the first book on child care in history was by Vallambert in 1565, centering its discourse on the good understanding required between the nursemaid and the infant, understanding necessary to maintain the balance between moods (Parrat-Dayan 1997). Thus, Vallambert wrote: "If the mother is delicate, if she cannot be available to bathe him, feed him and soothe him when the baby cries, if she cannot stand the child's odors, it is better to choose a wet nurse". We remember that Élizabeth Badinter had used the nannying of children by women from privileged backgrounds in those times to support her thesis on the non-existence of the maternal instinct.

In the 18th century, the time of Rousseau, the child was judged to be "good" and it was society that perverts it. Parents were made aware that the human being is "naturally good" and that doctors would be putting the accent on hygiene and disqualifying the nursemaids.

The 19th century was Pasteurian, the fight against microbes became the great cause and doctors took control over mothers to control hygiene. The phrase "child care" appeared, but at that time, the baby was considered only as a digestive tract that had to be protected. The medical establishment would supervise

3 We know Freud's famous saying, "Whatever you do, it will be wrong".

mothering, interfering in the mother–child relationship, and would judge body contact and attachment behaviors as being of no interest. Cleanliness was more important than affection and the child was, in fact, an object.

Then, finally, from the second half of the 20th century, the "child king" that we know today appeared, affection took precedence over hygiene, psychology became the theoretical body of reference for the education of children, the needs and rights of the child became recognized and the baby became a person, according to Dolto's famous formula. Painless childbirth, massages, songs and so on, all contributed to child well-being in the 1970s.

The child has thus progressively found himself at the heart of parental narcissism, as well as producing overprotection, preoccupations and guilt. The child's autonomy is theoretically a target, but do these parental positions really favor the subject's autonomy? These ambivalences are reflected in the choice of child care, interrupting the work of mothers (but not suitable for the new status of women), childminders and crèches.

To conclude, we can see how the conceptions of childhood, family, mothering and the place of the child in society have been, are and will be perpetually evolving social constructs. This will be evident again in the chapter at the end of this book on homoparental families.

1.7. Adolescent development and its contemporary evolution

The problem of adolescence is well known: theoretically at the optimum of health, the second decade of life, also called the "tumultuous decade", is characterized by significant mortality and morbidity, from avoidable causes related to behavioral problems, against which psychological interventions often have little effect. Yet, while adolescence is a period of vulnerability, it can also be a period of opportunity for prevention, thanks to significant skills in learning and plasticity.

1.7.1. *The (psychological and biological) "dual agenda"*

Youth vulnerability can be linked to what we have called a "dual agenda" (Assailly 2019), or, to be more precise, the coordination of two trends.

On the one hand, a purely biological, physiological tendency called the "secular trend in puberty", attested by biologists, physiologists and doctors. Compared with our ancestors, puberty, as observed by physiological and physical changes in the bodies of young boys and girls, appears earlier in life, on average two years earlier than in previous centuries, for both boys and girls.

This secular trend has stabilized and, although it is not completely explained, hypotheses are increasingly being put forward around hygiene, nutrition, chemical pollutants and endocrine disruptors, factors similar to the contemporary obesity epidemic. As puberty is mainly a hormonal triggering phenomenon, all of the factors affecting the hormonal life of the embryo (its first exposure to testosterone) and the adolescent (its main exposure to testosterone) may play a role in this earlier triggering.

On the other hand, a psychosociological phenomenon that can be described as the "increasing precocity of behavioral disorders", attested by educators and psychologists, among others ("what previous generations did at 14 is now experienced at 12"), and which is reflected in the earlier average age of onset of all kinds of problems (such as regular and excessive consumption of alcohol, tobacco, use of illicit drugs and antisocial behavior).

It is only recently that neurobiologists and brain imaging specialists have helped us to better understand the relationships and interactions between these two historical developments and how risk-taking in adolescence is being constructed in the confrontation between two neurobiological agendas.

According to the dual systems model (Steinberg 2010) and the related maturational imbalance model (Casey 2015), adolescent risk-taking can be understood in terms of two distinct dimensions – incentive processing and cognitive control – that mature on separate time scales and are underpinned by distinct neurobiological circuitry.

From puberty onwards, the subject becomes more sensitive to rewards, novelty and sensation seeking, due to changes in the functioning of the dopaminergic system, a "socioemotional" system that involves limbic structures, the amygdala, the nucleus accumbens and other areas of the brain associated with judgments about the attractiveness of stimuli.

This stimulus-processing system develops rapidly in early to mid-adolescence; adolescents show greater reactivity in the ventral striatum in response to rewards than do children or adults and the extent of ventral striatum reactivity correlates with real-world risk-taking.

This system is activated by a strong secretion of testosterone during puberty, which is, of course, much higher in boys than in girls. So this "reward system" is activated earlier now, from the beginning of puberty.

In late adolescence, self-regulation is enhanced by a second system, the "cognitive control decision system", located in the prefrontal areas (responsible for executive functions such as memory, attention, planning, inhibition and flexibility). This system regulates decisions about reward and peer pressure. Unfortunately, this control system does not mature until the age of 22, 23 or even 24.

For example, white matter volume increases until the mid-20s, particularly in brain areas involved in high-level cognitive control. Thus, this neural maturity gap is thought to result in increased sensitivity in adolescents to rewards and emotions without a concomitant increase in their ability to control their behavior.

The problem of adolescence is thus a problem of the agenda between these two systems, the first developing more rapidly than the second and producing that strong increase in the search for sensations and rewards that the adolescent can find in risk-taking, this being the means of satisfying this need. With the secular changes in the age of puberty, this also allows us to understand why risky behaviors and their potentially dangerous consequences are occurring earlier today.

Thus, the issue is not that adolescents are more impulsive than adults or that they seek more rewards than adults; the issue is that they do not sufficiently understand the associations between behavior and consequences (and the balance between benefits and costs: "If I have one more drink, I will be more euphoric but I might also get my license revoked"). This has been shown using functional brain imaging: the synaptic chains connecting the limbic to the prefrontal regions are not "finite" ("myelinated", to use the technical term), so there is not enough synchronization between cognition and affect.

Brain imaging has also shown the influence of this coordination on resistance to peer pressure, a highly significant factor in risk-taking in young people. Adolescents who are more sensitive to peer pressure are those who activate the areas most involved in the perception of others' actions, whereas subjects who are less sensitive to peer pressure are those with better connectivity between these areas and those of cognitive control in decision-making.

The transition from adolescence to adulthood thus seems to be a period of "tuning", thanks to a better connectivity between the prefrontal and the limbic, which allows a better cognitive control of emotions. For as long as this adjustment is not made, adolescence will be a period of vulnerability, because the two cortical systems are in conflict during decision-making and risk-taking, and when one system predominates over the other – for example, the socioemotional system – immediate rewards will be too prevalent.

To conclude on this neurobiological agenda, it leads to the idea that risk-taking is a question of tempo, or, more precisely, of two different tempi, between the rapid socioemotional system of reward and the much slower system of cognitive control. Adolescents will (fortunately) not take risks all the time, but there will be times when emotions and peer pressure will activate the emotional system to such an extent that it will overwhelm the adaptive capacity of cognitive control.

This helps to explain why early puberty and early initiation of substance use behaviors are predictive risk factors, which occur at a time in life when the prefrontal and executive functions are not yet controlling the reward system.

However, adolescent behavior also depends on the social and relational context. To take just one example, English adolescents are killed half as much on roads as their French counterparts, with the same number of individuals and cars. While biology is the same, it is culture that explains the differences.

Furthermore, the discovery of the dual agenda by neurobiology may lead actors to two conflicting conclusions:

– some may argue that the lack of maturation of prefrontal control means that nothing can be done and that adolescents must be protected in spite of themselves, by measures to reduce exposure to risk;

– others will argue, on the other hand, that adolescence is a time of maximum plasticity for learning and experience and that intervention is needed. Furthermore, testosterone also increases social status sensitivity at puberty, not just reward sensitivity; this could allow for status to be played out in peer intervention and prevention.

1.7.2. *Questioning the existence of adolescence*

The concepts used to categorize individuals between the ages of 10 and 30 (such as "pre-adolescent", "post-adolescent", "adolescent", "Tanguy[4]", "early adolescence" and "late adolescence") have little scientific validity; this led René Zazzo to his provocative formulas: "childhood and adolescence do not exist".

4 "Tanguy" was a very popular French movie 20 years ago, Tanguy being a nearly 30-year-old son showing his desperate parents no intention of leaving the family home…

Indeed, a dual variability is highly characteristic of the second decade of life and casts considerable doubts over the validity of categorizations:

– a strong “interindividual” variability: subjects at the same age are very different from one another (girls are two years more advanced than boys in terms of maturation and, within the same sex, boys with very early puberty or very late puberty can be very different);

– a strong “intraindividual” variability: at this period of life, the individual can change rapidly and strongly.

On the other hand, one phenomenon will affect all young people in France the extension and precariousness of youth, as shown by the statistical data in Table 1.1.

Year	1930	1970	1990
Age	15.8	20.3	21.5

Table 1.1. *Average age at end of education in France*

This extension, which is desirable, is sometimes even decided politically, when a minister declares that 80% of an age group must obtain their baccalaureate. The price to be paid is the prolongation of dependence on parents. Thus, 72% of 18–24 year-olds live with their parents (EU average).

Another consequence is the delay of parenthood (see Table 1.2).

Another negative consequence is that many people enter the world of work in a precarious way; previously, it was done in a way of integration, but today, it is more a question of experimentation (the archetype of the trainee).

Year	1974	2019
Age	24	29

Table 1.2. *Average age of mothers at first child in France*

As a result, unemployment is twice as high among young people (23% compared with 10% for the general population) and 20% of young French people live below the poverty line, a reality that the country does not dare to face.

Experimentation is therefore what specifically characterizes this period of life: experimentation with work, roles, psychoactive products and so on.

Still, within this cohort, the university dropout rate is massive: 30% in the first year.

Another contemporary phenomenon strongly influences adolescence today: the rise of "individualism", the disappearance of traditional solidarities and therefore the autonomization of identity constructs and "intergenerational transmissions deficit". The loss of influences such as family, religion and communism will disturb identity construction, a fundamental developmental task of adolescence, hence the "uncertain individual".

1.7.3. *Risk behaviors and rites of passage*

From birth to death, the individual passes through a certain number of states and statuses and, since the beginning of humanity, societies have created rites to frame and operate these passages. These rites can concern the stages of life (such as burial to pass from the state of life to that of death), changes in religious status (baptism to pass from the profane to the sacred state), temporal markers (seasonal rites) and so on.

Each society has developed its own rites, but we owe to ethnologist and folklorist Arnold van Gennep (1909) the idea of an anthropological structure common to all rites in his work *The Rites of Passage*, a systematic study of the rites of "passing through the door and over the threshold" of, for example, hospitality, adoption, pregnancy and labor, birth, childhood, puberty, initiation, ordination, coronation, engagement and marriage, funerals and the seasons.

The duration of the rites of passage between childhood and adulthood can vary in traditional societies (from two weeks to several years), but a temporal sequence and common meanings emerge; this sequential structure unfolds in three stages: the first is organized around the separation, the second around the intermediary and the margin and the third around acknowledgment of the initiation and the passage.

From the Latin etymology *limen*, which means "threshold", van Gennep created three concepts:

1) preliminary rites, or rites of separation from the previous state;

2) liminal rites, carried out during the intermediate phase, putting in play testing or symbolic death;

3) postliminary rites, or rites of reintegration with the acquisition of a new status.

In traditional societies, these rites would allow for a harmonious passage from childhood to adulthood: prepubescent subjects were separated from the rest of the social group, isolated in places devoted to liminal rites and underwent a certain number of physical or moral tests, “symbolic markings” at the end of this intermediate phase. At the end of this intermediate phase, the young person was reintegrated into the group with full adult status, without restrictions.

Moreover, these rites of passage were initially different for boys and girls in traditional societies:

– in boys, they were public, exercised in groups; the period of testing was essentially applied to boys, meaning the necessary separation of the boys from their mothers, in order to reach adult, paternal or reproducer status, subject to the order of seniority; in addition, physical testing during the liminary phase was more perilous in order to make them affirm their masculinity;

– in girls, the rites were more private, less collective, more intimate, such as pregnancy, for example; there was no separation from the mother, but transmission of the procreative function, there was continuity and non-breakdown.

In our modern societies, many rites of passage have lost their meaning and validity: military service no longer exists, the baccalaureate no longer guarantees a job, marriage often leads to divorce and religion has lost its influence. In this context, which rites remain and are still functional? Can we still speak of rites of passage in modern societies?

The use of psychoactive products is currently used by many young people for this purpose (as was traditionally the case with the first drunkenness of young men), but while this use fulfills the first two functions of the rite (it symbolically separates from the world of adults and from the norm and constitutes a test of the body and mind), it seems to be of little use for the third function, reintegration with the acquisition of a new status, since this use may, on the contrary, lead to a certain marginality or even to exclusion or homelessness.

Piercings and tattoos, very in vogue at present, are indeed an equivalent of the symbolic markings of the body and the scarifications, but is that enough to confer on them a value of insertion? Running away, wandering, cars “speeding runs” and extreme sports, among other activities, do not seem to be very effective either.

A number of differences between traditional and modern rites have been identified in this regard (Jeffrey 2008):

– In traditional societies, rites were framed and supervised by adults; in modern societies, young people are much more left to their own devices. However, the test must be recognized by the community to allow for reintegration (as with school exams), particular examples being the raids or boat trips that are proposed to young offenders to reintegrate them, to learn about life in a group and to understand their limits.

– In traditional societies, rites had a transmission function concerning the fundamental question of death; today, although death is no longer part of life, our contemporaries want to be invincible and immortal, so there is a forgetfulness, an avoidance, a concealment, in short a denial of death, a sequestration of the experience. Sometimes, young people play with death in ordalic behaviors, but, today, men no longer live with death, it can no longer give meaning. Should young risk-takers be put in contact with people at the end of life, so that they become aware of the finitude of all human life?

– In traditional societies, it was enviable and recognized to become an adult; is this still the case today? Will the phenomena of endless adolescence, of "Tanguy", of adults who constantly regret their lost youth, make people want to become adults? What do we "gain" from becoming adults today?

Because of this loss of meaning, young people recreate "marginal" rites without adults, which causes a third-phase deficiency, aggregation, hence the extension of these marginal rites and therefore of initiatory and dangerous practices.

1.7.4. *The evolution of festive practices*

In relation to this evolution of rites, we are witnessing a "festivalization of society" (Moreau and Sauvage 2007): the festive events of today no longer correspond to the votive festivals of yesteryear, they are becoming more everyday occurrences (such as Thursdays on Rue de la Soif in Rennes, Fridays in the Bouffay district of Nantes and all-nighters in Paris), and therefore the periods of exposure to risks are more significant.

We should value the festivals, the music and the culture against boredom, so that they do not simply become drinking parties, but moments when we live together. The night as a space of political intervention.

1.7.5. *Changes in product consumption*

In relation to the above-mentioned phenomena, changes can be observed in consumption norms, from chronic, daily consumption of wine to episodic consumption of strong alcohol on weekends, "binge drinking" and a reduction in the distinction between gender behaviors.

Beyond these developments, alcohol and cannabis consumption among young French people is among the highest in the world, a phenomenon that would fill the contents of a book its own right (Assailly 2017), but which will be covered in the chapter on health.

1.8. The family and its contemporary evolution

> Parents are like lighthouses at sea for children: they play in the area lit by their presence (Anne-Marie Fontaine).

The main developments have been:

– the influence of the transformation of the status of women in society: access to education and then to salaried employment from the 19th century, to equality and then to contraception in the 20th century. This has led to a drop in the birth rate (two children per French woman today compared to 2.47 in 1970);

– the outdated institution of marriage: since the abolition of marital control and of the distinction between legitimate and natural children, more than one child in two (59%) is born today to unmarried parents, compared with 6% in 1972; the number of marriages per year has fallen from 400,000 in the 1970s to 240,000 today. Couples who marry do so much later in life (37 years for men, 35 years for women). Finally, the development of civil unions (*Pacte Civil de Solidarité*, PACS) and the facilitation of divorce are two recent elements of marriage being seen as an outdated concept;

– changes in the status of the child: the popularization of child psychology since the 1970s (Dolto's "the baby is a person", "the king child", etc.) has modified parental educational strategies and parent–child relationships.

To conclude, fewer children, who are more wanted, and more autonomous but more fragile couples, hence:

– the increase in divorces and shared custody: with feminism, we have seen an increase in the rights and involvement of fathers and, after a separation, we accept that the father–child bond should no longer be broken; shared custody judgments are now pronounced in 21% of divorces and, in the other cases, an agreement is obtained between the father and the mother on custody;

– the persistent inequality of paternal and maternal roles: despite these societal evolutions, mothers continue to assume the parental role for 30 minutes more per day on average than fathers;

– the diversification of the family model (such as mixed, single-parent, homo-parent and multi-parent families).

There is therefore no naturality of the family, as there is with animals; we are in the symbolic and the cultural (abandonment, adoption, heritage, name).

With these evolutions, what will remain of the Oedipus Complex? This was built around the father–mother–child relationship, but already in 1921, the ethnologist Malinowski had questioned its universality, by observing the numerous variations of family structures, the influence of patriarchy and the lines of transmission, for which the Oedipus Complex is only valid within the framework of Roman law, Christian morality and the Viennese bourgeoisie. Thus, in certain cultures, the prohibition of incest does not relate to the mother but to the sisters.

Thus, from 1950, Lacan, in his structuralist perspective, no longer spoke of the father in the sense of *pater familias*, but of the paternal function. This function is present even in the absence of the father and can be very well assumed by the mother. In certain traditional father–mother–child families, however, this function is not assumed at all.

Then, in the 1970s, Lacan added that "there is no sexual relationship", nothing allows *a priori* the harmony of complementarity between men and women. Would the Oedipus Complex finally only be the impossibility of jouissance and the obligation of lack? In single- or homoparental families, inseminations and surrogacy signify this as being impossible. The Oedipus Complex is only one of the possible forms of the impossible.

1.9. Social class, family income and poverty

Child poverty is a serious public health issue. For example, over 13 million young people under the age of 18 currently live in poverty in the United States and 20% of French youth live below the poverty line.

The impact of social background on educational performance is now well known following sociological studies in the aftermath of the Bourdieusian theory of social reproduction, so there is no need to belabor it here.

Decades of research have also highlighted the adverse effects of child poverty on multiple dimensions of mental health, including depression, anxiety, behavioral problems and substance abuse. Indeed, children and adolescents from low-income families are two to three times more likely to develop mental health problems than their more affluent counterparts.

The Millennium Study showed a significant protective effect of higher family income on behavioral problems at age 11. Maternal distress is an important mediator in the relationship between income and child behavior and explains the maintaining of the effect through childhood and adolescence because of its impact on the child's emotional self-regulation.

1.10. Parenting and parenting styles: how do we find the "right balance"?

The French term "parentalité" appeared in the 1990s, to correspond to the American "parenting" and the "parentage" of Quebecers, to define the way that parents educate their children, their educational styles. Since then, thousands of scientific studies have been devoted to it, countless manuals since the famous Dr. Spock in the United States and numerous radio (since Françoise Dolto in the 1970s) and TV shows ("Les Maternelles"). It is hard to find a more relevant and media-friendly subject. Finally, support for parenting is a concern and a worry for political leaders, because it is obviously assumed that if parents are failing in their educational missions, other institutions will have a hard time redressing the balance.

There is a consensus in this field that "extreme" educational styles, the Charybdis of authoritarianism and the Scylla of laxity, both result in negative consequences for the child's socialization, health, safety and education. As Buddhism teaches us, we must again find "the middle way".

We propose to call this "middle way", described as "authoritative" in Baumrind's (1985) three-dimensional classification, "negotiated authority": "this is what you should do and I will explain why". Persuasion is achieved through dialog, not physical punishment; these parents provide love and limits. Negotiated authority is a combination of affection and behavioral control, because authoritarianism also involves behavioral control, but without the affection.

Authoritarianism, itself, can take two forms: physical (coercion through beatings, physical punishment and very severe discipline) and psychological (psychological control and intrusion into the child's autonomy through blackmail, manipulation and lying). In mothers, physical punishment may be associated with a perceived lack of control over the child: those mothers who "cannot do it anymore" will stick to this defensive educational style.

Overprotection and psychological control of the child, which block his or her autonomy, play an important role in the genesis of anxiety in children and adolescents; they induce the idea that the world is dangerous; they reinforce avoidance behaviors and impair children's skills and self-confidence. Sometimes the measure of overprotectiveness is more related to the anxiety level of the mother than to that of the child.

The educational style adopted by a parent depends on beliefs that are in turn dependent on their own gender and educational background. Fathers tend to have more traditionalist views than mothers, especially when the child is a boy. The higher the educational level, the more likely the parent is to adopt negotiated authority and progressive views.

The educational style adopted by parents also obviously depends on their personalities. For example, parents with weak internal personality cohesion and low emotional control skills are less likely to adopt negotiated authority.

On the other hand, a parent's educational style is also an effect of the child towards the parent: the parent reacts to what the child is. Thus, the "norm" in modern Western families, at least those of the middle class or bourgeoisie, is negotiated authority, since the media and their environment now tell them that this is the best strategy. Parents therefore prefer to use this strategy, at least as long as they are not confronted with a type of child that thwarts it (e.g. a child with a difficult character), in which case they will then be forced to change their strategy.

This is probably why, while ordinary physical violence (slapping, spanking, etc.) is decreasing, because it is more stigmatized, more serious physical abuse does not follow this trend (when parents are overwhelmed). There is an interaction between the parents and the child: parents using the authoritarian strategy most often have children with difficult characters (at least in the middle and upper classes). Meta-analyses on this subject show that the relationship between the mother's educational style and the child's temperament is a two-way street: the parent's perceptions and attributions strongly influence their educational style.

The longitudinal relationship between parenting and child behavior problems is thus bidirectional, so negative parenting can influence behavior problems as much as the reverse. For example, maternal emotional rejection at kindergarten entry predicts an increase in behavior problems at the end of kindergarten, and then behavior problems at the end of kindergarten in turn predict an increase in maternal emotional rejection at the beginning of first grade. For fathers, there is a bidirectional relationship between hostility and behavior problems. These phenomena are analyzed as "developmental cascades"; we have also proposed the concept of "spiral causality" (Assailly 2017).

Furthermore, the reciprocal influence between practices and problems evolves differently in mother–child and father–child dyads, depending on the dimensions studied.

In terms of "affective rejection", the relationship would be bidirectional in the case of the mother, but unidirectional in the case of the father (affective rejection that predicts behavioral problems); the father's expression of affection would be more important as the child ages, whereas for mothers, the affective bond is linked to the child's adaptation from the preschool period. It is recognized that mothers are more involved with their children and spend more time with them than fathers, especially when the children are younger. Fathers, on the other hand, feel that their emotional bond with their young child may not be as strong as that of the mother, but they say that this bond will grow stronger as the child grows.

Conversely, with regard to "hostile practices", there is a bidirectional link between fathers' hostility and behavioral problems, whereas for mothers, this link is unidirectional; the more intense affective investment of mothers towards younger children could also explain why behavioral problems only seem to predict an increase in the use of hostile practices in a unidirectional link. Indeed, the nature of the particular mother–child emotional bond might somehow delay the use of more hostile practices toward the child.

Indeed, maternal hostility predicts an increase in children's externalizing behavior problems in the period between 11 and 13. The strength of the emotional bond between mother and infant may explain why mothers employ fewer hostile practices when the child is younger, but when the child is older and exhibits increasing behavior problems, the protective effect of the emotional bond disappears.

Another type of interaction studied is that parents are more authoritarian with their daughters and give more autonomy to boys. Similarly, pubescent girls have more autonomy than non-pubescent girls. Finally, the sexual composition of the siblings plays a role in the difference in treatment between boys and girls. These differences are strongly dependent on parents' adherence to gender stereotypes in their educational practices.

Various studies (Assailly 2007) have allowed us to understand the impact of parental educational styles on the child's future: coercive styles produce anxiety in children, permissive styles produce aggression and transgression, as well as feelings of loneliness in girls.

Authoritarianism is linked to poorer moral judgment in children and lower self-esteem, smoking and illicit drug use by adolescents. Certainly, many interaction effects exist. In the example of tobacco use, the effects of authoritarianism are mediated by peer smoking; it has more negative effects on Caucasian children than on African American children, for instance.

Similarly, the correlation between authoritarianism, coercive educational styles based on physical punishment and externalized child disorders is observed in the United States in privileged environments, but not for African American families. In other words, the same family characteristic does not have the same effect depending on the family's background. It also indicates that smacking may not be experienced in the same way: it will be seen as aggression for children from privileged backgrounds, but a norm that does not imply rejection of the parent in disadvantaged backgrounds. Conversely, the absence of physical discipline in disadvantaged environments does not necessarily indicate an advantage: it may come from an abdication of the parental role. This remains true only when physical discipline remains within a certain range; beyond that, when faced with abuse, the negative effects are the same in all settings.

The negative effects of authoritarianism have also been observed in a population of Beijing children (Assailly 2007); this authoritarianism is related to poor control (ability to inhibit habitual responses) and a disposition towards anger/frustration. Permissiveness or *laissez-faire* also results in various negative effects: impulsiveness, aggressiveness and irresponsibility.

The relationship between negative parenting practices in mothers and fathers and the presence of externalizing behavior problems in children from kindergarten to grade 3 has evolved over time. While the link between these two variables is no longer in question, questions persist as to the direction of their influence and their evolution over time, especially in the case of father–child dyads. Indeed, while some authors assert that, in order to fully understand the externalized problems in young children, it is necessary to look simultaneously at their individual characteristics and the educational practices of their parents, many authors strongly suggest that results that have been validated with mothers should not be applied unilaterally to fathers. In fact, it is increasingly recognized that fathers have an influence on their child's development that is different from and complementary to that of mothers. Moreover, both parents contribute in a different way to the development of their preschooler's behavioral difficulties.

Involvement in delinquency, substance use and early sexuality are therefore less common in families with negotiated authority. Negotiated authority is obviously a more complex model of parenting to make work: it requires parents to be sensitive both to the child's needs and to the persuasiveness of his or her arguments. In authoritarian families, parents make the decisions; in permissive families, children do. In negotiated authority families, decisions are negotiated.

1.10.1. *Knowledge of child behaviors*

While parents' knowledge of what their children do (such as their activities, behaviors and relationships), especially during adolescence when young people spend less and less time with their parents and more and more with their peers, is a protective factor against risk-taking, delinquency or addiction, it remains to be seen how parents acquire this knowledge.

This knowledge is a two-way, two-dimensional process: the parent must make the effort to know, and the child must want to communicate information. Trust is a key element in the process, and we consider that the child's willingness is the more essential factor of the two.

Greater parental knowledge predicts less child engagement in a given behavior, but less child engagement in a given behavior also predicts greater parental knowledge.

There are three types of sources of parental knowledge: the child's confidence, the parent's solicitation and finally the parent's control. In recent years, several studies (Assailly 2007) have insisted that the first source is by far the most influential. The parents would not play such an active, direct role in the development of externalized problems and the young person's adaptation would be more related to what they are willing to entrust.

That said, confidence is possible because parents create a climate that allows it. It is, in fact, more an indicator of the quality of the parent/child relationship than of educational and parenting behavior. Confidence and bonding are associated and reinforce each other: when we confide, the relationship improves, and vice versa. This has been observed in different sociocultural environments (e.g. in Holland, it has been observed as much in adolescents of European origin as in Moroccan, Turkish or Surinamese). This does not preclude cultural differences in the sensitivity to the detection of externalized disorders and hyperactivity (also in Holland, Moroccan, Turkish and Surinamese parents detect them less than parents of Dutch origin).

Three causal relationships are possible:

– Indirect: the parents' educational style predicts their child's confidence, which, in turn, predicts both the parents' knowledge of their child's problems and, ultimately, their child's problems.

– Direct: the educational style determines the parents' level of knowledge, whether or not the adolescent confides in them; parents obtain this knowledge by other means (observation, solicitation of the spouse or other adults).

– Direct relationship between style and behavior: whether they know it or not, parents influence their children simply by the way they raise them.

For example, applying this model to substance use and delinquency, we see that both causal models exist. Some effects are direct, from parental behavior based on their knowledge of what their child is doing. Parents who are invested in controlling the behavior of the young person manage to gain knowledge without their child even confiding in them, by other means. Some effects, however, are indirect, through what their child is willing to tell them about what he or she is doing; this is true for both mothers and fathers.

Thus, we see the interplay between control and connection: sensitivity promotes the young person's confidence, intrusiveness inhibits it. The warmth of the relationship and the absence of intrusive strategies provide the relational basis for the adolescent's trust and confidence, which then enhance parents' knowledge of what their child is really doing. This is what protects against affiliation with deviant peers and the development of externalized problems.

As for the prevention implications of these phenomena, we know that addressing this relational dimension is most important in family environments that are not too "at risk". In contrast, in very disadvantaged environments, the direct effects of behavioral control are more important.

Other works (Assailly 2007) highlight a more complex modeling of sources and their influences, distinguishing between paternal and maternal functioning. Fathers have more indirect ways of gathering information than mothers, and the strategies are dependent on various factors, such as the number of hours at work. When fathers get information from mothers, this seems to be linked to a lesser involvement of the young person in risky behaviors. This is a system not only of communication between the child and the parents but also of how parents communicate with each other.

On the other hand, adolescents feel more compelled to disclose safety issues than more personal issues. Adolescent boys and girls confide more in their mothers than in their fathers, especially about personal matters: overall, 60% of adolescents confide in their mothers, 20% in their fathers and 20% in neither (Choquet and Com-Ruelle 2003). Girls confide in their mothers more than boys, but mothers overestimate the extent to which their daughters confide in them, which they do not do about their sons.

As for addiction, the paradox is that parents whose children actually use illicit drugs underestimate the phenomenon more than parents whose children do not use them. The former also overestimate the control they have over the phenomenon. The underestimation is even greater for alcohol.

We can see that awareness-raising activities should be carried out, because it is the parents who are most concerned who paradoxically feel the least concerned. When there is a discrepancy between what parents and adolescents report about risky behavior (sexuality, psychoactive substances, violence), there is a link between parents' overestimation of their child's real involvement in risky behavior at a given time and the child's greater involvement in such behavior later on. It is as if overestimation also acts as a risk factor.

Is it because young people, confronted with their parents' overestimation, see it as a lack of confidence, a factor that will push them into risk and make their parent's judgment "prophetic" ("since you think I am going to do it so much, then I am going to do it")? Or is it because parents have good intuition and "guess" in advance what their children will do later? Or even, do the characteristics of the family's social environment lead both to parents overestimating and young people engaging in risky behaviors later on?

Similarly, accurate parental knowledge is sometimes more harmful than underestimation if parents become more authoritarian and the relationship with their child suffers. We must work not only on this issue of the concordance between what the parents and the adolescent know but also on the parents' reaction modes to the disclosure of their children's dangerous behaviors.

For example, when their child does well in school, parents tend to underestimate his or her risky behaviors. Is it because of the "reassurance" of schooling that parents relax their control, which ends up being harmful? We know that teenagers who do well in school are not the ones who confide in others most.

We see how this issue of disclosure and secrecy is complex: parental knowledge can be a protective factor, but parents believe they know more than they actually do. Their knowledge depends on aspects of life, the age and sex of the child and differences between generations.

Thus, parental knowledge of various behaviors will determine their reactions. For example, there may be a lot of conflict about smoking, because smoking is not considered serious on either side, so it will be less hidden, whereas the young person will make much more of an effort to hide other behaviors related to illicit drugs or sex.

Conversely, parents, no doubt overly focused on the dangers of illicit drugs, will communicate much more about these and forget to communicate about the dangers of tobacco. These communication patterns are passed from generation to generation.

In conclusion, and contrary to the old maxim, “children should be seen but not heard”, we note that parental supervision must not be too rigid, fussy or intrusive, because, in this case, the child will no longer confide in them, and it is this absence of confidence that will become the causal factor of risky behavior. This is an environmental transaction and parents must be careful, in their words and actions, so as not to block their child’s communication with them.

1.11. Maternal employment in early childhood

Employment rates of mothers have increased substantially in recent decades, with this increase being particularly noticeable among mothers of young children under the age of five. Much of this growth occurred in the 1970s. However, the mid-1990s saw an increase in the employment rate of low-income single mothers.

The issue of mothers returning to work or entering the workforce shortly after childbirth has been a source of great concern to parents, policymakers and researchers and has prompted numerous analyses of the impact of early maternal employment on child development.

Developmental psychologists first voiced their concerns in the 1980s in a series of highly discussed and debated papers by Belsky (1988, 1990). In these papers, he highlighted that more than 20 hours per week of out-of-home day care poses risks to the infant–mother relationship and to psychological and behavioral adjustment during infancy, preschool and early elementary school.

It was against this backdrop of such dramatic changes in motherhood, employment, child care and a heated debate about its effects on child development and on society in general that a National Institute of Child Health and Human Development (NICHD) and an Early Child Care Research Network were established in the United States.. This network centered its work on the question of whether early child care before the age of five was associated with risks or benefits to child development.

At the same time, economists were focusing on how children are impacted by choices about employment, in particular on two resources important to children’s well-being: parents’ time and money. Economists suggested that parents may invest more in their child’s development, because more income from working is available to purchase material resources (such as books, toys or healthy food) and non-monetary goods (such as access to leisure activities). However, working longer hours may limit the time available for children (and thus the bond). This view therefore suggests that there will be trade-offs when mothers work, between increased income and reduced time with their children.

Together, these views suggest that mothers' entry into the workforce when their children are young poses particular challenges to their development. Consequently, the trade-off between maternal employment, particularly in the first year of a child's life, and the effects on children are important empirical questions.

Literature on the subject (Im 2018) suggests that young children in low-income settings are affected by maternal employment and that these effects differ according to paternal involvement; maternal employment in the early years is associated with adverse effects on aggressive behavior and internalized problems in young children.

Young children whose mothers begin or return to work in the first year after childbirth thus present internalized problems. Non-maternal care and maternal employment are certainly not identical but are assumed to be related.

Alternatively, the effect of early maternal employment on a young child's cognitive functioning may vary according to subgroup-specific characteristics, such as family income. Put another way, poverty could have a pre-weighted effect on the development of cognitive abilities. For example, there are many hypotheses that affluent parents talk much more with their children and use a wider vocabulary. Thus, for economically disadvantaged families, having mothers with their children may result in a weaker impact on cognition if children are still not receiving the stimulation (e.g. expressive and receptive language skills) that predicts later cognitive outcomes, even with their mothers.

According to the economic view of child development, the main idea was therefore that mothers' entry into the labor market would increase family economic resources, which would facilitate children's development, but would require a trade-off between increased income and reduced time spent with children. However, the work of psychologists does not support this hypothesis.

Rather, this work shows that mothers staying home to care for their infants in the first year, in conjunction with greater father involvement with young children, is a more beneficial solution than bringing more income into the household: children would thrive when high-quality parenting is available, even when the family is financially disadvantaged, and even though high income may facilitate good parenting.

Another important dimension of the problem is the involvement of fathers in bringing up children. Paternal involvement may offset the reduction in time spent by employed mothers with their children, thereby reducing the potential negative effects (on attachment insecurity) of maternal employment on child development. The moderating role of paternal involvement is associated with a lower incidence of internalized problems in children.

1.12. Child care

The EDEN longitudinal study analyzed a number of influences of child care arrangement (Gomajee *et al.* 2017).

1.12.1. *Child care and emotional and relational development*

Compared with children in informal care, those in group care had a lower likelihood of developing emotional and peer relationship disorders, whereas children in child care (maternal assistant) had a higher likelihood of developing behavioral disorders.

Children in group child care also had a greater likelihood of developing prosocial behavior. Children who, in particular, spent at least one year in group child care had the most beneficial effect, with girls benefitting more than boys. However, this association was not found among children from disadvantaged families.

Group child care thus seems to be linked to a protective effect against symptoms of emotional and peer relationship disorders and enables children to develop more prosocial behaviors, but not among children from disadvantaged backgrounds.

Group child care for young children can therefore have long-term benefits for their behavioral and emotional development, especially if it is of high quality and lasts at least one year.

1.12.2. *Child care and language*

Few studies have described how different infant care experiences may be related to later cognitive, language and motor function, with most analyses focusing on samples from industrialized countries. A Chilean study (Narea 2020) analyzed cognitive, language, motor and vocabulary sub-scores from tests of 7,564 24- to 48-month-old children from the Chilean Early Childhood Longitudinal Survey, which were compared on the basis of retrospective reports of child care arrangements during infancy.

Children who, as infants, had received one of four types of non-maternal care – center-based, grandparents, other relatives and non-family – were compared with those who had received exclusively maternal care.

Compared with those cared for by their mothers, children cared for in centers or by grandparents had higher total cognitive and language sub-scores, while those cared for by grandparents also had higher motor sub-scores. In contrast, children in non-relative care had lower vocabulary scores.

So to conclude:

– group child care is positively associated with the child's global and linguistic development;

– grandparent care is positively associated with the child's global, linguistic and motor development;

– non-parental care is negatively associated with the vocabulary of children;

– household poverty attenuates the association between non-maternal modes and child development.

1.12.3. *Child care arrangements, academic success and gender*

Gender differences in academic achievement have long been a societal and scientific concern. Recent trends indicate that, on average, girls outperform boys in grades and verbal performance in school and that boys' averages exceed those of girls in spatial and mathematical tasks.

Such differences have been documented in many countries, but have been found to be particularly prevalent in North America and economically developed countries.

In the vast literature on this topic, relatively few studies have considered differences in the non-parental child care settings where boys and girls spend their early years. Yet more than three-quarters of preschoolers in the United States attend some type of non-parental child care and attendance is correlated with school readiness and achievement.

One study (Gordona 2020) showed gender differences in child care arrangements among preschoolers in the United States: in families of high socioeconomic status, boys were more likely than girls to attend centers, but the reverse was true in less affluent families. Parents' general perspectives that center- or home-based child care is better for preschool development and safety also differed depending on whether the child studied was a boy or girl in families of varying socioeconomic status.

Given that center-based child care attendance for preschoolers has been associated with school readiness, it is important to understand and address these gender disparities. It would be interesting to obtain data on this topic in France.

1.13. Ranking among siblings

The first psychologist to study the influence of sibling rank was a psychoanalyst, Adler, who placed the feeling of inferiority at the heart of the creation of neurosis. He believed that sibling rivalry and the dominance of the eldest sibling are at the root of psychological differences between siblings. Freud, on the other hand, attributed little importance to sibling rank, as he gave much more importance to the emotional relationship with the parents. It must also be said that Adler lived at a time when the eldest sibling was indeed very much favored, particularly with regard to inheritance, so that there was no indivision.

These privileges have disappeared today. On the other hand, what has not changed is the role of "opener", to borrow a mountain metaphor, played by the eldest child and the task of inclusion into an already formed relational universe that falls to the youngest child. Sibling rank is therefore the variable that comes most naturally to mind when we think of the evolution of the structure and that of the non-shared family environment: the eldest is first alone, then has to "make way" for the youngest, the parents have more experience and so on.

It has long been assumed that first-borns were first spoiled and then "dethroned", which would constitute a form of trauma. In order to overcome this trauma, they would reinforce the imitation of their parents and the feeling of responsibility towards the younger children. They would thus put more emphasis on rule, discipline and become more conservative. First-borns who do not overcome this battle for the "lost love" of the mother become angry or resigned.

For a long time, a different hypothesis was also assumed, that for first-borns, parents are inexperienced and are more anxious and more demanding in their parenting behavior. This would make the older children more fearful and more dependent (and possibly therefore more dependent on psychoactive substances?). The younger children would be more open, more independent and more rebellious, and the older ones would be more conformist, more ambitious, etc. The feelings of an only child would be closer to those of an older child than a younger one.

However, what do 50 years of research on sibling rank show? Well, they show that there is no correlation between sibling rank and personality, in particular, that we do not find the above associations with openness of mind. In fact, the results of the studies go in all directions, and analysts have not been lacking in imagination when explaining completely opposite results, based on the use of popular theories about the effects of rank, when it suits the reasoning.

Associations with the subject's personality traits are only found in descriptions by parents or siblings. In fact, the influence of sibling rank would only be subjective: the way others see you, the way you behave at home because "an older child is supposed to behave like this or like that", but in no case does this translate objectively into measurements when taking personality tests.

1.14. Sibling size

There is a stereotype of the only child (egocentric, tyrannical, etc.), but does this cliché correspond to reality? Studies on this topic have not found any particular characteristics of only children (Almodovar 1981). It is true that childhood experiences are different for only children, but we can imagine that relationships with parents and then with peers would create a strong psychological variability among these children.

In China, the one-child policy in particular led to the belief that these only children were "little emperors", corresponding to the stereotype.

Male only children received fewer positive evaluations than female only children. In particular, they were found to be at greater risk of obesity.

Evaluations of only children are better after the implementation of the one-child policy in 1979 than before, but the policy has just changed.

1.15. Twins

The birth of twins is always a phenomenon that arouses curiosity. It is known that there are two types of twins: dizygotic twins resulting from the fertilization of two ovocytes by two different spermatozoa, and therefore have a different genetic heritage, like brothers and sisters; and monozygotic twins resulting from the division of a single embryo and therefore have an identical genetic heritage.

The prevalence of twin births has increased over the past 40 years in France:

– 1972: 9 births out of 1,000;

– 2000: 15 births out of 1,000;

– 2013: 17 births out of 1,000.

This increase is mostly related to dizygotic pregnancies, the prevalence of monozygotic pregnancies being stable at around 1 to 3 per 1,000 births.

Prevalence varies according to culture: in Europe and the United States, the rates are between 10 and 20, in Asia 6 and in some African countries 40.

Why this increase? Two factors have been put forward:

– the increase in the age of the mother at first child, that we mentioned above;

– the developments in medically assisted procreation. Thus, the proportion of twin births is 17% following *in vitro* fertilization, 9% following intrauterine insemination with the spouse's sperm and 11% with donor sperm.

1.15.1. *Aspects of vulnerability*

Twins have greater morbidity and mortality than other children:

– from the fetal period: intrauterine growth retardation (average weight of twins under 600 grams), TOPS (Twin Oliguria Polyhydramnios Syndrome, or acardiac twin, an anemia related to hemodynamic and hormonal imbalance in 5 to 15% of cases), congenital malformations (mainly heart disease, relative risk of 1.7), prematurity (in 43% of cases, or 7 times more frequent than for single pregnancies), perinatal anoxia (especially for the second twin);

– higher neonatal mortality: in the EPIPAGE cohort study of low gestational ages (2,773 premature infants, before 32 weeks), the risk of death in hospital was increased for twins, after adjustment for gestational age and sex, and their survival at five years was decreased. Some factors influence this mortality, such as birth order or weight discrepancy (relative risk of 2.9 in the EPIPAGE study);

– sudden infant death syndrome has been observed to be more frequent in twins, but this correlation no longer holds when birth weight, prematurity and sociodemographic data are controlled.

These increased neonatal and perinatal risks in multiple pregnancies are no longer observed later in life (cancers and cardiovascular diseases are not more prevalent in twins).

Regarding development during childhood: there is no delay in psychomotor development according to the EPIPAGE study; there is no difference in IQ when prematurity and birth weight are controlled.

1.15.2. *How can we explain the differences between two monozygotic twins?*

Monozygotic twins are described as identical, but this is a simplification and there are usually differences between them.

These differences may come from:

– genetic factors (alteration of genes by DNA mutations, or of chromosomes by postzygotic mitotic errors, polymorphisms);

– epigenetic factors (differential DNA methylation and histone modifications, X chromosome inactivation, genomic imprinting);

– mitochondrial inheritance (mitochondrial DNA mutations);

– differences in intrauterine environments.

1.15.3. *The psychological consequences of twinning*

1.15.3.1. *On parents*

Multiple pregnancies can, from the start, be a risk factor for psychological difficulties and ambivalent attitudes.

Depression is five times more common in mothers of twins: the care and housework associated with the arrival of twins has been estimated at 12 hours per day, resulting in sleep and time deprivation. Hospitalization of one or both twins may also delay attachment mechanisms.

Concerning the father, his help during a multiple birth is often important at the beginning, but decreases with time.

1.15.3.2. *Regarding children*

As was well described by Zazzo (1960), twins have a specific psychic development, which he named a "screen effect". Each twin acts as a sort of "screen" between the world and the other twin: mutual inter-identification, leading to a partial fusion between the self and objectal representations, which causes the two individuals to merge. This can cause delays in individuation and body image disorders such as recognition in the mirror at about three to four years of age instead of two and a half.

Zazzo thus considered twins as a "couple", not as doubles, which explains the differences between twins, especially monozygotic ones. The personality is formed and transformed in and by the couple, each creating its roles according to those of the other, resulting in two complementary personalities. Thus, we see personality differences such as dominant/dominated and extravert/introvert.

Environment also causes differences: the parents of twins tend to appreciate the character of one always compared to the other.

With respect to friendship, monozygotes share 50% of their friends, same-sex dizygotes 25% and opposite-sex dizygotes 5%.

The twin relationship becomes stronger around the age of 36 months, once the separation–individuation process is completed. During adolescence, the traditional revolt against the parents may also be directed towards the other twin, which shows ambivalence between the desire for differentiation and that of twinning, which will produce an increased frequency of psychological disorders in monozygotic twins with psychosomatic and depressive disorders in the dominated twin and behavioral disorders in the dominant twin.

That said, ambivalence is not specific to the twin relationship, it can be observed in all sibling relationships: in the same way as "ordinary" siblings, twins develop relationships of closeness and conflict, of love and hatred, two complementary aspects called for in the definitions of sibling relationships. Proximity and conflict are present in twins in the same way as in ordinary siblings; ordinary and twin sibling relationships seem to be built around these two central, common and complementary dimensions, "warm" and "conflictual" relationships.

Three characteristics inherent to twin pairs may influence twin relationships: type of twinhood, gender and temperament of the children:

– monozygotes have higher scores on positive aspects of the relationship, such as companionship and empathy; dizygotes, on the other hand, have higher scores on aggression, rivalry and avoidance, although this difference has been observed in adolescence, not in infants;

– girls score higher than boys on empathy, companionship and guardianship, while boys score higher on avoidance;

– emotivity negatively impacts twin relationships in adolescents averaging 12 years of age, while sociability and activity have been associated with positive aspects of twin relationships.

Finally, there are differences in the perceptions of twin relationships between children and their parents. Indeed, the more children emphasize warm and conflictual relationships, the less their parents perceive them. Similarly, mothers value the positive aspects of the relationships, whereas adolescents are more critical.

It could be that a fundamental difference exists between what happens within the twinned pair and what the pair actually shows to outsiders, including their parents.

2

The Fetus and Fetal Life

2.1. Conception and medically assisted procreation: children born through medically assisted procreation

In order for a child to be born, there must first be procreation. Since the beginning of the 1980s, medically assisted procreation (MAP) has become increasingly frequent: in 2018, more than 25,000 births, or 1 child in every 30 (which is still modest compared to the 800,000 annual births in France), were conceived by MAP (IVF, DAI[1]). This increase in recourse to MAP could be explained in part by an alteration in fertility. Studies point in particular to smoking, obesity, sexually transmitted diseases and endocrine disruptors.

With regard to testicular dysgenesis syndrome (TDS), studies have observed an overall change in male reproductive health, probably since the 1970s, consistent with the sperm quality data observed internationally.

These trends appear to be more consistent with environmental changes (such as increased ubiquitous exposure to endocrine disruptors since the 1950s and increased female smoking) than with genetic variations in the French population.

Following up on the health of these children could constitute a major public health issue since the follow-up of the infants reveals increased perinatal complications (prematurity, hypotrophy and neonatal mortality) and an increased risk of congenital anomalies (cardiovascular, metabolic or urogenital system) compared to naturally conceived children.

However, many confounding factors exist, such as multiple pregnancies. There is an increase in birth weight after frozen embryo transfer compared with fresh

1 IVF = *in vitro* fertilization and DAI = donor-assisted insemination.

transfer, an increase in epigenetic diseases and certain solid tumors among children conceived by MAP, regardless of whether the IVF or ICSI techniques are used. However, the absolute risks remain moderate and the prevalence of these pathologies remains low.

After adjusting for confounding factors, the data is reassuring, with stature-weight, cognitive and psychomotor development equivalent to that of naturally conceived children. It would seem that the occurrence of chronic pathologies in adulthood can be attributed to an embryo-fetal origin, hence the need for long-term follow-up of these children, who are still under-studied, as well as the investigation into the causes of these observations. In this context, the information from couples initiating MAP treatment on the risks for the unborn child must be a major concern.

2.2. The issue of genetic screening

Genetic diseases represent one of the leading causes of infant mortality (20%) and are responsible for approximately 20% of hospitalizations in children. Among these genetic diseases, a large number occur through a recessive mechanism (there are more than 3,000 known recessive genetic diseases). In the case of autosomal recessive diseases, the parents, carriers of an altered allele of the "recessive" gene, do not become sick because the second allele is normal. It is the meeting of the two mutated alleles of the same gene that will be responsible, in one in four cases, for the birth of a child affected by the genetic disease linked to the alteration of this gene.

It is estimated that 2% of couples (or 1 in 50) are affected by this risk of autosomal recessive or X-linked genetic disorder, which represents approximately 3,000 births per year in France.

The evolution of genome-wide high-throughput sequencing means that it is now technically possible to screen couples at risk for a large number of recessive genetic diseases. In the current state of knowledge, genetics makes it possible to predict high risks of certain diseases and to develop screening or prevention strategies for predisposed individuals.

However, in some cases, prediction concerns diseases of particular severity, for which treatment and/or prevention are still limited. In these cases, prenatal diagnosis may be proposed to the parents with a view to a termination of the pregnancy for medical reasons if reliable genetic markers are identified in the parents and the fetus. The characterization of the genetic anomaly can also justify the proposal of a pre-implantation diagnosis, which allows the couple to avoid the medical termination of pregnancy by selecting the unaffected embryo.

Cystic fibrosis and infantile spinal muscular atrophy are among the most serious of genetic pathologies from autosomal recessive transmission in France in terms of frequency, with 1 person in 32 and 1 person in 40, respectively, carrying a predisposing genetic variation within a general population.

Infantile spinal muscular atrophy, in its major form (Type 1, which affects 60% of patients), is a disease that is most often fatal before the age of two. In milder forms, the amyotrophy develops in early childhood but the prognosis is often life-threatening before adulthood.

From a technological and medical point of view, it is now possible to identify a large proportion of people who are healthy carriers of a genetic variation that is deleterious for these pathologies. This type of screening is called preconceptional screening.

For autosomal recessive diseases, union with another carrier provides a 25% probability of having an affected child. In this case, several proposals can be put forward to the parents: pre-implantation or prenatal diagnosis, egg donation or adoption.

Currently, in France, preconceptional screening is limited to genetic counseling of parents and relatives of patients with severe recessive genetic diseases (or a known heterozygote). Genetic analysis looks only for genetic variations of the gene involved in the family disease.

The current question posed by advances in knowledge and technological progress, mainly linked to the deployment of high-throughput sequencing technologies, is therefore essentially ethical: should the proposals for preconceptional screening of some or all identified recessive diseases considered serious and incurable be extended to the general population for couples who wish to have children?

2.3. Knowledge of the child's sex

In France, thanks to the use of ultrasound in genetic screening, according to the ELFE (*Étude Longitudinale Française depuis l'Enfance*, French longitudinal study since childhood) survey, 9 out of 10 mothers across all sociocultural environments ask to know the sex of their child before birth.

This survey also shows that more than 40% of parents declare a preference, with mothers slightly more likely to prefer a girl and fathers a boy. Knowing the gender in advance will also allow them to overcome any disappointment and become "good parents" who will eventually adapt to the child's gender.

Knowing a child's sex is therefore considered important in preparing for parenthood. Even before birth, the fetus is gendered. The mother anticipating playing with dolls with her daughter, or the father playing soccer with his son, are preparations for parents that start well before the birth.

Purchasing baby clothes or decorating the bedroom is the start of preparations for conformity to sexual stereotypes. There is an anticipated socialization of the gender, the parents want to avoid any possible confusion, the masculinity or femininity of the baby must be able to develop from the beginning… and let us not forget that the choice, the purchase or the exchange of the clothes before and after the birth are activities exclusively operated by mothers.

The gendered relationship to clothing is also contemporary: until the beginning of the 20th century, little girls and boys up to the age of six or seven were dressed in a fairly similar way (Rollet and Morel 2000), in dresses. The little differentiated appearance of the small child was not considered problematic as long as the social roles between women and men were clearly defined. Today, at school or in leisure activities, the roles of women and men are a little more permeable. Maintaining very early forms of sexuation through physical appearance is a marker, mobilized very early on, to signify the difference in sex, reminding us of the gender order and preparing us for differentiated educational practices (Clément and Hamelin 2019).

2.4. The sensory and psychological functioning of the fetus

The fetus has the spirit of the origin and is the origin of the spirit…

The sensory system of the human being begins well before birth: skin sensitivity begins as early as 10 weeks after conception, the vestibular system of balance as early as 8 weeks, taste as early as the 12th week, smell as early as the 9th week and hearing around the 20th week.

2.4.1. *Taste*

The fetus detects the aromas and flavors of the mother's diet: the sweet tooth appears as early as the 20th week of pregnancy, and as early as the 32nd week, food aromas from the mother's diet are detected, which constitutes a sort of gradual familiarization with her future food culture (e.g. curry in India and garlic and olive oil in the Mediterranean). These aromas are not only detected but memorized because, after birth, a baby will prefer an aroma (such as aniseed) to which it has been exposed.

Boris Cyrulnik reported the following experience: when you put garlic mayonnaise on the tongue of a New York baby, it makes a face, but on the tongue of a Marseille baby, it smiles. The taste has therefore been memorized, and this memorization takes place during REM sleep, a task made all the easier by the fact that a fetus spends most of its time dreaming.

2.4.2. *Sleep*

We now know more about fetal sleep. The proportion of REM sleep, and therefore of dreaming, increases between the 32nd and 40th week, which corresponds to a phase of rapid maturation of the brain, in which dreaming plays a role.

The preponderance of REM sleep during the fetal period could be explained by the immaturity of the brain (Dugas 2019): its small size would be intended to facilitate the mother's delivery; in return, REM sleep, which is more agitated, would allow for both the accelerated multiplication of the neuronal circuits necessary for the development of the central nervous system and the facilitation of learning. Finally, it could be used for genetic programming (the main basic behaviors are learned *in utero* and at the very beginning of life (Jouvet 2000)).

2.5. Stress and maternal psychopathology

Exposure to maternal psychopathology, or stress, during pregnancy is associated with prematurity and low birth weight and, in the longer term, with behavioral, emotional, cognitive and motor problems in childhood and psychiatric disorders in adolescence. This intergenerational transmission of psychopathology and stress would be due to a combination of intrauterine environment, genetic factors and postnatal environment.

The fetus and then the infant adapt in response to the health and physical state of the mother, modifying important physiological and metabolic processes that can last into adulthood: for example, the HPA[2] axis plays an important role in many of the body's homeostatic systems and in the body's response to stress, with HPA axis activity being measured by cortisol levels.

2 The functioning of this system will be described later in the chapter on emotions.

For example, maternal psychopathology during the prenatal period is associated with increased cortisol in the child's hair at age six years (Molenaar 2019). Thus, maternal psychopathology and stress during pregnancy are associated with the child's long-term HPA axis activity.

2.5.1. *Prenatal maternal cortisol*

Structural and functional brain imaging data have shown that higher levels of prenatal cortisol are associated with amygdala hyper-reactivity and increased amygdala volumes in girls only; an elevated concentration of prenatal cortisol has also been positively associated with affective problems in girls only, an effect that has in part been induced by right amygdala volume and increased amygdala connectivity.

Thus, there is an association between prenatal stress and HPA axis function, postnatal HPA axis regulation and offspring anxiety and depression behaviors in both rats and humans, linked to sex.

Consequently, the low antisocial behavioral problems observed in girls compared with boys during childhood and the increase in anxiety-depressive symptoms, particularly depressive symptoms observed in girls after puberty, could be due to the same cause.

2.6. Prenatal exposures

2.6.1. *Exposure to alcohol*

Twenty percent of French women continue to occasionally drink alcohol during pregnancy. Fetal alcohol spectrum disorder (FASD) refers to all the effects (such as physical, cognitive and behavioral) that may be observed in a person whose mother drank alcohol during pregnancy.

It includes a set of conditions representing a "continuum", from the most characteristic, most severe and easiest-to-diagnose form – fetal alcohol syndrome (FAS) – to so-called "incomplete" forms, which are much less well known and will reveal themselves later on through occasionally severe learning and/or behavioral disorders, the causes of which are far from always being identified.

In France, the collective expertise of Inserm "*Alcool, effets sur la santé*" (Alcohol, effects on health), published in 2001, estimated that 700 to 3,000 children, out of 750,000 annual births, would be affected by this syndrome, with a higher incidence on the island of Reunion, in Nord-Pas-de-Calais, Normandy and Brittany.

The effects on the central nervous system that have functional implications are now well known and include, among others, cognitive, motor, memory, executive function and communication impairments.

Longitudinal studies of alcohol in young adults have also shown that prenatal alcohol exposure is related to adult drinking problems. Exposure to one or more drinks per day during the first trimester of pregnancy has been significantly linked with increased levels of alcohol use at age 22, while controlling other predictors of alcohol use (Goldschmidt and Richardson 2019). These results indicate that individuals exposed to a single drink per day during gestation are at risk of increased alcohol use and alcohol problems at age 22.

2.6.2. *Exposure to tobacco*

Thirty percent of women smoke before their pregnancy, and 17% still smoke in the third trimester. France ranks seventh out of 50 countries most affected by active smoking during pregnancy. It must be said that some doctors advise smoking more than stress (see previous chapter). This active smoking behavior is more frequent in Brittany than in other regions.

The risk factors for smoking during pregnancy are: young age, poor education, low socioeconomic level, primiparity, geographical origin in metropolitan France, lack of occupation, a smoking spouse, a lack of spouse or associated depression. Multiparity is a risk factor for withdrawal failure during pregnancy.

Prenatal exposure to tobacco has short-, medium- and long-term effects, such as: placental abruption, fetal growth disorders, low birth weight; then poor visuomotor integration, poor verbal skills, poor school performance (not found in the United States, or when confounding factors are controlled) and attention-deficit hyperactivity disorder.

A recent Icelandic study (Kristjansson 2018) examined the relationships between exposure and academic achievement at ages 4, 7 and 10 using data collected at birth, during the neonatal period and at each grade level in the study's birth cohort. Exposure influenced achievement scores, was negatively associated with math achievement at baseline and continued to negatively affect math achievement over time after controlling for gender, income, cohabitation and baseline math and science scores.

Thus, children whose mothers smoke in the first trimester of pregnancy are, on average, at greater risk of poor school performance over time than children whose mothers do not smoke in their first trimester.

In the EDEN study (Melchior and Hersi 2015), maternal smoking during pregnancy predicted only hyperactivity/attention-deficit through epigenetic mechanisms. By controlling confounding factors, only exposure throughout pregnancy was significantly associated. This correlation was not observed for paternal smoking during pregnancy. This is inconsistent with genetic transmission. Continued maternal use during pregnancy could also be a marker of social and environmental difficulties and poor parenting, with use also associated with more insecure mother–infant attachment (Melchior and Hersi 2015).

Smoking during pregnancy causes a transgenerational effect. Thus, an increased risk of asthma is observed in the grandchildren of maternal smokers.

Finally, children whose mothers continued to smoke during pregnancy are more likely to become smokers, 15 years later. In a way, the mother makes the fetus addicted to tobacco when he/she is building their nicotine receptors.

In conclusion, regardless of the various influences and consequences, it is clear that smoking cessation during pregnancy must be an issue for tobacco prevention workers in the general population, coupled with actions on parental behavior and screening and support for smoking cessation before or at the beginning of pregnancy.

2.6.3. *Pollutants and endocrine disruptors*

Pregnant women are exposed to a large number of chemicals through their diet, so the fetal period is more sensitive to the effects of these products. The influence of these products is increasingly being cited in phenomena such as the "obesity epidemic", that is currently affecting children, or the precociousness of puberty.

Various works have shown associations between prenatal exposure to environmental contaminants that cross the placental barrier (particularly endocrine disruptors) and postnatal growth (Traoré *et al.* 2018). Heavy metals also have an impact, particularly on intellectual development.

In most cases, chemicals are studied individually and potential interactions or additive effects of substances are not taken into account. However, some recent epidemiological studies have identified relationships between exposure to mixtures of substances and their effects on health: the EDEN and ELFE studies have identified the main mixtures to which mothers are exposed, based on the 441 substances analyzed in the second French Total Diet Study[3] (Traoré *et al.* 2018).

Exposure systems and substance composition were identified from co-exposures: individuals were grouped together to define clusters with similar co-exposure patterns. Six clusters associated with eight mixtures were identified. For example, in ELFE, cluster 2, comprising 10% of the population, was characterized by mixtures "Pest-1", which contained mainly pesticides, and "TE-F-PAH", which contained trace elements, furans and polycyclic aromatic hydrocarbons. Similar results were observed in the EDEN study.

This work enabled prioritization of mixtures for which it was crucial to investigate possible toxicological effects and to recommend epidemiological studies regarding health effects (Traoré *et al.* 2018).

2.6.4. *Exposure to acrylamide*

Acrylamide is a known neurotoxin to humans and animals and has been classified as "probably carcinogenic" in humans. It does not occur naturally and has been produced since the 1950s for use, for example, in water and wastewater treatment, as gels in laboratories, or in tile grout. In these cases, the main routes of occupational exposure are inhalation and epidermis. Acrylamide is also found in cigarette smoke and diet is the primary source of acrylamide exposure in non-smokers. Acrylamide crosses the placental barrier.

In the EDEN study, dietary acrylamide intake during pregnancy was assessed by combining maternal food frequency questionnaires with data on food contamination nationally, provided by the second French Total Diet Study. The study showed a relationship between increased maternal exposure to acrylamide and fetal growth, both in weight and length.

2.6.5. *Cadmium exposure*

Cadmium is a metal found in batteries, pigments and plastics; its toxicity on health is known (bone disease, certain cancers); exposure can come from two

3 To overcome the lack of precision of routine food health surveillance, total diet studies (TDSs) are national cross-sectional surveys designed to analyze a large number of substances in defined food samples to be representative of the diet of the study population. They are based on food surveys. TDSs allow the identification of substances for which there is a risk of excess in the population and the food vectors contributing most to exposures (Traoré *et al.* 2018).

sources, food and tobacco use, and its percentage through ingestion can increase during pregnancy.

In the EDEN study, blood cadmium concentration was associated with fetal growth restriction and low birth weight; the strong association between cadmium and tobacco use indicates that blood cadmium concentration may be a good biomarker of tobacco toxicity on fetal development.

2.6.6. *Exposure to caffeine*

Data from animal studies suggest that maternal caffeine consumption during pregnancy has adverse effects on the subsequent brain development of the offspring. However, human data in this area is limited.

Multivariate modeling was carried out on the EDEN cohort, using data from 1,083 mother–child pairs (Bernard and van der Waerden 2016). Measurements included estimated maternal caffeine intake during pregnancy, child IQ at 5.5 years and individual and family characteristics.

Prenatal caffeine exposure was common in the sample (91%), with 12% having intakes ≥ 200 mg/day, which is a high intake. There was a significant negative relationship between caffeine intake and child IQ at 5.5 years. In particular, children of mothers consuming ≥ 200 mg/day were more likely to have borderline or lower IQs compared with children of mothers consuming <100 mg/day.

2.7. Microbiota

The term "microbiota" refers to all the microorganisms that live on us or in us. The intestine is the most densely populated, but other organs such as the skin or the respiratory tract are also home to them.

So-called new-generation genetic sequencing technologies have improved our knowledge of the microbiota and identified a much larger repertoire (bacteria, fungi, viruses and parasites) than was previously known.

Thus, some authors suggest that the human being should henceforth be considered as a "holobiont", that is, a biomolecular ensemble associating the human host with a set of microbes, the whole constituting a single ecological entity.

Several theories attempt to explain the effects of microbiota on the child: hygiene theory assumes an inverse relationship between the frequency of allergic pathologies and exposure to microorganisms (greater circulation of microbes and prevalence of asthma, eczema and urticaria); the "Old Friends" or host-microbiota symbiosis theory assumes that microbial agents associated with the rural, or even ancestral, way of life provide protection against allergic pathologies; Dysbiosis and Biodiversity Loss theory, which assumes that the loss of diversity of the microbiota, favored by the Western lifestyle, leads to a disruption of the balance between microbiota and host, and to perturbations in the immune system leading to the breakdown of tolerance and the appearance of atopic[4] diseases.

The first 1,000 days (from conception to the end of the second year) seem to be a very sensitive period for biological influences, such as the microbiota. An undernourished or malnourished microbiota will have long-term consequences on the development of the child and greatly influences the risk of chronic disease. A dialog between the microbiota and the immune system will be established, strongly linked to the environment, to stabilize around the age of three years.

Various environmental factors influencing the microbiota have been identified: the mother's diet and prenatal exposures influence the immune system of the newborn and the mode of delivery and breastfeeding can also strongly influence the microbiota.

Thus, the analysis of a newborn's first stools could reveal certain clues about the risk of obesity at the age of three years. This prediction is based on the nature of the bacterial species in the gut. The first stool, or meconium, is essentially composed of material ingested during intrauterine life.

Similarly, the administration of antibiotics to newborns alters the microbiota. Thus, babies who receive antibiotics during their first year have a smaller actinobacteria population at age one than those who received an antibiotic just after birth, or whose mothers used antibiotics during pregnancy and, of course, those who did not receive antibiotics at all.

4 Atopy is a genetic predisposition to the cumulative development of common allergies.

3

Perinatal Care and the Infant

3.1. Perinatal care

3.1.1. *Low birth weight*

Low birth weight or being small for gestational age has been associated with increased risk of mortality and morbidity and may have major implications for later health: low birth weight may be associated with elevated systolic blood pressure and risk of cardiovascular disease in adulthood. As we have seen, various environmental exposures, such as smoking, air pollution or chemicals, affect fetal growth.

Low weight may be associated with psychiatric disorders and autism, but the results are not yet consistent. The risks of motor, cognitive, emotional and behavioral problems may be even higher in disadvantaged social settings. For example, in Brazil, one study (Torres Pacheco 2019) compared 100 children (47 adequate weight and 53 low weight) with the Child Behavior Checklist for behavioral and emotional problems and the Autism Behavior Checklist for autism symptoms. The results showed no difference between the two groups (low and adequate weight) in terms of behavioral problems and autistic characteristics.

3.1.2. *Prematurity*

Prematurity, defined as any birth before 37 weeks of amenorrhea (WA), affects 15 million children per year worldwide and about 60,000 children per year in France (7.5% of live births).

It may be subject to historical variations. For example, child birth weights may depend on when they, their parents and even their grandparents were born.

Moderate preterm (32-33 WA) and late preterm (34-36 WA) infants account for approximately 85% of preterm infants, very preterm (28-31 WA) infants account for 10% and extremely preterm (< 28 WA) infants account for 5%.

3.1.2.1. *Long-term follow-up of premature babies*

Preterm and low-birth-weight children are at higher risk and higher rates of motor, cognitive, behavioral and emotional problems.

A recent study (Gire 2020) assessed the quality of life of school-age children born before 28 WA who had no major disabilities. The mean birth term was 26.2 WA (± 0.8), the mean birth weight was 879 grams (± 181) and the mean follow-up age of the children was 8.4 years (± 0.8).

Forty-eight percent of participants had minor or moderate cognitive impairments. Working memory, attention and mental flexibility had a low mean compared to the reference group. Aside from family relationships, quality of life ratings were significantly lower from both child and parent perspectives.

Children reported significantly decreased quality of life in the areas of friendship, self-esteem and leisure time, while parents reported psychological well-being, schoolwork and vitality.

The quality of life of a child born extremely prematurely at school age without serious challenges is therefore inferior to that of a reference population of children born at term, from both the parents' and the child's point of view. This assessment should enable a better understanding of the long-term outcome and to offer appropriate support to the child and its family.

3.1.3. *Brain changes in mothers*

In mothers, birth is associated with a high reinforcement value that motivates maternal care. This occurs through the release of dopamine in the nucleus accumbens, a central component of the brain's reward system located in the ventral striatum, an area known to respond to infant cues.

There was a reduction in the right ventral striatum and a trend toward a decrease in the left ventral striatum in pregnant women between sessions compared with non-pregnant women. Furthermore, volume reductions during pregnancy are associated with infant-related responses in the *postpartum* period, with more prognostic volume decreases predicting stronger functional activation of offspring signals.

Thus, the transition to motherhood promotes the strong reactivity of a mother's reward system to her child's signals.

3.1.4. *Postpartum depression or the "baby blues"*

Postpartum depression is a significant public health problem, with studies showing that between 3% and 35% of women suffer from major or minor depression in the first year after giving birth, with an average value of 15%. It negatively affects women's functioning, personal relationships and the social and cognitive development of children.

Regular physical activity has been recognized as an effective treatment modality for major and minor depression in the general population, and the potential benefits of exercise on perinatal depression are also beginning to emerge. Several systematic reviews and meta-analyses have shown that exercise may be effective in reducing depressive symptoms during pregnancy and *postpartum* (van der Waerde 2019).

Using the two French birth cohorts, EDEN and ELFE, the relationship between physical activity (including sedentary leisure time behavior) during pregnancy and the occurrence of *postpartum* depression has been analyzed (van der Waerde 2019).

Participants in the ELFE cohort (n = 15,538) completed the pregnancy physical activity questionnaire (PPAQ), which assesses the following physical activity/sedentary behavior domains: household/caregiving, work, sport/exercise, transportation and leisure time sedentary behavior in the third trimester of pregnancy. In the EDEN cohort (n = 1,745), women completed the Baecke Questionnaire (BQ) measuring work, sport/exercise and leisure activity during the first trimester of pregnancy.

Depressive symptoms in the first year *postpartum* were measured using the Edinburgh Postnatal Depression Scale in both cohorts.

Associations of physical activity/sedentary behavior with depressive symptoms were determined using logistic regression analysis, adjusted for potential confounding factors. In the adjusted models, higher levels of household/caregiving activities and sedentary leisure time behavior during the third trimester of pregnancy were associated with an increased risk of depression. No significant association was found for domains of physical activity in the first trimester of pregnancy. Higher levels of household and caregiving activities and sedentary leisure time behavior in the last trimester of pregnancy appear to increase the likelihood of *postpartum* depression.

In conclusion, purpose and context must be considered when encouraging physical activity as a strategy to help prevent *postpartum* mental health problems from pregnancy. Reducing sedentary behaviors could be a complementary strategy (van der Waerde 2019).

3.1.5. *Self-harm*

Self-harm is most common among adolescents and young adults, especially women, but thoughts of self-harm can also occur during pregnancy and the year after birth. However, little is known about perinatal self-harm, its effects on the fetus or the infant, or whether these behaviors predict suicide.

Evidence suggests that self-harm during the perinatal period is rare in the general population; however, in women with severe mental illness, it is more common, with some studies reporting a prevalence of up to 20%.

Untreated maternal mental disorders can negatively impact infant development. Perinatal self-harm may therefore be a marker of untreated illness.

3.2. The infant stage (0–2 years)

3.2.1. *Introduction*

This is the period of life when development is most rapid: neuronal connections are established at a rate of at least 1,000 per second. We therefore "learn" as much between the ages of 0 and 2 as we do during the rest of our lives. We go from the visible (motor skills) to the invisible (thought) because "infants" do not talk. However, perception develops much faster than motor skills at this age.

Biological and social interactions continue to produce individual differences; there are as many differences between infants (between the tonic and the contemplative) as there are among adults.

This period of life conceals an important epistemological issue: recent research on the perception and cognition of infants questions the Piagetian theory of assimilation (the child understands the world through his actions, but the infant does not act, or only does so to a limited extent).

3.2.2. *The issue of breastfeeding*

Breastfeeding is the most suitable diet for children, regardless of the economic and health level of the country concerned. It contributes to the child's growth and the strengthening of the immune system, as well as helps to reduce the prevalence of health problems, such as obesity and atopy. There are also benefits for the mother, such as the reduction of the risk of breast cancer. This practice is therefore promoted.

In the EDEN mother–child cohort, a protective role for breastfeeding against diarrhea in the first months of life was suggested, but not against other childhood infections or allergic symptoms in infancy.

Since the seminal 1929 study, numerous studies have shown that breastfeeding is associated with better language ability in childhood and that breastfed children have higher scores on intelligence tests than children who have never been breastfed (Bernard and De Agostini 2013). However, some authors have suggested that these results were due to confounding factors (differences in social, economic and cultural levels between breastfeeding and non-breastfeeding mothers).

In the French EDEN mother–child cohort study, breastfed (by duration of breastfeeding) and non-breastfed children were compared in multivariate linear models, controlled for a wide range of potential confounding factors. It was observed that longer duration of breastfeeding was associated with better cognitive and motor development in 2- and 3-year-olds and a dose–response relationship was suggested (Bernard and De Agostini 2013).

Polyunsaturated fatty acids (PUFAs) are naturally found in breast milk and colostrum[1] and are necessary for fetal and infant brain development. In the EDEN study, the duration of breastfeeding and colostrum PUFA levels were associated with child IQs (Bernard 2017). This data supports breastfeeding and adds evidence for the role of early PUFA exposure on infant cognition.

3.2.3. *Taste*

There is little doubt that sweet, sour and bitter trigger very different reactions, as does olfaction, although it is more unstable.

---

1 Colostrum is produced by all female mammals for the purpose of feeding the newborn from birth. It is a thick yellowish liquid secreted by the mammary gland during the third trimester of pregnancy and the first days after delivery. Since breast milk is not rich enough in antibodies, colostrum occurs within the first few hours of life to pass on the immunological resistances acquired by the mother to the infant (Bernard 2017).

Taste depends on how the baby is fed. For example, breastfeeding decreases the likelihood of neophobia (the rejection of new foods, this topic will be discussed later in the chapter on feeding behavior) because breast milk has a greater variety of flavors than substitute milks. These influences can be very long-term. For example, the presence of vanilla in milk will influence taste for vanilla foods into adulthood (Streri 2018).

3.2.4. *Thought before language*

Can we think before and without language? The answer in the past has often been No. As a result, developmental psychologists have had to develop new observational methodologies to assess without language (Streri 2018), such as the "transgression of expectations" or "impossible situations" (e.g. one object crossing another, we see if the child is surprised; *ditto* for the notion of number: when a situation is impossible using subtraction or addiction, the infant looks for longer. Even the notion of probability: they look longer at an impossible solution).

Thus, the debate is about representation, attributed very late by Piaget, more precociously by the intuitionists, even from birth. Intuition is what the infant possesses before cognition: "Does this situation correspond or resonate with my brain, or not?"

3.2.5. *Perception*

No, infants are not blind, nor are they a digestive tract. It is assumed that their vision is blurred, but in fact the contrast polarity of their eyes (from the iris, knowing what the eye is really looking at) shows that newborns see like adults.

Since newborns do not move much yet, they watch. They have been called "baby astronomers". The observation and the analysis of what they see and of their visual fixations bring us new knowledge on their intellectual function.

Thus, Piaget placed the onset of object permanence (understanding that an object always exists even if it is hidden) at about 8–12 months; with techniques not available to Piaget (video and the computer), this has been shown to be possible as early as four to five months (Streri 2018).

3.2.6. *The conception of number*

Piaget thought that the conception of number was not acquired until around six to seven years of age, because, before that age, a child would judge that the longer a row of tokens was, the more tokens there were (even if they were spaced further apart). Yet, more recently, it has been observed that children as young as two years old do not make this mistake with candy, rather than tokens (Streri 2018). Piaget had overlooked one important thing: motivation, in this case greed. Motivation will therefore improve the child's intuition and make him a mathematician.

Thus, children as young as two years old react differently to additions or subtractions giving correct or incorrect results (1 + 1 = 2 or 1 + 1 = 3), the expected number remains in their working memory.

3.2.7. *The perception and expression of emotions*

Infants discriminate between smiles, as well as pouting and surprises. Their cries of hunger, anger and pain are different (they are therefore to be differentiated by the attachment figure). The melody of the infants' cries presents similarities with the mother tongue (due to the fetal impregnation of the language).

3.2.8. *The perception of the social world and social cognition*

Newborns perceive agency (understanding that people act with a goal directed toward an object and interact with others or the object) and perceive this difference with inanimate objects.

Infants are referred to as having a "fundamental visual bias", which indicates the newborn's preference for human faces without prior learning: nine minutes after birth, a newborn spends more time looking at a paddle with a human face drawn on it than at a paddle that is blank, or one where the facial features are distorted (e.g. the mouth over the nose). Similarly, 5-day-old subjects look longer at human faces than at other stimuli (Streri 2018).

A neural network would therefore take charge of the geometric "mouth/nose/eyes" shape: a face photographed from the front attracts more attention than a face photographed in profile, with eyes open rather than closed.

Recognition of the mother's face appears at between 12 and 78 hours, depending on the time spent with her, and this at a time when the infant is sleeping most of the time. However, voice is also important: only mothers who speak to their child are recognized, because the voice is already perceived *in utero*.

However, in fact, this interaction between gaze and language also works with people unknown to infants: they only recognize people who speak to them.

From the first days of life, it is therefore the eyes that attract children to a face. Following the movements of the gaze testifies to the development of a skill coming from a phylogenetic inheritance across three hierarchical levels: the intention detector, the gaze direction detector (between 9 and 18 months) and the theory of mind (concept explained later in the book).

3.2.8.1. *The perception of ethnicities*

It is well known that members of an ethnic group differentiate better between members of their own group than between members of other ethnic groups.

At birth, infants do not differentiate; at three months, they differentiate between members of their own ethnicity but not members of another ethnicity; at 10 months, they also differentiate between members of other ethnicities. Chinese children stare much more into the eyes of Chinese than Caucasian adults. Next, performance depends on the experiences (confrontations or otherwise with strangers).

3.2.9. *Imitation*

It was by chance that Zazzo discovered that his 25-day-old son was imitating sticking his tongue out. However, according to Piaget or Wallon, imitation should not have been possible before the age of two. They then interpreted this as contagion or echolalia, because imitation assumes representation, which they believed impossible in a newborn.

Regardless of their status, facial, gestural and oral imitations are common in newborns (Streri 2018).

3.2.10. *The moral sense*

At six months, the child chooses a "nice" figure in a "comic book"-type scenario (helping or not helping someone climb a hill), but at 10 months, he chooses the "bad guy" (Streri 2018). At maybe 10 months, he chooses "the strongest".

4

What's New in Cognition?

4.1. The child's brain

"The child is not a miniature adult…" (Jean-Jacques Rousseau)

As Rousseau intuited, "children are not just little adults": the developing brain is not only quantitatively different from adults, but also qualitatively different.

Three types of relationship between cognitive and neural development have been analyzed:

– mature models, when children and adults rely on similar neural mechanisms or call on the same regions of the brain for a particular task;

– in contrast, immature patterns identified in adult neural substrates, when children and adults differ in amplitude, temporal configuration, localization or extent of activity;

– a third, rarely studied structure is "child-unique" neural activity, in which children may exhibit patterns of neural functioning during periods of early learning that do not exist in adults.

4.2. The question of universality

According to Piaget, the sequence of cognitive development during childhood and adolescence is universal, in other words, the same for all individuals, regardless of the social, cultural, economic and other aspects of their lives.

However, comparisons of children living in different countries, in different social conditions within a country, or even in the same institution, show differences in the developmental stages.

For some authors, it is only the rate of acquisition that may be different in certain environments; according to others, cognitive content and structure may be different.

4.3. The theory of mind

This concept, which was first discovered in chimpanzees, refers to the ability to attribute mental states (intentions, perceptions, knowledge, beliefs) to others and to ourselves, and to understand that everyone may be different.

Developmental psychologists have therefore sought to identify when children acquire this skill. It is, in fact, a developmental sequence: as children age, they understand, in the following order, perceptions, intentions, knowledge, false beliefs and finally the hidden emotions of others.

For example, in the false belief tasks, the child is asked what someone thinks about the location of an object when it has been moved without this subject being able to see it. Three-year-olds often incorrectly respond that someone will look for it where the object arrived, whereas four-year-olds will more often respond that someone will look for it where the object was before the move.

This progression could be related to the development of other cognitive abilities, such as language, or to certain executive function abilities, such as inhibitory control, attention, working memory and planning.

There is also a phylogenetic aspect to this skill: chimpanzees understand the visual perceptions of others better than their knowledge, but do not seem to understand the false beliefs of others.

Traditionally, it was thought that understanding the intentions of others would not be possible until around 18 months. However, estimates of the onset ages of these skills may depend on the techniques employed: with implicit tasks; it has been observed that children can understand a false belief earlier than previously found.

In order to better understand the ontogeny and phylogeny of the theory of mind, we need to uncover environmental factors (such as competitive or cooperative contexts) that may have previously functioned as selective pressures by providing adaptive advantages to individuals with better theory of mind abilities.

It is so vital and adaptive for children to understand the intentions and thoughts of others close to them that we might wonder if this skill, like language, would be under genetic programming. It is this module that would be deteriorated in autistic children.

4.4. Metacognition

"I know that I know nothing..." (Socrates)

Metacognition, or the ability to monitor our own mental states and processes (memory, attention, errors and so on), is a cognitive function of the prefrontal areas that allows for flexible and adaptive behavior. It is a good predictor of cognitive development and, in particular, of academic performance.

Different aspects of metacognitive monitoring develop at different ages. A distinction is made between implicit metacognition – measured by its effect on behavior, potentially present from infancy – and explicit metacognition, which is measured by the accuracy of explicit verbal judgments, emerging in the preschool years.

For example, three- and four-year-olds are able to recognize that they do not have information by choosing not to inform a third party; the ability to realize that we do not know something and report it explicitly, or meta-ignorance, emerges after about five years.

4.5. Mirror neurons

Mirror neurons, which were discovered by the Italian neurologist Giacomo Rizzolatti in monkeys, are activated, not when we perform a behavior, but when we observe others performing that behavior.

When you take the fingers of a 15-month-old baby and bring them to the adult's mouth, the baby opens its mouth. When someone experiences pain or disgust, the same mirror neurons are activated in the observer and the observed.

Mirror neurons in monkeys appeared 80,000 years ago but are much more developed in humans, thus greatly increasing imitation abilities.

They exist from birth but in limited numbers, and their number will develop through learning: a baby who does not yet walk does not activate mirror neurons when observing a child walking. It is only when he/she can walk himself/herself that these mirror neurons will develop. This has also been observed in adults in relation to dancing.

Mirror neurons are therefore dependent on socialization, on the observation of others; everything that in the current societal evolution (isolation in the virtual world of children, transfer of "real life" to screens) deprives interactions with others will prevent the development of mirror neurons.

4.6. Embodied cognition

This new approach, which can be positioned in the filiation of the Wallonian school, considers that cognition is at all times influenced by the morphology of our body and by its sensorimotor systems. Cognition is no longer differentiated from perception and action.

In traditional cognitive approaches, the brain processes information from sensory information, transformed into representations, and then sends messages to the body effectors; with embodied cognition, the sensorimotor system is part of the cognition. Thus, to describe a lemon, we traditionally speak of its matter or its shape; with embodied cognition, the concept of lemon corresponds to all the associated sensations, such as its bitterness, when we reactivate the concept.

This new theoretical approach may also have important implications for child education if we are to include sensorimotor processes, action, emotion and interoception in order to accurately describe how children process information (e.g. the role of hand movements in learning to solve different types of mathematical or reading tasks).

Unlike Piaget, who thought that the child's thinking started from the concrete and became abstract, this embodiment approach shows that the concrete always remains present throughout development and that this could help overcome the difficulties that many subjects have with abstraction.

4.7. The issue of programming, "starter kits", neuroplasticity and the need for an integrative approach

We know since Chomsky that the human child does not "learn" to speak, he/she "learns" to speak French or Chinese depending on the language bath in which he/she is immersed, but the brain's capacity to produce language is innate, programmed. The child's brain "waits" for visual stimuli, language and social relations from birth. What does the adolescent brain "wait for"? Two things essentially: social and sexual relationships and the quest for identity.

The neuroplasticity of the brains of children and adolescents requires an integrative approach, including, for example, developmental and clinical psychology, medicine, educational sciences, neuroscience, sociology, biology and anthropology.

It is about creating a "developmental science", a transdisciplinary developmental psychology, and rewriting the old story of nature and nurture, as epigenetics has revolutionized the way we understand the interactions between genetics and environment.

Bottom-up connections of the senses are myelinated before top-down connections, which is consistent with behavioral observations: infants' perceptual abilities exceed their ability to perform voluntary actions.

The application of brain imaging technology has changed our understanding of cognitive development through many new observations about information processing in the brain. For example, brain areas that were known from adult neurology and neuropsychology to be associated with functions such as language, facial recognition, arithmetic skills and mentalization appear to be associated with these functions already in childhood.

Thus, the future of cognitive functions is already "mapped out", even though these functions do not yet exist. The child's brain prefigures the adult brain. Finally, children's brains may still be adult brains in miniature form!

Moreover, development is not linear, there are sensitive periods, and younger children can sometimes "outperform" older children, such as in the acquisition of phonology distinct from the mother tongue.

The study of developmental disorders also provides important insights by analyzing a missing cognitive precondition in the causal chain, as in the case of autism and dyslexia.

In autism, the failure of automatic mentalization, the difficulty in understanding false beliefs and in understanding deception, has been used to explain the characteristic difficulties in reciprocal social interaction and communication.

In dyslexia, the phonological processing deficit hypothesis has provided an explanation for the difficulty in acquiring a phoneme–grapheme code and the expected difficulties in speech processing tasks.

One of the most encouraging findings when monitoring the behavior of children with neurodevelopmental disorders is that behavior improves with "compensatory" learning, even without targeted intervention or teaching.

4.7.1. *Starter kits*

The starter kits that developed with evolution are now the source of our cognitive abilities: some stimuli that were once crucial for survival have acquired and now maintain the ability to trigger actions in the organism. A good example of an unlearned predisposition is the ability to detect animosity, using only self-propulsion as a cue, which has been demonstrated in newborn chicks as well as in newborn humans.

The starter kits for social abilities, such as sensing, affiliation, mentalizing, empathy and group loyalty, appear to be independent of abstract reasoning abilities. Asperger's autism and psychopathy tell us that one or more of the basic social predispositions may be absent without general intellectual abilities being impaired.

4.8. Vygotsky and the zone of proximal development model

REMINDER.– *The zone of proximal development concept, proposed by Vygotsky, refers to the gap between what the child is capable of doing on his/her own and what he/she is capable of doing with adult supervision.*

According to Vygotsky (1980), developmental changes are generated by learning located in this zone of proximal development. The educational interventions of adults evolve with the child and, as the child's capacity for internalization increases, they play an increasingly important role in determining behavior.

Therefore, we need to understand the nature and specificity of the tutor's interventions that enable the child to progress in solving a problem.

Two situations are distinguished: a region of sensitivity to instruction, in which the most effective tutors solicit performance just above that already mastered by the child, and a use of the contingent change rule (the most effective tutors adjust their interventions to the type of performance of the child, providing more help after a failure and less help after a success).

Mothers provide more direct and explicit information at the beginning of the child's second year of life and less explicit, less concrete and more verbal information at the end of the second year. In addition, by the second year of life, mothers solicit autonomous functioning by encouraging the child to function one step above their current capabilities, while providing assistance if the child fails.

Fathers are even more likely than mothers to want their children to independently function by the second year.

These interventions, which are intended to give the child an opportunity to note or correct their own mistakes, may be ineffective when they increase the child's estimation of the difficulty of the task and decrease their enthusiasm for accomplishing it. Another hypothesis would be that effective support does not consist of developing assistance strategies that are inversely proportional to the child's level of performance, but rather in maintaining a high level of intervention even after several successive failures, thus giving the child an additional chance to solve the problem independently and to attribute the success to himself/herself.

4.9. Contributions from the mother and father

It has long been known that favorable environmental experiences, particularly those rooted in early relationships, have a positive impact on a child's cognitive development. However, while this influence is well known for the mother, less is known about the association between father–child interactions and the development of cognitive abilities in children.

Although mothers continue to spend more time with their children, paternal involvement in caregiving has increased, particularly among the middle classes. As a result, we can study not only the amount of time fathers spend with their children, but also the quality of their interactions. Indeed, while parents have similarities in their interaction styles, father–child interactions have a distinct quality: more vigorous and challenging than mother–child relationships.

Thus, a positive association has been reported between paternal involvement in caregiving tasks (from the first month of infancy) and cognitive development from the first years of life: supportive, responsive and stimulating paternal behaviors during infancy are positively associated with cognitive development after controlling for various demographic and socioeconomic factors.

As a result, children whose fathers exhibited more withdrawn or depressive behaviors during father–child interactions at three months had lower IQ scores at 24 months. At 24 months, children whose fathers were less authoritative in their interactions had higher scores. These observations are independent of maternal sensitivity effects.

Research on parenting behavior has generally focused on three main aspects, sensitivity, structuring and intrusion, as indicators of similarities and differences between mothers and fathers. Some research has found no differences between them, while other studies have shown significant differences such as less sensitivity, less structuring and more intrusion in mothers.

Fathers tend to spend more time with their children in play activities than mothers; in fact, play is a typical orientation for fathers, meaning that they tend to spend more time playing with their children than any other activity.

Mothers are generally more responsible for caregiving and routine activities, thus forming more "vertical" interactions; they tend to structure, guide, teach and engage in empathetic conversations when interacting with their child. Fathers spend more time on play, creating more "horizontal" interactions.

Winnicott (2005) suggested that play and creativity occur in a "transitional space", linking the inner and outer worlds. Play leads to a state of mind in which the individual can flexibly think and allow creative thoughts to emerge. Play is the interaction most typically characterized by a reciprocal nature, and is based on the principle that children and parents can cooperate with each other and seek common goals. Thus, fathers, more than mothers, encourage their children to take the initiative in unfamiliar situations, to explore, to take risks and to overcome obstacles.

Fathers therefore create a more horizontal interaction when playing with their children, which is often referred to as homologous interaction (as evidenced by their more physical behavior, their play behavior is similar to that of the children); they continue the parental role, but with the authority of a stronger play partner, such as when they challenge their children during play. For a father, a successful play interaction occurs when he can maintain the balance between challenging his child and letting them "win".

4.10. Intelligence, its definition and measurements

For a very long time, philosophers and scientists have been dealing with the nature of human intelligence, resulting in multiple definitions of intelligence.

A scientific consensus currently exists (Pereira Da Costa 2019) to define intelligence around hierarchical models such as Cattell's model, which is based on factor analyses, identifying factors that contribute to the success of a cognitive task in three strata: the first corresponds to numerous factors that are fairly specific to a task or situation, the second to broader factors common to a type of task and the third to a factor labeled "general intelligence".

The analysis of individual differences in intelligence has become a central preoccupation in many fields, including cognitive neuroscience and developmental psychology, since intelligence plays an important role in academic and then professional success.

A classic measure of intelligence is the variance shared across multiple cognitive tasks, such as: fluid reasoning, executive function, processing speed, working and short-term memory and spatial reasoning.

The relative ranking of individuals on this measure remains remarkably stable over the life course, but the absolute differences increase during development between children and then adolescents.

The unitary notion of intelligence that developed at the beginning of the 20th century, around the general intelligence factor concept (Spearman's G factor) led to the calculation of a unique score that enabled the characterization of the level of intellectual efficiencies of the adult and the child, whether by measuring mental age on the Binet–Simon scale (the child's performance is evaluated in relation to children of a given age) or by measuring their IQ using the WISC (Wechsler Intelligence Scale for Children, where the child is compared to children of his or her own age).

The Wechsler scales remain the most widely used tools: the WPPSI (Wechsler Preschool and Primary Scale of Intelligence) for children under 7 years of age, the WISC, for children between 7 and 16 years of age, and the adult version, called the WAIS (Wechsler Adult Intelligence Scale), where raw scores are transformed to be interpreted on a statistical scale that has a mean of 100 and a standard deviation of 15.

Having an IQ of 100 means that our performance is identical to the average performance of other subjects of the same age; to be significantly different, the result must differ by 15 points (the standard deviation) above or below this value. Above 130, or two standard deviations above the mean (2.2% of the population), we speak of high potential.

Recently, the fifth version of the Wechsler scales for children and adolescents, the WISC, has become available. The evolution of the test has led to the differentiation of the measures according to the main categories of cognitive processes. The first versions comprised two categories, measuring verbal and performance (or non-verbal) IQ, whereas there are now five main categories: verbal comprehension, visuospatial, fluid reasoning, working memory and processing speed. We are therefore moving towards the notion of profiles and not a single score.

4.10.1. *The cerebral locations of intelligence*

Classical localist theories that analyze lesions or plasticities of cognitive function have defined the dorsolateral prefrontal cortex, the anterior cingulate cortex, the parietal lobe and the medial temporal cortex as the "locations" of intelligence.

However, recent developments in neuroscience emphasize the role of interactions between brain regions: the brain is described as a network of brain region nodes, which are linked by edges that exhibit white matter connections or statistical associations between brain signals. A consistent finding is that networks with shorter connections between any pair of nodes in the network are associated with higher scores on assessments of general intelligence in children and adults.

White matter maturation is thus an important aspect of postnatal brain development, with a prolonged trajectory extending up to the third decade of life, and is associated with individual differences. For example, in a comparison of typically and atypically developing children white matter connectome efficiency was strongly associated with intelligence and educational attainment. In addition, intelligence partially mediated the relationship between connectome efficiency and educational attainment. These results underline the importance of the properties of distributed brain networks in cognitive and educational ability in children.

4.10.2. *Intelligence and mortality*

High IQ children have lower mortality rates in adulthood. One possible explanation for these associations is mediation through adult health behaviors, which explains why child IQ scores are higher and linked to lower rates of smoking, higher levels of physical activity and increased consumption of fruits and vegetables.

Although high child IQ has generally been associated with health-promoting behaviors, it has also been associated with alcohol dependence, more frequent drinking and binge drinking in adulthood.

Since IQ is closely associated with socioeconomic disadvantage, illicit drug use and mental health problems, these factors may be important contributors or mediators of the IQ–use relationship.

The 1958 National Child Development Study followed a large cohort of births with assessments of child IQ, illicit drug use and a range of other risk factors to investigate potential confounding factors or mediators in the relationship between drug use and IQ.

The participants were 6,713 members of this study, whose IQ was assessed at age 11 and whose lifetime illegal drug use was measured at age 42. An increase in IQ of 1 standard deviation (15 points) was associated with an increased risk of illegal drug use in women: cannabis use, cocaine, amphetamines, amyl nitrate and hallucinogenic mushrooms. These relationships were less strong in men.

4.11. The question of the "drop in level" of French children

This question is a "chestnut" (frequent topic for newspapers) in the media: periodically, we are alarmed that "the level is falling". One source of valid data is provided by the French DEPP surveys (*Direction de l'Évaluation, de la Prospective et de la Performance du ministère de l'Éducation nationale*); these surveys (2016, 2019) focused on the reading, spelling and arithmetic levels of students aged 10–11 for the years 1987, 1999, 2007 and 2017.

In calculation, the average score evolved as follows:

- 1987: 250 points;
- 1999: 210 points;
- 2007: 202 points;
- 2017: 176 points.

In spelling, skills measured through dictation also declined:

- 1987: 10.6 errors on average;
- 2007: 14.3;
- 2015: 17.8.

These cuts affect all social classes, so they are democratic…

	1987	2017
Children of executives and higher intellectual professions	278 pts	206 pts
Children of the middle class	263 pts	188 pts
Children of the working class	238 pts	166 pts

Table 4.1. *Historical trends in average reading scores*

Today, 80% of young people attain the baccalaureate, but probably not at the same level as their parents or grandparents. When 27% of the French population attained "Bac plus 2" in 2000 and 44% in 2016, we suspect that it was not because they became twice as intelligent in such a short time.

We will see later in the book that the question of time spent in front of screens (from the calculator that no longer allows us to calculate, to the influences of television, tablets, smartphones, video games and so on) is perhaps not unrelated to this evolution. Without going as far as Alain Finkielkraut's declinism, developmental psychology researchers must not bury their heads in the sand in the face of these statistical developments. Indeed, this drop in level occurs at the moment of maximum plasticity of the human brain, between 0 and 10 years of age, and learning becomes less efficient later in life.

The first generations for whom the DEPP measured this drop in the level of calculation, reading and spelling will be 40 years old by 2030, in a world that will undoubtedly be very complex, but if it becomes a world of images and machines, will these "traditional" skills still be useful (Todd 2020)?

Finally, it should be noted that these declines in "traditional" school skills are observed in all European countries, in the north as well as in the south of the continent (but that overall, in international comparisons with other countries on other continents, French children are generally poorly ranked).

4.12. Children with high potential ("giftedness")

Giftedness, defined as a high IQ (above 130), is an adaptive advantage for problem solving and an ingredient for educational and professional success, but it can also be a burden, leading to difficulties in the emotional, behavioral and social domains, difficulties that may begin as early as kindergarten.

A number of child characteristics are associated with, or predictive of, giftedness, according to Vaivre-Douret (2019): a higher percentage of boys, right-handedness, a high frequency of elders, a higher sociocultural family environment, an average body weight that is very much higher than average and advanced psychomotor development (including acquisition of walking that is one month ahead of average, language learning that is 3.5 months ahead of average and early learning to read).

Neurobiologically, we can therefore hypothesize a neuromotor precocity of myelination maturation, and consequently a faster and earlier signal propagation rate, related to the insulation thickness due to the early onset of myelination (Vaivre-Douret 2019). In addition, these children have reduced energy expenditure with lower glucose consumption; faster conduction will save energy and may result in greater connectivity in a minimum of time and at a lower cost. This is also useful for encoding, especially for memory. This may explain why these children are not easily fatigued.

Two new intelligence theories have addressed the description of high potential and are the foundation of educational programs dedicated to high potential children, with the objective of facilitating their school career and reducing the number of students who are below their potential, or even in a situation of dropping out of school and who Renzulli (2003) calls underachievers:

– Sternberg's Triarchic Theory (1985) describes three forms of intelligence: analytical, practical and creative;

– Gardner's Theory of Multiple Intelligences (1983) describes seven forms of intelligence: language, visuospatial, logical–mathematical, kinesthetic, interpersonal, intrapersonal and musical.

Several high potential development models have aimed to reduce the phenomena of under-achievement observed in certain individuals. Renzulli's model (2003) is particularly interesting from this perspective. This model, known as the "three rings" model, brings into play cognitive abilities, creativity and involvement in the activity, which includes non-cognitive factors such as motivation, self-confidence and self-demand. By combining these three dimensions, which he considers complementary in the description of high potential, he broadens the identification beyond a simple intellectual performance and makes us question the reductive approaches we might be satisfied with (Pereira Da Costa 2019).

Analyses by the CNAHP (*Centre National d'Aide aux enfants et adolescents à Haut Potentiel*) show that they may paradoxically present proven academic (including academic failure: 7.5%) and socioemotional problems related to their high intellectual potential, including, in particular, anxiety disorders associated with high verbal potential (Tordjman and Kermarrec 2019).

Indeed, giftedness has often been associated with a variety of negative emotional states in children and adults, including symptoms of depression and anxiety, attention difficulties and a range of relationship difficulties.

These findings are frequently interpreted in light of Dąbrowski's (1972) theory, which links high intelligence to overexcitability; giftedness can also lead to a sense of being different and thus to problems of emotional and social adjustment.

Nevertheless, the results of works, particularly on anxiety, are not consistent and this may reflect the existence of confounding factors:

– The variability of definitions of giftedness: although the most common definition is based on a high IQ score, many authors include creativity, academic achievement, leadership or any combination of these in their definition. Those who base it on IQ have chosen several thresholds (120, 125, 130, 145 or even 160), although the most common choice remains 130. Sometimes, the definition of giftedness used by the authors is not even made explicit in the article.

– Sampling bias: some work relies on teacher screening, a method that biases the sample towards stereotypes shared by teachers. Other work has been conducted by clinical psychologists or even in psychiatric wards, resulting in an increased rate of observed psychiatric disorders. Some have used special education school samples for both gifted and overachievers, in which case gifted underachievers are likely underrepresented.

What does the EDEN Study say? Behavioral, emotional and social problems have been measured using questionnaires distributed to parents; IQ scores were based on the WPPSI-III at 5–6 years of age.

No significant differences in behavioral, emotional and social problems were observed between gifted children and children with normal IQs ($\geq$ 70 and $\leq$ 130). The conclusion of the EDEN study is that during the pre-school period, gifted children do not appear to exhibit any more behavioral, emotional or social problems than children with normal IQs.

Finally, the situation of high potential children who present academic or emotional difficulties can be improved if adequate therapeutic responses are provided, such as discreet identification in the school environment or by pediatricians without, however, labeling the child as gifted very early on. Indeed, the announcement of an early diagnosis of high potential can also have perverse effects, which may lead to behavioral problems in view of the stressful expectations of the environment, or the child can have an over-inflated image of omnipotence (Vaivre-Douret 2019).

4.13. Learning disabilities, the "dys" disorders

Specific learning disabilities are part of neurodevelopmental disorders and are thought to affect 5–15% of school-aged children according to the DSM-5, the Diagnostic and Statistical Manual of Mental Disorders (5th edition), which was published in 2013 in the United States.

These specific disorders are part of the "dys" category – dyslexia, dysorthographia, dysphasia and dyspraxia – and may also be associated with another neurodevelopmental disorder, ADHD, an attention deficit disorder with or without hyperactivity.

These disorders impact the acquisition, organization, retention, comprehension or processing of verbal and non-verbal information, and interfere with basic academic learning, including: reading, writing and arithmetic.

For the diagnosis, it is obviously necessary to exclude a mental disorder, one or more sensory disorders (hearing, vision), a proven neurological disorder or a lack of education.

The consequences of the "dys" disorders can be harmful for the child, leading to academic failure, disengagement, dropping out of school, failure complex, lack of motivation, escapist behavior, blocks, anxiety, feelings of guilt, reacting aggressiveness and depression. We understand the importance of treating these disorders early.

4.14. Creativity

In our society, until very recently, skills put forward were mainly related to technical competencies, in other words, "hard skills". However, our ever-changing society requires the development of other skills that are increasingly sought-after in people's profiles, called "soft skills".

These cross-cutting skills are useful in different domains because they allow for greater adaptability of individuals, so it is important for children to learn to master a set of cognitive, social and emotional skills in which communication, cooperation, critical thinking and creativity play a very important part, whether in the academic environment or, later, in the professional field.

Creativity corresponds to the capacity to produce new and adapted content in its context. It is not always easy to distinguish conceptually between the notions of creativity and intelligence, although in reality and in the way these concepts are handled, it is quite possible to dissociate them.

Correlations between measures of creativity and measures of intelligence such as IQ are often weak, around 0.17. The same is true for academic achievement: creativity and divergent thinking are poorly correlated with academic performance (0.22). We have seen that this has led Renzulli (2003), in his three-ring model, to distinguish between high intellectual potential and high creative potential.

Indeed, creativity includes several components: cognition (mental flexibility, knowledge), conation (risk taking, motivation), emotion and the subject's environment.

The pedagogy that children are exposed to in elementary school has an effect on the development of their creative potential (Lubart 2006). Predictably, children educated in Montessori and Freinet schools perform better in divergent and convergent thinking tests in the graphic and verbal domains.

Since 2015, the OECD has been conducting research in 10 countries, in which the creative potential of children is assessed at the start and end of the year. Between these two measurements, creativity actions either are or are not implemented in order to verify if it is possible to develop creativity in children through specific educational practices.

4.15. Moral development

Historically, the psychology of moral development in children has been dominated by the cognitivist perspective, explaining moral development through theories of cognitive development:

1) Piaget's theory (1928), often considered the first cognitive-developmental theory of moral development, describes four stages of logical reasoning and two stages of moral development: heteronomy and autonomy; children in the heteronomous stage feel obliged to follow external rules set by adults and, when they reach the autonomous stage, understand that rules deserve respect and are based on mutual consent. By age six or seven, opportunities for peer cooperation facilitate the development of mutual respect and the child moves away from egocentric thinking.

2) Kohlberg (1973) extended Piaget's theory beyond childhood to adolescence and adulthood and argued that, since moral reasoning is clearly reasoning, advanced moral reasoning depends on advanced logical reasoning. This author proposes six stages of moral judgment, grouped into three levels, preconventional, conventional and postconventional:

– the preconventional level is characterized by egocentrism, in other words, the child is only concerned with their own interests; rules do not apply and the child only perceives them through punishment and reward (Stage 1: obedience and punishment. The child adapts their behavior to avoid punishment. Moral standards are not integrated. Stage 2: self-interest. The child integrates rewards in addition to punishment);

– the conventional level sees otherness take on importance; the child learns to satisfy expectations and obey laws and general rules (Stage 3: interpersonal relations and conformity. The child integrates the rules of the restricted group to which they belong. The child's main question is: what will people think of me? Stage 4:

authority and maintenance of social order. The child integrates social norms and respects laws even if not in his/her interest and knows how to escape punishment);

– the postconventional level begins with adolescence, early adulthood, or is not reached by some. The individual bases their moral judgment on rational criteria and attributes value to democratically accepted law, generally considers that respect for the law is necessary, but may recognize conflicts between laws and values. They understand that there may be conflicts between respect for the law and the needs of the individual. They are willing to break a law if they think it is wrong, or are, conversely, willing to morally condemn certain activities and then refrain from them, even though the law allows them (Stage 5: social contract. At this stage, the individual thinks that the law should be respected, but that some conflicts exist between the law and the individual. Stage 6: universal ethical principles. Moral judgment is based on the moral values of universal scope and is adopted personally by the subject following ethical reflection, including equal rights, courage, honesty, respect for consent and non-violence). These moral values of the subject take precedence over respect for the law. Thus, the person is ready to defend a minority moral judgment and is capable of judging an illicit action as good or, on the contrary, of judging a lawful action as bad. According to Kohlberg, only 13% of the adult population would reach stage 6.

Like Piaget, Kohlberg emphasized the importance of role taking (taking the perspective of others) in moral development and proposed that the child's social environment provides opportunities for role taking and that participation in this promotes moral development. This author saw these six stages as sequential, one at a time. Progression to the next stage occurs when cognitive imbalance is created, or when a person's perspective is not sufficient to deal with a moral dilemma. This imbalance causes a person to reflect on the inadequacies of their reasoning and to seek more adequate reasons. Kohlberg's theory has been the subject of notable criticism; some have pointed out that his theory is masculine in perspective and there is strong reason to doubt that the higher stages of moral development are culturally universal.

By focusing on the development of logical reasoning, early moral development theorists therefore assume that moral decisions are reason-driven, in the cognitive domain. However, other authors have proposed that moral decisions are based on emotionally driven intuitions and that moral reasoning is constructed after the decision is made to explain a decision that was made intuitively.

This, of course, evokes Damasio's Somatic Marker Hypothesis (1994). This hypothesis is based on the role of emotions in decision-making and proposed that when we think of a bad outcome related to a given response option that comes to mind, we experience an unpleasant internal feeling, which is a "somatic marker".

This then forces our attention onto the negative outcome and can lead to the rejection of that option. Somatic markers can be stored in memory as affect-event links, which facilitate future decision-making because they can guide it by anticipating future events, even when they are not consciously recognized.

Finally, the domain theory, referred to as social-cognitive domain theory or moral domain theory, views morality as one element among many in children's growing social knowledge (Turiel 2015). This theory draws on the important distinction between the various domains: personal, moral and social. It is proposed that these follow different developmental trajectories, with knowledge being constructed through reciprocal social interactions. The majority of research based on domain theory has focused on whether children of different ages can distinguish between moral and social conventional acts.

4.16. Language

Up to eight months of age, a baby has a universal ability to discriminate the sounds of all the world's languages; then, from eight months, they lose this ability and can only focus on their native language. As with many aspects of development, this learning is therefore "unlearning", or "learning by loss". The child renounces the universal to concentrate on the specific prosody of his/her mother tongue.

Next comes the babbling, "pre-language" period, between 8 and 18 months, where the child practices reproducing syllables; then after 18 months, a verbal explosion, where the child learns more than 10 new words a day.

Even before the age of two, the child understands many more words (200) than they are able to produce: comprehension requires both hemispheres, production mainly the left hemisphere.

The field of language acquisition is transdisciplinary in nature since the theoretical foundations are located in developmental psychology, linguistics, pedagogy and in the interaction between these disciplines.

Verbal expression in early childhood is an established predictor of later language development in children and positively predicts their literacy[1] and academic performance; longitudinal studies, such as the EDEN cohort, effectively show that children who start school with stronger language skills continue to outperform their peers throughout their schooling. Conversely, early language deficits play a role in later maladjustment.

1 Ability to read, understand and use written information in daily life.

Social gradients in lexical development have been reported as early as 18 months, and gradients in child vocabulary according to socioeconomic status are well established by the time children start school, persisting throughout school years with differences in vocabulary – exacerbated by knowledge – becoming apparent as the child progresses through learning.

Socioeconomic level is actually a composite variable that is most often indexed to child development according to the mother's educational level, which is a distal factor in its influence on language development and is thought to affect expressive vocabulary in children through proximal processes, such as talking more with them and providing more varied vocal input.

In fact, in a "Bourdieusian" logic, the mother's educational level corresponds to various forms of capital, including (1) human capital, which can be thought of as skills, knowledge and abilities; (2) cultural capital, defined as preferences and behaviors relevant to academic success; (3) social capital, which is the set of maternal networks and resources that can be used to support academic effort and success.

Low maternal sociocultural levels are associated with many health-damaging behaviors that impair child development and may plausibly impact child language development through both direct and indirect pathways.

For example, pregnancy planning is correlated with maternal educational attainment and is an important predictor of maternal investment in the child; planned pregnancy is associated with improved nutrition and diet during pregnancy and being aware of not smoking during pregnancy; smoking is toxic to fetal development and has been associated with reduced school performance later in life. Similarly, high levels of alcohol consumption are associated with fetal alcohol syndrome and language impairment.

In addition, the level of maternal education is correlated with higher occupational status and higher income, which may enhance child language development by providing access to resources. Family income is an early source of inequality in cognitive performance in children, with income having the greatest impact on early childhood up to age four.

Mothers with higher levels of education also tend to be older when they give birth and are more likely to practice the types of language associated with improved language in early childhood.

Finally, better educated mothers are more likely to have stable, long-term relationships. Having a partner in the home predicts better cognitive outcomes in young children and may influence language development through educational capital, better access to financial resources and quality of father–child interactions.

Early social experiences are thus an important source of language acquisition. A social feature of interaction that has been implicated in child language development is parental sensitivity. In particular, it has been shown that parental sensitivity, or responsiveness, promotes communication skills in children from the first year of life. For example, when mothers were instructed to respond to their child's babbling, the phonological structure of infants' babbling reflected the mothers' input (Bornstein 2020).

Numerous studies have documented the relatively short-term positive effects of parental sensitivity on language acquisition in children, including in the second and third years of life (Bornstein 2020).

Attachment may mediate this relationship between maternal sensitivity and child language: children who are confident that the world around them and those who care for them are reliably responding are more likely to regularly engage in intentional communication, knowing that their intentions are likely to be heard and acted upon (Bornstein 2020).

A three-wave longitudinal study of 50 mother–infant dyads (Bornstein 2020) showed that maternal sensitivity and language at five months each uniquely predicted child language at 49 months, controlling for maternal age, education and verbal IQ, as well as the presence of maternal support at 49 months.

4.16.1. *Bilingualism*

The robust relationship between a mother's educational level and her child's language, presented above, is not always observed in bilingual immigrant children. One factor in this exception may be the language with which mothers complete their highest level of school education. For example, in the United States, the mother's English schooling is correlated with the child's English vocabulary level, but not with their Spanish level; conversely, the mother's Spanish schooling is correlated with the child's Spanish vocabulary level, but not with their English level. Thus, the mother's education may benefit the child's language, or it may not, depending on whether or not it changes her language use when her schooling ends.

5

Attachment

The theme of love of the mother or father – and the difficulties linked to their uncertain presence or absence – haunts mythology, feeds literature and fills the offices of psychoanalysts. Let us briefly recall, from the point of view of our discipline, the three main stages of the psychology of attachment between the child and the parent.

5.1. The concept of attachment

In 1969, an English psychiatrist, John Bowlby, in a book entitled "Attachment and Loss", presented his theory of attachment, which is based on ethological work: the observation of the similarity of the reactions of rhesus macaques (Harlow's experiments) and human infants (Spitz's experiments) to the loss of the mother (sequence of reactions in three phases: protest, despair, detachment) and the long-term consequences of separation.

The other ethological dimension supporting attachment theory is the observation of attachment behaviors (behaviors aiming at obtaining or maintaining a certain proximity with the maternal organism or its substitute: screaming, crying, moving towards, embracing, smiling), which have a protective function. This protection is a function for the individual in question, as well as more generally, in a Darwinian perspective, for the survival of the species: it is necessary for the young to reach the age of reproduction.

These behaviors are obviously reminiscent of a concept from animal ethology, more precisely Lorenz's Imprinting Theory relating to birds, that is, the innate behavior of pursuit and recognition of the mother, or whatever takes its place. However, the difference lies in the fact that, while imprinting works immediately, attachment is constructed.

From these observations, the conclusion is that attachment is a primary, innate need, not based on feeding or sexuality, as Freud thought. For example, Harlow's rhesus macaques prefer the touch of a soft cloth to food. Children die in orphanages even though they are properly fed and cared for.

Attachment is innate. The parent's behavior will determine the type of attachment that is formed, but not the existence of attachment *per se*; all children become attached, even to a parent who mistreats or does not love them. We could even go so far as to say that mistreatment increases attachment since, initially, it activates attachment behavior. The abused child seeks the love of the parent even more. But what will the child do with the feelings experienced in such a situation? This is the whole question, and we will return to it.

We should distinguish between two notions. On the one hand, attachment, the disposition to seek the proximity or contact of a certain individual, a durable disposition that does not depend on the situation and evolves only very slowly over time. On the other hand, the attachment behavior which covers all the various expressions and behavioral modalities that the individual implements from time to time, in order to obtain or maintain this desired proximity.

Attachment behaviors can follow one another in sequence: crying first when the mother is not nearby, followed by clinging. As development progresses, attachment behaviors become more diverse and complex (clinging, crying, following, talking, offering a bouquet to the wife, flattering the office manager), but they all fulfill the same function: protection. At first, we crawl towards the attachment figure, then we talk to them, but both behaviors have the same objective.

We have thus been able to distinguish the child's primary strategies, namely the manifestation of attachment behaviors. When the mother does not respond to these manifestations, the child implements secondary strategies: either amplify the signals in order to finally attract her attention, or give them up and focus attention on something else, for example, the environment. We will see later how these secondary strategies gradually turn into counterproductive defense mechanisms. Indeed, when faced with the absence of response from the attachment figure, the attachment is never completely deactivated, and we have to deal with negative emotions.

Diet or sexuality interfere with attachment behaviors, but they do not condition their existence or structure them. On this point, Bowlby's thinking departs from Freud's since, for the latter, when the mother's breast is absent, the child tries to maintain the "hallucinatory satisfaction of desire", by reactivating the memory traces of pleasure, by sucking his/her thumb, for example, which constructs the oral stage and impulses.

The concept of attachment is very close to the psychoanalytical concept of objectal relations, with the difference that the latter is built on fantasies, whereas attachment is built on real experiences. However, we will see that in adulthood, these two concepts come closer together.

This attachment behavior is gradually matched with exploration behavior. There is a pendulum movement between these two innate impulses, and only when the need for attachment is satisfied does the subject explore the inner and outer worlds, the self and relationships with others. Like the "base camp" that provides security for mountain climbers, we will evoke Bowlby's concept of a "secure base" or Winnicott's "good enough mother".

Attachment is "secure" when we are sufficiently confident in the availability of our attachment figure, but "insecure" when we are not sufficiently reassured about it. In general, the mother is "good enough" because of her particular state in the first months of the child's life, which Winnicott called the "primary maternal preoccupation" and which allows her to adapt to the infant's individual needs. A "good enough" maternal environment gives the baby a certain amount of experience of mighty power, of omnipotence, and it is this feeling that is paradoxically necessary for the child's acceptance of reality.

When the child has experienced trust, a "psychic space" is created between him/her and his/her mother, this space constituting the basis of socialization and, more generally, of everything that will constitute development, such as: emotion, language and cognition. Two systems of behavior act in complementarity. When the maternal organism becomes absent, the attachment system is activated and the child will seek to return to its "security base". When the maternal body is present, the exploration system is activated and the child will seek to explore. This pendulum movement has also been observed in rhesus macaques.

From the innate need for protection, attachment will progressively constitute the matrix of our emotional life and socialization. The attachment figure is not only a refuge but also a "springboard" for exploration and risk taking, if we consider the ratio between the percentage of time spent exploring and the relational configurations around a child between 18 and 24 months: 97% for child + mother, 86% for child + mother + unrelated carer, 61% for child + father, 45% for child + father + unrelated carer, 35% for child alone and 4% for child + unrelated carer. A similar phenomenon has been observed in relation to swimming babies: the baby's initiative in such a risky situation is linked to parental stimulation. To a certain extent, the parents play an early part in the game with limits.

This pendulum movement continues until the end of life, even though adult attachments are less dependent on physical proximity to the attachment figure and may use more symbolic means (such as letters, telephones and gifts). The dialectical interplay between the need for security and the need for stimulation is expressed from the cradle to the grave. Only the amplitude of the pendulum movement varies over the course of life: it seems to be particularly important, if not maximal, between the ages of 15 and 25. Therein lies the paradox of adolescence: if the pendulum theory is correct, then the maximal need for sensation, risk and novelty will result in a "pendulum swing", a great need for reassurance. However, it is precisely at this moment in life when we would need the reassuring gaze of others the most that this gaze becomes the most threatening, because we have become a "problem" and are no longer that docile and charming little thing that we were as a child.

As the child grows, they no longer need the actual physical presence of the attachment figure. They build "internal operating models" based on the behaviors of the attachment figures and the expectations of others' behaviors towards them. The term "operating" means that these models act on the child's perception of his/her environment and therefore on their behavior. These models are, in a way, prototypes, lenses or glasses through which the subject will then look at future interpersonal relationships.

At the beginning of life, these patterns are simple: the infant plans sequences of actions that restore homeostasis when he/she feels a need. At this stage, the mother can only be "Kleinian", in other words, good or bad. Then, progressively, these models become scripts, move to the level of representation and the subject anticipates sequences of events in order to try to predict the behavior of others. The subject is then less dependent on the environment, on its stimuli and more nuanced (they realize that it is the same person who is both "good" and "bad", depending on the moment).

Each of us has a "template" of attitudes and reactions that is "ready to be used". This is the concept of repetition, which is dear to psychoanalysts. If a subject changes partner, then he/she keeps the same type of relationship and the potential inconveniences that this brings to him/her change nothing. These models are sensitive to intergenerational reproductions and are translated on the level of personal identity, of our own self-image; a satisfactory functioning of the attachment will promote a positive self-image. What is at stake in the pendulum movement and the cybernetic game between the search for protection and exploration is also the construction of autonomy, a construction that is easier for individuals with secure attachment. Attachment does not create dependence but, on the contrary, autonomy.

5.2. The biological bases and correlates of attachment

We now know more about the biological mechanisms of internal operating models: physiologically, the perceptions of safety or threat influence the autonomic nervous system (ANS) with its sympathetic and parasympathetic branches. An infant's internal attachment pattern continues throughout life, as does the individual variability of the ANS, and thus adaptability to stress. Both influence physical and mental health later in life (Rodera 2020).

Various brain imaging studies of mother–infant interactions have identified hypothalamic–limbic–paralimbic–cortical circuits as the neurobiological basis of attachment.

In recent years, the study of neural synchronization has been greatly facilitated by advances in simultaneous multi-brain neuroimaging, known as hyper-scanning. A growing number of hyper-scanning studies have examined neural synchronization in adult dyads during imitation, free verbal conversation and cooperative or competitive interaction. Conversely, adult–child and more specifically parent–child neural synchronization has only recently become the focus of developmental research (Cui and Nguyen 2020). The results emphasize neural synchronization as a biomarker of the quality of the mother–infant interaction.

5.2.1. *Oxytocin*

Oxytocin is in fashion. It is even sold in spray form to improve sexuality.

It is the regulator, the modulator of our social behaviors: it is associated with childbirth, lactation, attachment and sexuality. A deficiency in the release of this hormone results in disorders in all of the areas mentioned above, both in humans and in animals.

It is, above all, the hormone of the link more than of the sex. Unfortunately, the consequences of this deficiency in the mother–baby relationship will only be observed much later in life. Autism, social phobias and domestic violence have been linked to this deficiency. There is, therefore, a growing interest in the therapeutic value of oxytocin administration in the early treatment of mental health disorders.

It also plays a role in prosocial behavior, altruism, empathy and cooperation, but studies on oxytocin in child populations are still rare and sample sizes are limited.

5.3. The mother's response to the need for attachment

In 1978, an English psychologist, Mary Ainsworth, translated Bowlby's theory into behavioral and developmental psychology. Her work began in 1954 in Uganda, where she observed children in situations of separation (work published in 1967 in the book "Infancy in Uganda"). Then, in 1963, she followed 23 children from their birth in Baltimore. She noted very few differences between the attachment behaviors of Ugandan babies and those of American babies.

In order to verify her observations, she created a standardized (at home and in the laboratory) experimental situation, the "strange situation" consisting of episodes of separations and reunions between mothers and their one-year-old children, a situation intended to activate attachment behaviors in the children by involving, at times, a person unknown to them. The differences between children in terms of their reactions during the reunion with their mother had already been noticed at the end of the London Blitz during World War II by Robertson, a collaborator of Bowlby.

The type of mother–child attachment is essentially constructed from the second six months of life. Before the age of six months, the child shows few differentiated reactions to its attachment figure or to other people. It is true that olfactory and auditory recognition of the mother appears earlier, from the first days, even before, based on studies of the embryo. However, at this period, the child does not show fear or distress in front of the stranger.

During the first six months of life, we observe a three phase progression: distinction between the animate and the inanimate, then between the familiar and the unfamiliar and finally the selective search for certain proximities. After six months, the child manifests his/her need for contact differently depending on the adult present.

Mary Ainsworth initially distinguished three types of attachment:

– "Secure" attachment (about 66% of children): the child protests at the moment of separation, is quickly consoled, expresses joy at the return of the mother and then returns to his or her activities, especially to explore. The attachment figure provides a secure base for exploration, with the attachment being more activated in the laboratory than at home or in the presence of an unknown person.

– "Insecure avoidant" attachment (about 22% of children): the child does not protest much at the beginning and does not react much to the return. We will see later why this type of child, whose behavior might seem the easiest, is said to be insecure. This indifference reflects the child's effort to deactivate their attachment behavior; the very high heart rate of these children during the strange situation effectively reveals the distress they are experiencing.

– Insecure ambivalent or resistant attachment (about 12% of children): the child protests but is not comforted, is not soothed upon return and clings to the mother while exhibiting angry reactions. The attachment figure cannot provide a secure base for exploration, resulting in contact seeking and resentment; these children cry the most.

The child's reactions to the mother's return are thus the criterion for defining the quality of an attachment. It is the reunion behaviors, rather than the separation behaviors, that reveal its quality. Ainsworth, who began her work in Uganda and finished it in Baltimore, assumed that the strange situation activates attachment behavior in the same way for all children across all cultures; however, certain subgroups of children may react, not because of their attachment style, but due to the fact that their attachment behavior has not been activated because the situation is not experienced as anxiety-provoking.

Mary Ainsworth's description of attachment types will be remembered as a major discovery in the 20th century developmental psychology. Hundreds of studies have since confirmed it. Some authors had objected that the strange situation measures, not the attachment, but the way in which the child manages their anxiety during the mother's absence, and that the mode of care would play a role in this behavior. However, various studies have shown that attachment distributions are similar in children raised full-time by their mothers and those in day care. Similarly, children do not react differently when they are in a situation that is normal for them, such as at home, or on the contrary, when they are stressed and exceptional, such as when they are hospitalized in an emergency department.

A residual 5% (up to 15% in some studies and clinical populations) of children are difficult to characterize because their behavior is very unstable: they seek contact with the mother and then immediately ignore her. Mary Main and Kaplan (1985) thus created a fourth category, "disorganized" or "disoriented" attachment (typical of abused children or children with developmental disabilities). Rather than being worried about the strange situation, the child appears to be worried about the parent.

The majority of abused children (up to 80% in some studies) are said to have this type of attachment where the parent's behavior conflicts with the need for protection. The child's strange and incoherent behaviors reveal the stress and anxiety generated by an insoluble paradox: the attachment figure is both the source of the anxiety and the only possible refuge from it.

Since this group is very heterogeneous, subgroups have gradually been identified: the "securely disorganized", the "avoidant disorganized" and the "ambivalent disorganized". Although confused and disorganized behavior was observed in all three sub-groups during the confrontation with the attachment figure, it was the degree of regulation of emotion that differentiated the three groups, with the "securely disorganized" managing to overcome their distress during the reunion, whereas the other two sub-groups did not.

Mary Ainsworth's other contribution is to have shown the link between the parent–child relationship during the first year of life and these four types of attachment. What strongly determines the type of attachment is the mother's sensitivity to the child's requests. It is not only the physical proximity between mother and child that is important, but also the psychological proximity: correctly perceiving the signals coming from the child and responding to them in an appropriate manner, having empathy and understanding the motivations underlying the child's behavior and their emotional experiences.

Crying is the first means by which the child attracts the attention of their attachment figure, and Ainsworth observed that the children whose demands are met most quickly during the first trimester of life are those for whom we observe the greatest decrease in their crying during the second trimester. This clearly shows the psychogenetic role of attachment.

This is in line with the Winnicottian notions of holding (physical support, the way the child is held) and handling (care, the way the child is handled), which refer to the real care given to the child, to parenthood, to a preverbal love. These functions are carried out correctly, regardless of the parent's knowledge or educational level. They simply need to understand what the baby wants. Occasionally, this adaptation between mother and child is so strong that it can continue up to an identification, or even be perceived as a threat by the mother, a fear of not finding her own self, a factor that can lead to the so-called baby blues.

5.3.1. *Mothers of "secure" children*

They react quickly to the child's requests. The main feature of this model is the child's confidence in the availability and type of response of their attachment figure in case of need, in other words, during negative or threatening experiences. The role of intimate and tender body contact between mother and child in the first months of life seems to be a central factor in this type of attachment.

When body contact is not "necessary", it is more generally the sensitivity of the mother (or substitute attachment figure), the "interactional synchrony" between requests and responses (e.g. for feeding) to the child's signals, when they are seeking protection or comfort, that will also induce this type of attachment. This is evidenced by the "still face" experiment. Mothers are asked to have a totally inexpressive face when interacting with the child after a period of play. Very quickly, this causes distress. The child smiles, then adopts a more negative facial expression, cries, looks away, holds out his/her hands, sucks his/her thumb and so on, all behaviors that are intended to regain the adult's attention and/or relieve their own distress.

Very early on, the child understands the reciprocal nature of the social bond. This concept of sensitivity is very close to that of empathy and to the concept of insightfulness: the capacity to understand the motivations of the child's behavior and to do so quickly, as indicated by the cognitive meaning of the concept of insight (immediate, sudden understanding, without the need for learning).

Various studies have shown that this ability of the mother to "decentralize", to understand things "from the child's point of view", was predictive of secure attachment. However, the concept of maternal sensitivity as a behavioral antecedent of attachment cannot always be translated into observable interactions. It has been the subject of controversy, particularly when maternal reports have not matched observed behaviors. The more we push into "micro-semiology" and the more we multiply behavioral measures, then the weaker the relationship between maternal sensitivity and attachment quality becomes, whereas global measures of maternal sensitivity produce the strongest correlations.

It seems, however, that interactional synchrony is the antecedent of dyad functioning, the basis of attachment quality: synchronous dyads produce secure attachments, while asynchronous dyads produce insecure attachments. The attachment relationship is thus based above all on a question of tempo. Even if we remain in a musical metaphor, the construction of a secure bond can be likened to a tuning of the interactions between the child and the mother.

5.3.2. *Mothers of "insecure avoidant" children*

They react abruptly, but without affect, neither positive (affection) nor negative (anger). The main feature of this model is that the child has no confidence in the availability of their attachment figure because they expect, instead, to be rejected. From this rejection, the child will gradually build up expectations about their relationship with others and will try to live without the love and support of others. This pattern is induced by a parent who regularly rejects the child's requests. The child will "do without" an affective relationship with their attachment figure, the more the parent encourages them to do so.

Another characteristic of maternal behaviors leading to avoidant attachment is intrusion, the mother soliciting the child when the child is not available, then interrupting contact. The child is "pushed" at a very early age towards self-escape, to avoid the relationship as a defense mechanism, in order to deal with distress and anger and to avoid a serious disorganization of its functioning. In the case of intrusion, the child may choose to adopt a secondary strategy, namely, to develop the most superficial relationship possible, in order to keep the mother at a distance, an "all's well with you", so to speak.

This pattern of avoidant attachment is adaptive at first because it protects against frustration, but it will have harmful effects in the long run. When we avoid and block all contact and feeling, we also block positive contact and feeling. There is a risk of generalizing anxiety, distrust and resentment towards people other than the parents. As the child is "encouraged" by their parents to value the cognitive, academic success, sports performance and so on, to the detriment of their emotional life, these defensive idealizations can only be overcome later by working on themselves and distancing themselves from their parents.

Finally, the construction of this type of attachment is reminiscent of Winnicott's concept of the "false self": the child will substitute what they really feel for what they think the mother wants. The "false self" is a facade that some individuals construct to face the world, to protect the true self that has been traumatized and must not be found again.

5.3.3. *Mothers of "insecure ambivalent or resistant" children*

They react in a contrary manner: indifferent when they should, intrusive when they should not. The main feature of this model is that the child is not sure of the availability and the type of response of their attachment figure in case of need, negative or threatening experiences. Because of this uncertainty, they experience strong separation anxiety, tend to "cling" to others and feel anxious to explore their environment. This pattern is induced by a parent who is available and supportive at times, but not at others, or by a parent who uses threats of abandonment or guilt as a strategy to control the child. The child is constantly confronted with unpredictability and will "overreact" to defend against anxiety or settle into ambivalent positions.

We recall the baby macaque of the ethologist Harlow's experiments, who, by the intensity of his clutches, of his clings, will try to become the "therapist" of a mother who rejects him. The human child will also always try to please others, seeking distress signals in the environment and exaggerating their own signals in order to attract the mother's attention. The attachment behavior is permanently hyper-activated, the child always favors the affective over the cognitive; in short, ambivalence creates dependence.

When comparing insecure attachment types, the mothers of avoidant attachment children tend to be overly stimulating and intrusive. Is this so, or is it the image of themselves they want to portray to the observer? This is consistent with the defensive idealization they show when asked to reflect on their own childhood. Mothers of ambivalently attached children are rather unchallenging, insufficiently stimulating and unavailable (is this so, or do they place less importance on the image they want to give of themselves to the observer?).

5.3.4. *Mothers of "disorganized" children*

They have histories of abuse, trauma or unresolved grief from their own childhood, even when they do not abuse their child. When the mother has suffered a trauma relating to her own attachment figure, and there has been no resolution or "perlaboration" of this problem, her behavior towards her child can be frightening for them, without necessarily being abusive, confronting them with an "invisible fear" (we could just as easily say that the mother is frightened by the child), making it impossible to distinguish the threat from the game.

A mother who responds to the child's anxiety with that of her own cannot provide a secure base. Both mother and child then proceed to a "defensive exclusion of affects", notably anxiety, which makes them vulnerable when a separation situation arises. The term "parentification" of the child is also used to describe this role reversal, with the child attempting to control the parent.

In short, the child is confronted with a paradox: what should reassure them becomes a source of threat. The organizational strategies mentioned above cannot be used, hence the disorganization.

Finally, the transmission of relationship systems across generations is now well documented in various studies and in various countries; thus, the attachment security between the child and their mother is correlated with the attachment security between their mother and grandmother.

5.4. The father and attachment

Another theme focuses on the interactions between the various attachment figures: originally, theorists in this field spoke only of the "maternal body" and the "relationship to the mother". As the education of children was for a long time totally entrusted to the mother, attachment was assumed to be "monotropic", a concept close to Lorenz's imprinting, and dependent on a particular cultural structure (the child–father–mother nuclear family, where the father is much less present).

Moreover, the mother–child dyad is a culturally determined preference; in other cultures, the child is simultaneously raised by several people.

Currently, while the mother remains the main attachment figure, the contemporary evolutions of the family structure, the family recomposition and the status of the women mean that the father, other members of the family and educational staff are no longer completely neglected and can compensate for a "failing" mother. Thus, we know that today's fathers spend more time with their offspring than fathers of the past. Whatever the amount, this time spent between the father and the child appears today as important for the child, for the mother and for the father himself.

Attachment theory was developed during the 30 years following the end of World War II, with regard to the "baby boomers". The full-time availability of the mother at home was then considered by Bowlby to be "as important as vitamins", a view that would today seem conservative, to say the least.

On the other hand, we should note the role of industrialization and the two world wars that took fathers away from their children. At the end of these wars, the politically correct view was that women should "give back" their jobs to men and return to caring for their children.

Moreover, what Darwin, Munch and Bowlby have in common is that all three lacked maternal affection. It is probably because of this that Bowlby maintained, until his death in 1990, very strict positions on the availability of the mother, which were criticized by feminists. The question of parenthood may be very ideological, as well as reflects the personal histories of scholars.

Faced with criticism from feminists, Bowlby and then Main accepted the notion of an attachment hierarchy, with attachment to the father being considered as secondary. Thus, in strange father–child situations, the father can play a securing role just as well as the mother. The prediction of the quality of father–child attachment based on the types of interactions during the first year, paternal sensitivity and the time spent between father and child are just as strong as the prediction of the quality of mother–child attachment based on the same criteria.

We also observe intergenerational transmission phenomena in the father: his attachment to his child depends on the type of attachment he had with his mother. The role of the father has been progressively more studied. In separate observations of mother–child and father–child dyads, the child seeks proximity to the father as much as to the mother, but when father and mother are together, the child seeks proximity to the mother more.

However, the child may show affiliation behaviors (smiling, holding objects) with the father, rather than attachment behaviors. Similarly, when the child is stressed, he/she will direct his/her attachment behaviors towards the mother. On the other hand, when he/she is not stressed, the child will solicit the father more. This seems to indicate that each attachment figure has its function. The father–child relationship is more concerned with affiliation needs than with security needs.

The father, as a play partner and socializing agent, provides the child with social and cognitive stimulation distinct from that of the mother. Fathers cannot be confined to a playful or instrumental role. Like mothers, they have an affective, consoling and reassuring power. Simply put, in daily life, during "normal" functioning, their consoling power is as strong as that of the mother, but when life becomes difficult (e.g. in cases of fatigue, illness and intrusion), the maternal preponderance takes over.

Men are just as well "equipped" as women to respond to a child's signals, but it is the social role expectations that will create the differences in attitudes and behaviors between men and women. A man can hear a baby crying at night just as well as a woman. Another hypothesis is that women generally sleep more lightly than men; to test this hypothesis, the sleep of women and men without children should be studied.

In short, while studies point to a differentiation of the roles of the mother and the father, this does not mean that the father cannot play the role of "base camp" when the mother figure disappears.

We also have evidence of differences in the two parenting behaviors: mothers spend more time with the child, and are responsible for care activities, while fathers spend more time in play activities; fathers play in a more emotional, physical, idiosyncratic, stimulating way, whereas mothers tend to play in a less stimulating, more verbal way, involving more conventional toys and games.

For example, studies of baby swimmers have shown that children respond more to the father's incentives for exploration and risk taking than to the mother's incentives. These differences are not related to the amount of time spent with each parent, as they have been observed in children raised on kibbutzes, where there are no differences between mothers and fathers in this respect.

The child attaches to both parents in this way, but differences in experiences will "color" the type of attachment: the mother would be more sensitive to the need for security, the father to the need for exploration. A consequence of these distinctions is that each interaction will influence different aspects of the child's development. For example, physical play with the father will be important for the development of emotional and social skills, such as communication and interpretation of emotional states. Paternal characteristics are related to the emotional quality of social interactions with strangers, or, later, with members of the adolescent's social network.

The child's behavior towards their father is more predictive of child–stranger, rather than child–mother interactions, In this sense, attachment psychology "confirms" Lacanian psychoanalysis: the father is "the third party", in other words, the father–child relationship has a particularly important influence on the child's social relationships outside the family.

5.5. The concordance between attachment types

Concordance between the mother–child and father–child attachment types is not the rule. It is not uncommon to observe children who are securely attached to one parent and insecurely attached to another. Meta-analyses on this theme conclude that there are modest correlations, of the order of .17, with correspondences in only 60% of cases. This is true for both organized and disorganized attachments.

The internal operating models relating to the father and mother may be different. Like a half-empty or half-full bottle, this 60% is likely to be interpreted in two different ways. For attachment theorists, the child's temperament is not as influential as the relationship, because otherwise the concordances between mother and father attachment types would be more important. Each bond is the product of a particular history; attachment is the property of a relationship, not of an individual. For temperament theorists (see below), this 60% concordance indicates the existence of a factor specific to the child.

On the other hand, certain situations (such as when the child is alone with a stranger) will generate more consistency in the child's reactions. While the type of interaction organization reveals the specificity of each relationship, other aspects, such as emotional control and the intensity of crying, reflect more permanence of the behavior across the two relationships. Concordance between the two attachments could very well come from the fact that the two parents influence each other, that they learn how to raise the child and to react to the child's needs together, and the fact that they both initially had the same type of attachment.

Thus, when parents have the same attachment style, concordance between the child's attachments to both parents is 77%, but when they do not have the same attachment style, concordance is only 23%. If we consider only the father–child relationship itself, we find the four attachment types observed for the mother–child relationship in the same proportions. Furthermore, studies show that two secure attachments are better for the child's development than one, which is a predictable result.

Finally, attachment systems are better understood within the concept of triangulation. In the same way that psychoanalysts discuss disturbances in triangulation, notably in relation to the law (the Lacanian concept of foreclosure), it is also possible to consider it in relation to the construction of attachment and the subject's relationship to security and danger: the father and mother can be cooperative, stressed or in competition, for instance, during these constructions. In any case, these constructions are dynamic phenomena and cannot be reduced to fixed traits or dispositions of one or the other parent.

Similarly, when we observe the behavior of babies, we quickly notice that they can tell the difference between a dyadic and a triadic situation as early as the third month.

To conclude on this point, the family is a system, and the functioning of each element of the system must be analyzed in relation to the other elements. For example, the mother–child relationship seems to function one way when studied in isolation, but seems to function quite differently when viewed in the context of the interactions of that relationship with the father–child relationship.

Similarly, the father's influence on the child can be direct (depending on the characteristics of the father and those of the child) as well as indirect (through the father's influence on the mother).

In this systemic or triadic perspective, the relationship with the father either enhances the mother–child relationship or, on the contrary, degrades it. Our role will be to understand how the child integrates the two relationships and the two histories, which are sometimes contradictory. Indeed, these contradictions can lead to disruptions, even disorganizations, of the attachment bonds. To conclude, we have two different models of the self, as William James assumed: we come from our relationship with our mother, the other from our relationship with our father.

5.6. Paternal behavior

Paternal behavior can be predicted from a variety of variables: psychological (mental health, gender identity, relationship with our own father), marital (quality of the marriage, the mother's attitudes towards paternal behavior), sociocultural (employment, income, leisure time, ages of father and child) and parental (the father's previous parental experiences).

We saw earlier that the type of attachment established with the father does not necessarily correspond to that established with the mother, but we may wonder whether the secure/avoidant/ambivalent classification covers the same realities for the father and the mother. According to some authors, attempting to analyze the father–child relationship with the same conceptual tools as the mother–child relationship is inappropriate and leads to denigrating the father's role.

The gender of the child is an influential variable: fathers are less involved with their daughters than with their sons. An interesting observation, corroborated by various studies, is that the quantity and quality of paternal behavior are not correlated. A father who spends a lot of time with his child does not necessarily take better care of him. From the increase in the amount of time spent by fathers today, it could be hypothesized that quantity plays on quality and that today's fathers develop stronger attachments with their children. This does not always seem to be the case.

For example, Swedish fathers are known to take parental leave more often and to care for children more readily than fathers in southern Europe. However, they have not been found to become more important attachment figures than their working wives or "traditional" fathers.

Among the psychological variables, the father's psychological autonomy seems to be an important predictive factor (ability to manage intimacy and separation); among the sociocultural variables, we should mention professional involvement and satisfaction in his work. This also explains the lack of correlation between quantity and quality of paternal behavior. Men who are highly involved and satisfied with their work generally spend little time with their child. It remains to be seen whether this initially positive situation is also beneficial for women and for children when they become adolescents.

Several indirect variables are important, including the amount of maternal behavior. When mothers want to spend as much time as possible with the child, especially in the case of a first-born, paternal behavior is "discouraged". We should also note the impact of sociocultural variables: the older the mother, the higher her level of education and the better her personal qualifications, then the less time the father spends with the child. This is related to the aspect of couple dynamics mentioned earlier: when an "autonomous" woman decides to stay at home to raise her child, she can act as a "barrier" between the father and the child.

As for the quality of paternal behavior, a correlation is observed between maternal and paternal skills: here, we see an effect of the "modeling" of the father's behavior by the mother, the father learning from the mother. In conclusion, we can see that we cannot isolate father and mother, but that we must globally study a family relational system where complementarity and identification between the two partners play a role.

5.7. Sibling attachment

Sibling relationships have long been a neglected area of research in developmental psychology. It is only in recent years that studies have been undertaken to better understand the characteristics of the sibling relationship (Troupel-Cremel and Zaouche-Gaudron 2006).

Elder siblings, in particular, can be caregivers, emotional supports, for the majority of children, but the hypothesis that the elder child could act as an attachment figure for the youngest child has been neglected because of the focus on the study of the bond between the child and the mother.

In fact, elder children can indeed be attachment figures for the younger child, with 52% acting to reassure, comfort and provide care for the younger child when their mother leaves them together, alone, or with a stranger. Big brothers are more active in reassuring a younger sister, while big sisters are more active for a younger brother. Big brothers proportionately respond to the demand for care, while big sisters provide more care than their younger sibling demands, with boys adopting more paternal and girls more maternal strategies (Troupel-Cremel and Zaouche-Gaudron 2006).

While only half of elder children play the attachment figure role, this brings attachment theory and theory of mind together: to understand that the younger child is stressed, we must be able to understand the emotions of others.

There is also a transmission of attachment: it is the securely attached elder children who act as attachment figures for the younger children.

Finally, the function of the older child also extends to the exploration side of attachment: younger siblings with secure attachment to their older siblings explore the environment more.

Attachment theory has thus been progressively extended: initially focused on the mother, it has been extended to the father, then to the siblings, but with different functions and practices. The mother is more competent for the reassurance aspect, the father and the older children for the exploration aspect. However, while attachments with the father and with siblings are considered to be of a different nature than the initial link with the mother, some authors prefer to speak of an "activation relationship" for the first two in order to avoid confusion (Troupel-Cremel and Zaouche-Gaudron 2006).

5.8. Attachment to objects

Children form strong emotional bonds with "comforters", teddy bears, blankets or pillows, for example, and become anxious if separated from them. In Guatemala, children are traditionally given "worry dolls" so that they can share their worries and place them under their pillows. Some children anthropomorphize their objects and refer to them as living beings.

Winnicott first described these objects as "transitional", reflecting his psychoanalytic perspective that they served as a mechanism for the child to develop emotional distance from the mother. Thus, separation from the object was a symbolic separation from the mother. Similarly, Bowlby called these objects "attachment objects" and suggested that they should be used as a maternal substitute in the mother's absence.

This behavior is not unique to humans; it is also observed in young dogs. Similarly, in Harlow's "famous" experiments that gave rise to the theory of attachment, infant rhesus monkeys attached to an artificial terry cloth "mother" rather than to a metal cage "mother" that dispensed milk. The infant monkey visited the wire cage mother only when it needed food and returned to the cloth mother when it was fed. Attachment occurs primarily as a function of tactile comfort, as opposed to food.

Attachment objects provide comfort and security by reducing separation anxiety: children who have their attachment objects in the room, when the mother is not present, play and explore for the same amount of time as children whose mothers are present, without showing signs of distress (Lee and Hood 2021).

This behavior usually occurs in the first year of life, at bedtime, but depends on the cultural practice associated with sleep. For example, almost all Korean children sleep in the same room as their mother, whereas most French or American children sleep alone or with their siblings after six months. This may explain why the use of attachment objects is much higher in western cultures, where children are separated earlier for sleep than in eastern cultures. For example, there is no use of attachment objects in India or Gabon.

However, within the same country, we observe differences in usage by region or social class: in Italy, 5% in rural areas versus 30% in Rome. Similarly, in the United States, it is more common among Caucasian children (77%) than among African American children (46%).

Children who sleep alone in their own rooms from an early age are more likely to develop use than those who share a bed or room with others, highlighting the partial role of socioeconomic status in this behavior (Lee and Hood 2021).

Behavioral genetic studies of identical and non-identical twins indicate that heritability is 48%, with the shared environment accounting for an additional 48% of the variation in attachment to an inanimate object.

Children were indeed more likely to attribute mental states to their toys if they were emotionally attached to them, although it is difficult to determine whether the emotional connection was formed after the children developed routines that included the object, or whether the object became part of the routine because they were emotionally attached to it. However, as these objects are often the ones placed in the crib by adults when children are very young and motor immature, it seems more likely that the routine with the toy is established first, before the emotional bond is formed (Lee and Hood 2021).

Object attachment can extend beyond childhood: according to attachment theory, if emotional attachment to the attachment object arises from separation anxiety, the need for that object should diminish as the child grows, leading to increased autonomy.

The average age of abandonment of the attachment object in different cultures is about seven years. However, for some individuals, this use may extend into adulthood. Retention of attachment objects beyond childhood is an indication that the individual has a degree of emotional vulnerability and a sign of psychological distress.

The tendency to accumulate objects has even been classified as a "hoarding disorder" in DSM-5. However, this differs from object attachment behavior in that it does not focus on a limited set of possessions, but generally involves any object, regardless of its monetary or sentimental value, leading to "the accumulation of possessions that congest and clutter active living areas", a frequent subject of discord between spouses.

Conversely, in the pathologically disturbed adolescent, having an attachment object may enable the individual to better resolve separation issues and help them develop a sense of self and others. Thus, while the majority of literature suggests that persistent attachment to objects beyond childhood is indicative of emotional distress, there may also be psychological benefits to not getting rid of these objects.

In conclusion, attachment objects are not only a source of comfort for children, but can also help them manage their anxieties and concerns. How and why attachment to objects persists into adulthood is not yet known, but it is notable that each object tends to be viewed as a unique and irreplaceable individual and this bias towards authenticity appears to influence adult attitudes about the value placed on collectibles (Lee and Hood 2021).

5.9. Attachment and child care

The contemporary evolution of the status of women is accompanied by a growing proportion (20% in the 1960s, 60% today) of mothers who quickly return to work after giving birth; this obviously contradicts the supposedly essential full-time availability of the mother, which Bowlby, in his time, advocated as being "as important as vitamins".

Moreover, maternity, female employment and child care systems are intrinsically linked; while French women have become the most fertile in Europe with a high employment rate, it is thanks to the quality of France's child care facilities.

Is the relationship between quality of attachment and time spent with the child quantitative and linear? Research shows that the type of child care does not affect the quality of mother–child attachment.

5.10. Attachment disorders

5.10.1. *Internalized and externalized disorders*

Numerous studies have shown the relationship between the type of attachment and externalized (risky behavior, running away, destruction, anger) or internalized (anxiety, shyness, withdrawal, fatigue, headaches, depression, sadness) behavioral disorders, as measured by the Achenbach Checklist.

The correlation between disorganized attachment and aggressiveness in children has been noted in multiple studies. These relationships can be observed very early on. For example, the absence of "normative" reactions to the "still face" experience (reactions that reflect the child's strategy to re-establish contact with the mother) at six months of age is predictive of externalizing disorders at 18 months.

Moreover, interaction effects with other variables are also noted: correlations between insecure attachment and behavioral problems are stronger among children living in high-risk environments (such as poverty and illness); similarly, social support may act as a protective factor with respect to the effects of insecure attachment.

For the study of psychosomatic disorders, the work of Pierrehumbert (2003) revealed an interesting association between the intensity of anxiety during the strange situation (whether the attachment was secure or insecure) and the frequency of psychosomatic disorders at age five. "Proximal" children are more at risk than "distal" children. The author links this association with alexithymia or operative thought (a concept from the French *École de Psychosomatique*).

In addition, a particular form of attachment disturbance, with a "psychosomatic transaction" (the attachment is organized around the child's symptoms), would lead to the "Münchhausen Syndrome" (manipulation of the doctor by maintaining the symptoms of the child), and to a proportion (30%!) of the sudden deaths of infants, due to abuse.

One of the most common associations with externalized disorders is disorganized attachment. In populations of "at risk" children, 83% of those characterized by teachers as having significant externalized disorders had disorganized attachment, compared with 13% of children without such disorders.

Disorganized attachment is more associated with antisociality, whereas insecure avoidant attachment and maternal depression lead more to internalized disorders, addiction or depression.

Another association observed is the predictive value of a slight deficit in verbal intelligence in childhood (when the verbal IQ is much lower than the non-verbal IQ) when it is associated with attachment disorganization. We can conclude that, for these children who are insecure about the question of attachment, the deficit in language skills "pushes" them towards aggressiveness.

From a preventive perspective of early detection of antisociality, these elements are important. The maternal expression of emotions (negativity, warmth, coldness) is associated with antisocial behaviors in the child; this has been observed cross-sectionally (at age five) and longitudinally (from age five to seven). This last point is essential, because it means that the link between maternal expression and child problems does not only reveal a directional effect from the child to the parent, that is, an effect of the child's behavior on the parent's treatment of them. There is a parent effect on the child, since, even controlling for the level of antisocial behavior at age five, maternal expression predicts increased problems at age seven.

Thus, when comparing British monozygotic twins (a nationally representative sample of 565 pairs of twins born in 1994–1995), we note that the majority of them display the same antisocial behaviors, but that 30% of them do not, which can be attributed to the influence of the non-shared environment. At this age, when peers and other adults are not yet very influential, it is above all the type of mother–child bond that will play differently on subjects who are as similar as monozygotic twins. Moreover, the correlation observed between mother and child is not under the influence of genetic factors since we are dealing with monozygotes.

Thus, we note a different evaluation by the mother of her own behavior according to the twin and a correlation between the maternal expression of emotions (negativity, warmth, coldness) and the child's antisocial behaviors, whether the information is brought by the mother or by a teacher of the child (this last point is also important because it means that we do not measure the representation of the mother and we avoid the bias of her distortion in the perception of the child): the "favored" twin exhibits less antisocial behavior than the "unfavored" twin. Appreciation is correlated with birth weight: the smallest weights receive less favorable appraisals.

Why do the mothers look at each twin differently? There may be a variety of factors: one of the twins may have been ill, which would lead to differences in parental behavior towards one twin and the other. However, the negativity is not always towards the one who has been ill, sometimes it is the other way around; in any case, it is a factor that influences parental behavior in one direction or another.

It may not be the child's illness *per se*, but the significance of that illness to the mother that disrupts the mother–child bond. Another possibility is that the mother believes in clichés or stereotypes about twin couples ("one should be dominant and the other dominated", "one should be more masculine and the other more feminine" and so on) and behaves according to this belief. Or the mother has identified one of the twins as being more like herself and have feelings more (positively or negatively) towards that twin. Or, finally, the mother, whose relationship with the twins' father ended acrimoniously, identifies one of them with her ex-partner and directs negative emotions towards that twin.

We are in the realm of projection here. These stereotypes apply particularly to twins, as well as, to a lesser extent, to siblings ("a younger child is like this, an older child like that") or to only children; this is the whole problem of tagging and labeling. As we have seen, behavioral genetic methods can also shed light on environmental mechanisms and causality arising from the mother–child bond.

Finally, in longitudinal studies that evaluate conduct disorders during childhood, when comparing three major types of trajectories (chronicity, strong resilience, moderate resilience), we see how maternal rejection and maternal depression are associated with chronicity; these studies once again point to the need for early intervention. Indeed, the lack of maternal sensitivity will constitute a factor of vulnerability for the child: they become less able to cope with stress.

5.10.2. *Attachment as a transmission factor between maternal and child psychopathology*

One study (Delbarre 2020) aimed to evaluate the relationship between indices of maternal psychological functioning and the quality of the child's attachment to their mother, using a child psychiatry clinical sample: 29 children (aged between 23 and 71 months) consulting a child psychiatry service and their mothers participated in the study.

Maternal depression was marginally related to avoidant attachment, whereas maternal anxiety was significantly related. Faced with an anxious mother, the child could adjust to her lack of emotional and behavioral availability by avoiding her in stressful situations.

The higher the level of stress experienced by the mother in her parenting role, the more disorganized the child's attachment was and the less secure it tended to be. The higher the level of maternal stress related to the child's difficulties, the more ambivalent the mother–child attachment tended to be.

5.10.3. *Attachment and alexithymia*

REMINDER – *The concept of alexithymia (from "a" privative, "lexi" read or name and "thymia" emotion) refers to the incapacity of a subject to recognize his/her own emotions.*

Securely attached children are better able to perceive the connections between their thoughts, cognitions ("what I know about myself") and emotions, especially negative ("how I feel"), because their family environment helps them to perceive these connections.

Children with insecure attachment will become more alexithymic: avoidant children will favor cognition over affects in order to defend themselves against the insecurity linked to the parent's rejection; ambivalent children will favor affects over cognition, because they are obliged to "exaggerate" the affective signals due to the ambivalence or inconsistency of the parent

Similarly, children with secure attachments to both parents are more empathetic than children with insecure attachments to one parent. We should also mention the fact that secure children play more willingly in symbolic games and are more available for imagination, because they are less preoccupied with the question of the mother's availability.

Finally, alexithymia can be studied in mirror image, not only in the sense that parents make the child alexithymic, but in the influences of alexithymic parents: it has been shown that alexithymia in parents is related to reduced emotion differentiation abilities in their three-year-old children, a phenomenon of intergenerational transmission.

5.10.4. *Attachment and developmental disorders*

The first year of life is a "sensitive" or "critical" period. Children who have benefited from attentive care allow themselves to explore more (protection, the first function of attachment, enables exploration, its second function), because they have internalized an image of the other as "loving" and an image of themselves as "loved". In a way, their attachment behavior (and thus their anxiety) is less activated and they can more easily explore.

In Piagetian terminology, securely attached children are more capable of decentering and, in Flavell's terminology, of engaging in theory of mind (the ability to understand others' intentions and thoughts and how they differ from their own). A secure attachment is thus a predictive factor of an earlier development of theory of mind because secure children have a more flexible self, more receptive to the intentions of others due to their better communication.

Another observation that confirms the influence of attachment on social development is that insecure attachment is derived from overprotection and the mother's intrusion will constitute a risk factor that the child will be a victim of peer aggression in preschool. The child will be perceived as "weak". Victimization also has its roots in attachment.

Of course, this factor does not play out in isolation. The relationship between insecure attachment and victimization varies according to the number of classmates that the child has: the more they have, the weaker the relationship. Securely attached children show more interest in exploration and socialization; avoidantly attached children will avoid situations where their attachment behavior might be activated; ambivalently attached children will tend to become dependent.

When the child feels that they cannot truly rely on the parent, they may either permanently deactivate their attachment behavior out of anticipatory fear of rejection in the case of avoidant attachments, or permanently overactivate it in an attempt to attract the parent's attention and love in the case of ambivalent attachments.

Regensburg's follow-up shows that, at age 10, securely attached children admit to having negative feelings and report being able to ask others for help; insecurely attached avoidant children report having no friends or claim to have friends without being able to name them.

Meta-analyses on maternal and peer attachment show that there is a correlation and confirm the internal operating model hypothesis. For example, it has been shown that the mother's mode of conflict resolution in mother–child arguments is transmitted to the child in their own mode of conflict resolution with their best friend.

This returns us to the "secure: certainty of being loved", "avoidance: certainty of being rejected" and "ambivalence: uncertainty" associations. A "good" relationship with the attachment figure will not encourage dependence on this figure but, on the contrary, the autonomy of the subject.

In the same way, and using the perspective of the psychoanalyst Melanie Klein, the presence of the attachment figure "deactivates" the negative emotions (fear, anger, hatred, ambivalence) of the child and, therefore, the consequences of these negative emotions on development. It deactivates them, but, conversely, a secure attachment allows the child to better understand negative emotions in others (such as sadness) than positive emotions (such as happiness).

Five risk factors related to attachment can already be mentioned with regard to the subject's future risk behaviors and addictions: early maternal deficiency (absence of an attachment bond between six months and three years of age); organized and unfortunately chronic forms of disorganized attachment; major separations from attachment figures; disorganized attachment following abuse; insecure attachment resulting from intergenerational effects (childhood trauma of the parent).

The DSM-IV (a reference manual for the classification of psychopathological disorders) distinguishes two types of reactive attachment disorders: inhibited attachment, corresponding to avoidant attachment, and uninhibited attachment, corresponding to resistant attachment.

Through the various revisions of nosographies over the past 20 years, a consensus has emerged that Reactive Attachment Disorder includes clusters of symptoms not found in other types of psychiatric disorders.

Thus, uninhibited attachment is particularly associated with children raised in institutions who, due to the lack of a personalized, individualized relationship with an attachment figure, will tend to show "all over the place" affectivity, diffuse attachments, indiscriminate sociability and difficulties in establishing selective attachments. It remains to be seen whether this is an "adapted" response to their situation in order to get the adult's attention, or whether it will cause a delay in the development of attachments. We might even wonder if it is still justified to speak of attachment in this regard, since these relationships are often very superficial.

Another typology of attachment disorders has been proposed:

– Absence of attachment: this profile is reminiscent of Tizard's institutionalized children or Bowlby's "tenderness-deprived" juvenile delinquents. The difference between these and insecure attachment avoidant subjects is that the latter experience separation anxiety.

– Non-selective attachments: similar to ambivalent attachments, these children "cling" to everyone and their demand for love or attention is never satisfied. The balance between exploratory and attachment behaviors is tilted too much in favor of the former because these subjects never really attach themselves and their risk taking is sometimes excessive. The attachment bond is not strong enough, and these subjects do not use the parent as a reference or as a source of information on the danger of a situation.

– Inhibited attachments: the balance between exploratory and attachment behaviors is too much in favor of the latter. These subjects are close to ambivalent attachment, with an excessive dependence on the parent. Separation anxiety is very strong, both in the child and the parent, which can lead to submissive attitudes, sometimes even to the point of accepting abuse.

– Aggressive attachments: aggression is integrated into the attachment behavior strategy in order to attract the parent's attention; it is more than just a consequence, as in resistant attachment.

– Role reversal: these are cases of "parentification" of the child, where the child seeks to protect the parent.

These last three categories have been grouped together in a more general dimension, the "*clinging attachment*" (Pierrehumbert 2003), strongly associated with substance abuse and eating disorders. Attachment disorders have not led to a hypotrophy of the latter, but, on the contrary, a hypertrophy. This hypertrophy will generate the addiction.

Moreover, attachment disorders and narcissism are strongly linked: narcissism is, in a way, a disorder of emotion regulation, of attachment activation.

However, it should not be inferred from this analysis that "everything happens before six months, three months, or even up to one year". When showing a correlation between parent–child relationships at t1 and a child's outcome at t2, we should also consider parent–child relationships at t2, as well as the interactions between parent–child relationships at t1 and at t2.

In fact, in most cases, a child keeps the same parents over the years, and unfortunately the relationship problems do not improve. It is not so much the initial condition itself that is a risk factor, but the fact that it predicts the chronicity of a condition. What is considered to be the prediction of a state at t2 by a state at t1 could, in fact, be only the observation of correlations of different aspects of the state at t2; if this state changes for various reasons, there is no future automaticity.

The impact of improved parenting behaviors was thus highlighted in a preventive study that sought to show how to break out of the vicious circle, the "spiral of transactions" leading to insecure attachment (Pierrehumbert 2003). The author followed a population of mothers of children with irritable temperaments, who were therefore at risk of insecure attachment (indeed, 78% of these children exhibited insecure attachment, compared to one-third of the overall population). The action was taken when the child was between six and nine months old in order to improve the mother's attention to the child's signals. When children benefited from this intervention, only 38% retained an insecure attachment (more similar to the frequency in the general population). Moving forward, the child will gradually establish other bonds that may be harmonious or, on the contrary, discordant with the original bond.

To conclude on the relationship between attachment and risk, the child's attachment to their parents fulfils the same function as that of love between adults, the search for certainty in a world (internal or external) of uncertainty, the search for predictability in events and in the reactions of others. As in marriage (!), this quest may lead to dependence and conformity or to the autonomy of the subject. Attachment theory allows us to understand how the family bond can become liberating or alienating.

5.11. Attachment, the individual and the family

Should attachment disorders be treated at the level of an individual who has an insecure attachment, or at the level of the family, which is provoking their insecurity? This is the debate between "traditional" psychotherapists, focused on the subject, and "systemic" or "transactional" therapists, who are focused on the family.

5.11.1. *Family styles*

An application of attachment theory to family functioning has been proposed by contrasting four typologies:

– *"Flexible" families*: parents and children are sensitive to communication and empathy, but respect each other's autonomy. This family characteristic of flexibility corresponds to the individual characteristic of attachment security. We can make a connection here with Lautrey's theory on flexibility and cognitive development: the more "agile" or "flexible" the parents' educational style is with regard to rules and family functioning, the better the child's cognitive development. The same is true for social and emotional development.

– *"Disengaged" families*: parents and children seem to cut off communication, avoid confrontational topics and avoid expressing their emotions. This family characteristic of disengagement corresponds to the individual characteristic of insecure avoidant attachment.

– *"Enmeshed" families*: intrusion, interference and lack of autonomy characterize the behavior of both children and parents. This family characteristic of enmeshment corresponds to the individual characteristic of ambivalent attachment.

– *"Chaotic" families*: this family characteristic of chaos corresponds to the individual characteristic of disorganized attachment in the child or the "disoriented" discourse of the mother.

5.11.2. *The place in the sibling group*

When two siblings participate in the strange situation experiment with the same parent, the observed concordance rates between attachment styles are about 60%. The sibling match is strong, but not perfect. Research has shown no influence of sibling rank on the quality of attachment. Elder siblings are not loved any more than younger siblings.

5.12. The character (or temperament) of the individual

A theme that has been grafted onto the field of attachment has consisted of seeking correlations between the type of attachment, the child's character (or temperament) and the parents' personalities. The notion of temperament comes from Hippocrates and Galen ("sanguine", "phlegmatic", "melancholic", "choleric"), and the temperament/attachment contrast is one of the expressions of the well-known innate/acquired theme.

Temperament is defined by inter-individual differences in self-regulation, motor, emotional and attentional reactivity and is expressed through behavioral responses.

Thus, conceptions about the etiology of childhood autism have evolved from Bettelheim's blaming of a "cold mother" in the 1970s to the genetic factors put forward by neuroscience in the 1990s. The debate is not only scientific, but also educational: parents often attribute the main influence on the child's development to their own education, to the first birth and then to the child's temperament towards the younger children.

The continuity debate applies as much to temperament as to attachment. Studies seem to show that there is not necessarily continuity; highly reactive children may become inhibited in adolescence, low-reactive children may become more sociable.

Research on child temperament distinguishes between "*easy*", "*difficult*" and "*slow-to-warm-up*" children. Parents of "difficult" children do not seem to differ from other parents at birth, which seems to be an argument for a constitutional temperament of the child.

For temperament theorists, what is expressed at nine months in the strange situation is not the history of the relationship with the attachment figure in the first year, but the "nature" of the child and, to use a fashionable expression, their "stress management" abilities.

Similarly, a different categorization of attachment security has been proposed by contrasting "distal" attachment behaviors (vocalization, smiling) with "proximal" attachment behaviors (need for physical contact) when the mother returns. "Distal" attachment behaviors can include "distal secure" and "insecure avoidant" attachment behaviors, while "proximal" attachment behaviors include "proximal secure" and "insecure ambivalent" attachment behaviors.

However, and unlike attachment security, as we have seen above, distal behaviors in the mother and the father are interlinked. This distal/proximal categorization revealed individual differences, linked to the child's temperament and not to the relational history. The results emphasize the notion of interaction: an "easy" child will strongly favor parental behavior, a "temperamental" or "difficult" child will not favor the construction of a secure attachment, but this can nevertheless be achieved according to the parents' educational style.

Increasingly, a "bidirectional" model is emerging between "parenting" and "child temperament" advocates. Thus, when parents are asked about the quality of the attachment relationship with their child, they often talk "instead" about characteristics of the child's temperament and place more emphasis on aspects that they consider "innate", forgetting the aspects of the relationship's construction. It is also significant that, to an extent, parents "forget" to consider the child's sense of security in order to focus on their temperament. It is true that attachment, which is more of an "acquired" dimension, involves their responsibility (and therefore their guilt) more than temperament, which is more of an "innate" dimension.

Attachment and temperament would thus be two independent dimensions that would be expressed at the same time and interact during separation situations. Depending on their temperament, the child will express their sense of security distally or proximally. For example, some children are very fearful, others not at all, and we understand that this trait will have an influence in separation situations. Also, depending on their temperament, the child will express their feelings of anxiety through avoidant or ambivalent behavior. Depending on their respective temperaments, the mother will treat each sibling differently and create different attachments. A difficult temperament will lead to insecurity, but only if it really affects the mother's sensitivity.

Conversely, the attachment style will gradually modify the child's temperament, and a secure attachment will gradually protect the child from developing antisociality. We are then in the presence of a transaction between the child's temperament and the maternal sensitivity.

Similarly, it is not only the child's temperament that influences mother–child attachment; the mother's temperament, for example, when she is emotionally unstable, can also contribute to insecure attachment. This also applies to the father: there is an interaction between the father's behavior and the child's temperament.

5.13. Attachment and the child's gender

There are no differences in the distribution of attachments between boys and girls, or between men and women, which seems logical. On the other hand, the same type of attachment would produce different effects depending on gender. An insecure attachment will sometimes be considered as a stress; however, in terms of vulnerability to stress, epidemiology has shown that the weaker sex is unquestionably the male sex.

The same biological, emotional or psychosocial stress does far more damage to a male body than to a female body, at least in the short-term. Since Rutter's seminal studies, we know that parental hostility is more closely related to behavioral problems in boys than in girls because, among girls, "conventionality" (the ability to adhere to norms) acts as a protective factor.

However, this does not mean that bonding pathology has no effect on girls. The relationship between attachment and interaction with others varies by gender; insecure boys are more aggressive than secure boys, insecure girls are less aggressive, but more dependent than secure girls.

The prediction of bonding consequences differs by gender and some gender differences might be related to differences in fate between two groups: insecure boys tending towards aggression and lawbreaking, insecure girls tending towards psychopathology and addiction to psychoactive substances.

Thus, female vulnerability to the harmful consequences of bonding pathology would be centered around the greater difficulty girls have in controlling their emotions. This difficulty will lead to a higher frequency of depressive states, with some depressive states leading to addiction.

5.14. Attachment in adolescence

Adolescence is a period of major transformations, and yet longitudinal follow-ups show that the adolescent is the heir to childhood experiences; adolescents who did not have problems in childhood generally continue not having them, those who did have them continue having them. The attachment type is thus associated with success and behaviors at school when the child becomes an adolescent. Adolescents who were secure children get better grades, are more attentive and engaged in high school and are less anxious about school.

Moreover, these correlations are observed independently of levels of prior achievement and problems – IQ, social class and gender. Attachment has an effect in itself, on self-representation and the ability to focus and interact with our environment. Attachment representations continue to have an influence at this time of life, when attachment behavior is no longer solely oriented towards the mother or father, but increasingly towards other individuals (such as peers and teachers).

Thus, the secure are described by their peers as less hostile, less insecure and more resilient, while insecure avoiders are seen as more hostile and less resilient and the insecure ambivalent as more anxious.

5.14.1. *The question of puberty*

Pubertal maturation is generally considered to be a negative element from the point of view of parent–child relationships. Maturation generates conflicts and has more negative effects in the middle of the pubertal cycle on relationships with mothers, but, for girls, conflicts continue beyond that, until the end of the cycle. From these observations, each author proposes his/her own psychoanalytical, psychosociological or ethological interpretation.

It has been suggested, however, that the causality also works the other way around, that increasing conflict accelerates pubertal maturation and that increasing intimacy slows it down. We know, in fact, how sensitive hormonal functioning is to psychological and social influences: menarche comes earlier in girls raised by a single parent, or with a step-parent, than in those raised in "intact" families.

Both effects have been observed: distancing (puberty creates a distance between the adolescent and their parents) and acceleration in girls (the distance between the young person and her parents accelerates puberty).

Distancing: for some adolescents, puberty creates conflict with the mother and a loss of a close bond with the father. In girls, it sometimes creates conflicts with the father; in boys, puberty leads to an increase in emotional and behavioral autonomy. According to epidemiological studies, relationships with the father deteriorate more often than with the mother during this period. These distancing effects mainly occur at the beginning of the cycle and are modest: pubertal status accounts for 5% of the variance in parent–child relationships. A 5% increase in distance should not be seen as a "storm".

Acceleration: distance in the mother–child relationship accelerates pubertal development in girls and intimacy in this relationship slows it down. No such effects are observed in boys. We see how development in girls is more sensitive to psychological and social influences. That said, these effects are modest: distance in the mother–child relationship accounts for 5% of the variance in pubertal maturation.

Furthermore, the link between family relationships and pubertal development presented above holds true, especially from the adolescent's point of view, but not if we ask the parents for their opinion. This is the subjective sense of interpersonal distance, as experienced by the adolescent.

The phenomenon of distancing can be understood from a psychoanalytical perspective (reactivation of oedipal conflicts in adolescence) or from a social learning perspective (the adolescent will look for models and rewards among peers). The acceleration (or slowing down) phenomenon is best understood from a psychobiological (neuroendocrine effects of stress) perspective.

A sociobiological perspective has also been evoked: since the dawn of time, puberty has separated the young from their parents (family emigration) in order to avoid consanguinity and a too weak diversity of genes. In contemporary times, where economic constraints are increasingly delaying this taking of autonomy and make it impossible at puberty, the conflicts of adolescence and the resulting distancing could be considered as an analogous protective mechanism.

Finally, the timing of puberty obviously has an important impact. For example, in a comparison of Finnish twins, it was observed that early puberty was a risk factor in early use (starting before the age of 13) of tobacco and alcohol; we also know how this early age is a risk factor in the development of abuse and dependence. Early puberty has an effect in itself, independently of the family composition and its problems. This statistical relationship is also influenced by contextual factors. For example, it is observed in urban areas but not rural (where there may be, for instance, differences in accessibility to psychoactive products, family control and attitudes).

5.14.2. *From attachment to autonomy*

The acquisition of autonomy is the primary developmental task of the adolescent. The subject must develop new relationships, friendly as well as romantic, without breaking pre-existing relationships with their parents. Secure adolescents have a better quality of friendly and loving relationships, and therefore a social support perceived by parents as more important; these subjects have more confidence in their friends or partners and experience fewer break-ups.

Similarly, in terms of the construction of a personal identity, of self-efficacy, secure subjects, who have more self-confidence, become mature fairly quickly, preoccupied subjects remain very immature and detached subjects are sometimes more precocious than autonomous subjects (because they are keen to cut ties with their parents). However, this maturity is a defense mechanism, which can give way when confronted with a difficult experience.

Indeed, and in keeping with their origin, differences in attachment organizations in adulthood are most apparent in stressful situations. In fact, both the detached and the parents of the detached tend to describe the subject as "autonomous" and "successful", but this may be a defensive, "stereotypical" portrait.

On the other hand, secure subjects have a better ability to establish intimate relationships, whether with their parents, friends or partners. Intimate relationships with peers do not develop at the expense of relationships with parents.

To conclude, in this phase of entry into adulthood, attachment organization plays mostly on the relational domains of development, less on other aspects such as self-esteem, but relationships with other domains of development vary according to the situations in which the subject is immersed. Secure subjects have more positive and generalized expectations regarding relationships and their own self (their internal operating model), stronger internalizations of social skills and more flexible and resilient emotion regulation, all characteristics that clearly favor friendships and romantic and family relationships.

Finally, the intergenerational transmission of attachment style occurs through a modeling of the child's thinking; the mother transmits her internal operating model to the child. How does the child organize thoughts about emotions based on their mother's narrative styles and scripts, and how does the mother's state of mind influence the way the dyad discusses and exchanges about the affective and emotional contents within the child's autobiography.

The conversations between child and mother during childhood are a fundamental element in the construction of the history of the self. As Vygotsky taught us, the adult will guide the child in organizing their memories into a narrative form: "with whom, what, when and where this happened to me", and so on.

5.14.3. *The fate of internal operating models from adolescence onwards*

In 1985, a Californian psychologist, Mary Main, passed attachment theory from behavior to representation by creating a tool, the AAI (Adult Attachment Interview), aimed at evaluating the relationships of an adolescent or adult subject with their parents and their reactions to separation.

It is no longer behavior that is evaluated, but discourse, the subject's state of mind, what Main calls "narrative competence", that is, a subject's ability to have access to his emotions and to build knowledge, a self-narration, which also refers to alexithymia and internal operating models.

Today, attachment theory and the work it generates are positioned at the precise point of a boundary between developmental psychology and psychoanalysis. Thus, the correspondences observed between attachment styles and self-narratives are as follows:

– Secure attachment is reflected in an *"autonomous" state of mind*: logical, coherent discourse on our past, no matter how difficult. Life is not a long, quiet river: even during a happy childhood, we can certainly experience separations, conflicts and so on. However, the subject has easy access to their memories and emotions and understands their impact, whether positive or negative. Trust in ourselves or in others is the main trait underlying the narrative. The subject values attachment, whether their experiences have been positive or negative, and, when a problem arises, then seeking an attachment figure remains a preferred strategy, with this figure expected to respond and help solve the problem. In the case of a difficult childhood history, we speak of an "acquired" security, through metacognition and work on our self; note, moreover, that self-narration evokes the beginnings of a psychotherapy. To explore inner worlds, we must not feel too vulnerable.

– Avoidant insecure attachment is reflected in a *"detached" state of mind*: poorly developed discourse, lacking in affect and memories of the parents. The subject presents himself as indifferent, independent and distrustful of others and the terms used to describe their parents may be at odds with the episodes recounted. This type of narration evokes processes of defensive exclusion and compulsive self-confidence. Deactivation of the attachment characteristic of insecure avoiders during childhood results in restricted access to memories. There is a split between cognition and affect: the subject will minimize the negative nature of experiences, over-idealize their parents or cut ties. The relationship between this attachment type and age (young detached subjects talk more positively about their relationship with their parents than older detached subjects) shows that idealization of the parent decreases with age or maturity.

– Ambivalent insecure attachment is expressed by a *"preoccupied" state of mind*: confused, emotional, reproachful or ambivalent discourse regarding their parents. The subject demonstrates, above all, a relational dependence. The lack of self-confidence or confidence in others is the main feature underlying the narrative. The attachment hyper-activation characteristic of ambivalent subjects during childhood is translated in adulthood by irritation, instability, agitation and persistence of parental control.

– Disorganized attachment is expressed by a *"disoriented", "unresolved" state of mind*: a discourse borrowing from the three other categories, with blocks when evoking traumatic experiences. It should be remembered that the disorganized may have initially been secure children, but abuse or bereavement may have caused them to "tip over" into insecurity. The subject reveals that their traumas have never been resolved, which leads to frequent inconsistencies.

This category of subjects is the one whose study clearly poses the relationship between attachment theory and psychoanalysis or trauma theory, which also refers to the phenomenon of post-traumatic stress disorders. Clinical studies show the correlation between unresolved state of mind and post-traumatic stress, the former multiplying by 7.5 the risk of a diagnosis of post-traumatic stress.

If we talk about alexithymia, we see that the autonomous have a fluid access to their emotions, the detached have a weakened access and the preoccupied have an unstable access.

The distribution observed in the general population corresponds to that of the strange situation: 56% autonomous, 27% detached and 17% preoccupied. A correlation with gender is mentioned by some authors: predictably, the preoccupied state of mind is more frequent among women, who are more likely to be looking for emotional proximity in relationships than men, and are therefore more likely to be disappointed.

The stability between attachment behavior in the strange situation during childhood and the representation of attachment later in life has been demonstrated in the Minnesota longitudinal follow-up: the concordance rates between behavior observed at age 1 and discourse produced at age 21 were 72% for all the children followed and 78% if we remove those who had lost a parent during this period.

On the other hand, this stability was not observed as clearly in the German Regensburg follow-up up to age 16: a concordance rate of only 50% was observed, emphasizing the influence of parental divorce on child–parent attachment stability; stressful life events, especially parental divorce, cause some subjects to "shift" from a secure attachment to a preoccupied adult representation. On the other hand, the absence of stressful events does not in itself increase the security of adult attachment for subjects who did not benefit from maternal sensitivity enabling secure attachment during childhood.

In conclusion, for secure subjects, we note a continuity that has been built up between the past and the present, between their childhood attachments and their representations as young adults. For insecure subjects, this continuity is broken, and the past can be superimposed on the present. For the secure, time and history continue, whereas for the insecure, time and history stop. Our temporality is our affectivity.

There is a high concordance between the mother's state of mind and the child's attachment, of the order of 70%, with maternal sensitivity mediating this association, whether the mother is biological or adoptive and regardless of the child's age at adoption. Attachment does not have to begin at birth.

5.14.4. *Maternal and paternal transmission pathways*

We have seen that, in childhood, concordance is far from perfect; in adulthood, we could imagine that the two representations become more "coalescent" and "integrated". From adolescence onwards, security is no longer the characteristic of a relationship, but becomes the characteristic of an individual and their thinking. The very notion of "state of mind" suggests this coalescence.

What about it? There is certainly a correspondence, but not systematic, in 68% of cases (correlation of 0.33). It remains to be seen what underpins this correlation: is it, for example, that the relationship with the mother is more influential and "pulls" the relationship with the father? In any case, the gradual creation of a coalescence of representations from different relationships is important, because we can assume that it will play a role in the way the subject will later deal with their own children.

5.15. Attachment and the Internet

Social interactions are increasingly becoming virtual, or even being replaced for some, because of the Internet. We might question if attachment types play a role in the involvement of the subject on the Internet. For subjects with an insecure attachment (especially the preoccupied), who fear close contact with others, social networks offer a kind of good solution.

For the exercise of parenthood, the Internet has become an important resource for seeking advice and information about pregnancy, health, child development, education and more. Blogs and forums also allow us to express our doubts and anxieties. Young mothers who are primiparous, single or from disadvantaged backgrounds are clearly more dependent on this resource.

One question remains: could digital technology enable an insecure mother to not transmit her insecurity to her child? This, of course, also applies to fathers.

One positive point is that the digital divide is now closing in disadvantaged settings. Are we therefore heading towards online interventions to improve attachment security? The first approaches in this direction, via personalized e-mails, seem to show promising results.

At a time when many young parents are in a situation of isolation (e.g. traditional solidarity networks are disappearing), digital technology could be an interesting resource for parenthood.

5.16. Attachment and risk taking

The assumptions that might be made about the link between attachment and risk taking are not necessarily unambiguous. While securely attached children are more comfortable in themselves, and while they are more likely to explore the environment, this does not tell us whether this is a protective factor. Children who are, for instance, more "securely attached", more "willing to explore" and bolder could also be those who have the most accidents because they expose themselves more.

Thus, children who have the best motor performance in terms of balance and agility, and whose psychomotor development is ahead of schedule, are also the ones who have the most accidents in everyday life, at home or on the playground, because they take too many risks.

The effect of attachment on risk taking is observed in its interaction with the individual's biological functioning: we know the association between high testosterone levels and risk taking. However, the parent–child relationship acts as a moderator of this biological effect: when the relationship deteriorates, the association between testosterone and risk taking becomes stronger.

An area close to risk taking, stress management, has been linked to attachment style. Securely attached subjects receive more social support (conversation) to cope with stress than insecurely attached subjects. Avoidantly attached subjects receive more cognitive than emotional support, which is logical since these subjects tend to restrict interactions in this domain. Ambivalently attached subjects cannot benefit from any support, because the cognitive supports, of the problem-solving type, refer them to an insufficiently good self-esteem.

Various studies have confirmed attachment theory: the emotional support of parents is linked to better self-esteem, less peer pressure and less involvement in risky behaviors (alcohol, illicit drugs, delinquency and, indiscipline at school).

By helping to build a better self-image, parental support enables less risky exploration of the environment. Secure attachment to the mother is associated with less risk taking and greater caution, for both boys and girls; the same is true for secure attachment to the father. However, there are some differences in the effects of attachment to the father for girls and boys. Indeed, risk taking in boys and girls is not perceived identically by the father. The father's adherence to gender stereotypes comes into play here.

5.17. Attachment and addictions

First of all, we need to remind ourselves that the link between mother–child separation and spontaneous alcohol consumption has been observed in mice: the links between attachment and addiction are not specific to the human species.

Several studies have highlighted the relationship between attachment style and substance use. Cannabis use (both in terms of early initiation and frequency of use) is related to insecure attachment to parents. Recent Australian research shows that the relative risk of cannabis use by young people is three times greater when attachment and relationship quality with parents deteriorate.

Longitudinal studies show that the quality of mother–child interactions at age 5 predicts the type of cannabis use at age 18 (experimentation or abuse). Mothers of abusers are said to have been cold, unresponsive and unprotective, offering little encouragement to their child, but exerting pressure to perform.

As for tobacco use, two vulnerability factors, attachment and depression, are associated with trajectories towards nicotine dependence in women. The difficulties of attachment to others, whether parents or friends, "push" girls towards tobacco dependence, and this is clearly more than for boys. Depression is also a factor in this relationship (possibly due to attachment difficulties).

It remains to be understood why this combination of attachment difficulties and depression produces tobacco dependence in girls but not in boys. In fact, in boys, the evolution towards addiction corresponds to other causes and follows other trajectories, those of antisociality, sensation seeking and self-escape.

When we study adolescents in psychiatric hospitals, we notice that it is mainly the detached who develop psychoactive substance dependencies. When we then extend the investigation to responses to psychotherapeutic treatments, the detached respond better, followed by the preoccupied and then the autonomous. This result may seem surprising, since the detached are characterized by the avoidance of recalling of affects, which is the basic principle of psychotherapy. It seems that psychotherapy allows them (at last…) access to their internal emotional world. This work would also have therapeutic implications, such as not only choosing a therapeutic strategy based on symptomatology.

A comparison of 114 young people in Lausanne, aged 15–25 and addicted to psychoactive substances, including 87 control subjects with no problems in this respect (Pierrehumbert 2003) showed that the addicted young people reported having been victims of violence (abuse, maltreatment, rape) during childhood four times more frequently than the control group (30%, as opposed to 8%) and of separations (31%, as opposed to 14%).

Statements such as "I only rely on myself to solve my problems", "I hate the feeling of depending on others" and "I never had a real relationship with my parents" highlight the defensive exclusion mechanism characteristic of detached bonds. Early experience of emotional violence is not directly predictive of addiction, but this influence is mediated by the defensive exclusion phenomenon; it is only when it leads to a “forced indifference”, to a blocking of emotions and to alexithymia, that it generates addiction.

The regulation of emotions is thus a mediating element between the traumatic events experienced by the child and the use of psychoactive substances. Sensation seeking, whose influence on different types of risk behaviors is well known, can be seen as a defense mechanism in relation to this problem of defensive exclusion: sensations would allow anxiety to be regulated without having to reactivate the emotions linked to attachment.

The use of psychoactive substances should be considered as a self-medication against insecurity in adolescence, an “anti-thought” (to use Philippe Jeammet’s expression (2007)), this period being characterized by a reactivation of separation anxiety and of negative emotions experienced during childhood. Helping the subject out of this vicious circle leading to addiction consists of helping them to build a reflective awareness of their emotions.

A concept is emerging from this analysis of the relationship between attachment and substance use, that of dependence; children with insecure attachments become more dependent on their mothers. We still need to verify, through longitudinal studies that the correlations described above reflect a causal link, a genetic relationship, and that children who are more dependent on their mothers become adolescents who are more dependent on products.

Within this relationship between attachment and addiction, we will distinguish between two “channels”, according to the properties of the substances and the characteristics of the behavioral dependencies:

– the detached will seek out “anesthetic” substances (such as heroin, high dose cannabis, tranquilizers, sleeping pills, work addiction and endurance activities);

– the preoccupied will seek out substances that cause emotional hyperactivation (such as cocaine, amphetamines, pathological gambling, compulsive shopping, kleptomania and compulsive sexuality).

In a way, the insecure will look for a product that “evokes” their childhood history. The question that remains is whether what is at stake with regard to psychoactive products would also apply to sports or recreational activities: are there sports for the detached and sports for the preoccupied? If we look at addiction from the point of view of intergenerational transmission, we would observe “toxicomanogenic” families, characterized by difficulty in coping with separations and by an inability to tolerate frustration, two characteristics that reflect a relationship of encroachment by the mother.

We frequently observe the difficulty that drug addicts have in separating from their parents and the lack of emotion in the parents. In this context, Olievenstein spoke of the affective fund of drug addicts as an “immense unspoken thing”, similar to the unspoken thing of the survivors of the Nazi camps. This unspoken fact concerns the traumas that have been repressed by the family over the generations.

We need to understand the genealogy of addiction. Among the secrets, the unspoken ones, there are often secrets related to filiation, the legitimacy of births, abortions, incest, offences and the trauma of the discovery of these secrets (“You are not my father!”). Addiction goes some way to “filling” the holes of our history. It can start, increase and (more rarely) decrease following the brutal revelation of a family secret.

5.18. Attachment and transgression

Attachment insecurity has been clearly linked to adolescent anger and hostility in both boys and girls. The quality of the parent–child relationship is the dimension that explains the genesis of adolescent antisocial behavior more than any other dimension of parental behavior.

Do attachment processes also influence the relationship with the law? Bowlby had assumed this, well before his attachment theory: as early as the 1940s, in his “44 Young Thieves” study (entitled like a fable), Bowlby noted the frequency of mother–child separations, compared with a control group. Among these young delinquents, 40% had undergone prolonged separations from their mothers and 70% presented a “detached” personality, “devoid of tenderness”.

These separations had provoked the defensive exclusion and compulsive self-confidence phenomena mentioned above in connection with addiction, phenomena that may even have persisted after the return of the mother. Deprivation would be the origin of the antisocial behavior: things going well, then going badly. It is the social connection to others that inhibits the manifestation of delinquent behavior. On this topic, Green spoke about a gap left by the imprint of the “dead mother” (“The lack is no longer a call to creation but a negative spiral, the loss becoming unworkable. It is then from this impossibility to the separation that the necessary annihilation of the other results, counteracting the annihilation of the self that threatens the horizon of the separation”).

The dysfunction of the parent–child bond, and the lack of cohesion perceived by the child, has often been highlighted in the genesis of delinquency. Conversely, the quality of the attachment has been associated with the prosocial orientations of the child and the adolescent, across quite different cultures.

There is therefore a general link between attachment and delinquent behavior, as well as specific categorical differences: violent offenders are distinguished from non-violent offenders by their higher level of insecurity and perpetrators of sexual violence are characterized by a more insecure attachment style than non-sexual offenders. Such differences are also found among sexual offenders: the detached attachment found among adult rapists compared to the significantly more insecure attachment found among perpetrators of sexual violence against minors.

Interaction effects between biological and psychological factors have also been observed. In a cohort of 4,269 Danish boys followed since birth, it was found that a birth with complications or with a neurological disorder in the child was not associated with involvement in delinquency 18 years later, but that, on the other hand, a birth with complications followed by rejection by the mother (4.5% of the subjects) was associated with involvement in delinquency 18 years later (18% of crimes). This risk factor was specifically related to violent crimes and not to non-violent offenses or recidivism, which confirms the idea of a specific relationship between affective links and violence.

This shows the importance of early prevention work by social workers after births with complications, so that these do not become a risk factor. It has been shown that these interventions in at-risk families with a focus on maternal behavior reduced the number of subsequent arrests (15 years later) due to the antisocial behavior of adolescents by half.

Finally, research on bullying, and the young people who are perpetrators or victims, shows that family conflict and difficult emotional relationships are strongly associated. It is interesting to note that this influence is true in both perpetrators and victims.

5.19. Attachment, antisocial behavior and hyperactivity

Hyperactivity/attention deficit syndrome during childhood has been considered (with the polemics that we know about "cube thieves"!) as one of the risk factors for antisociality and delinquency in adolescence. However, recent studies have shown that, among children with this syndrome, two factors play an important role in determining whether or not the trajectory towards delinquency will be followed: the mother's depression, which is a risk factor, and a good relationship between the mother and child in the first years of the child's life, a protective factor. Preventing the child's progression to delinquency means preventing and treating the mother's depression, probably as early as during pregnancy.

An intermediate variable would explain the link between attachment and delinquency, alexithymia. The frequency of alexithymia is much higher among young offender populations (47%) than among comparable control populations (22%); it is also similar to that of clinical psychiatric populations. Along with family dissociation, alexithymia is the other variable that is the most closely related to the emergence of juvenile delinquency. The lack of awareness of our own emotions seems to be one of the most important predictive factors and indicators of vulnerability to delinquency. These observations should have preventive implications for the rehabilitation of juvenile delinquents: it is necessary to help them to "mentalize", and for this purpose, group therapies are undoubtedly more suitable than individual psychotherapies.

6

The Differences between Boys and Girls, Gender and Stereotypes

The primary determining factor studied within developmental psychology is obviously age, but in many fields, it appears that gender can also play as significant a role in the differences between individuals.

Nature does things well and, from 120 male embryos for every 100 females, a few more boys are born each year than girls (100 vs. 95.2). Therefore, between the ages of 0 and 18, there are in France about 20,000 more boys per age group. Nature is compensating in some way for the significant excess male mortality (see below) due to factors such as miscarriage, sudden infant death syndrome, various types of illnesses, domestic and road accidents, suicides and homicides. Thus, there are more cohorts of boys than girls, although the difference will decrease with age; from adolescence onwards until the end of life, there are more cohorts of females.

Is having enough reproductive males as adults a Darwinian mechanism to help the survival of the species?

6.1. Developmental data

According to the EDEN Study, girls develop earlier and have better language skills than boys in most language domains (phonology, lexicon and syntax), but these differences can disappear between the ages of 3 and 5 (Peyre 2017, 2019).

In this study, children were assessed for language and gross and fine motor skills at ages 2, 3, 5 and 6, using parent questionnaires and neuropsychological tests. The main observations were:

– girls show better fine motor and language skills at ages 2 and 3;

– gender differences in fine motor and language skills tend to diminish or disappear by age 5–6.

Based on the studies of twins, we might think that gender differences in language skills at ages 2–4 would reflect gender differences in cognitive development, as indicated by results in non-verbal domains referenced in the Parent Report of Children's Abilities that measured fine motor skills and other cognitive dimensions, such as non-verbal intelligence (Peyre 2017, 2019). Dizygotic twins of different sexes presented greater differences in verbal skills than dizygotic twins of the same sex, which was not observed for non-verbal skills. Thus, individual differences in verbal ability may depend in part on some gender-specific factors.

Girls also perform better in fine motor skills up to age 6–7, in other words, activities requiring a high degree of precision and generally involving manual object manipulation activities.

In contrast, there are few gender differences in gross motor skills, that is, activities involving locomotion and torso movement during the preschool period.

How can these differences be explained? Three main types of factors can be put forward to explain these early gender differences in development:

– differential exposure to environmental factors known to influence development: these differential exposures between boys and girls may include life experiences related to gender role stereotypes and complications during childbirth that are more common in boys, perhaps because of their greater height and weight than girls. Nevertheless, this remains a hypothesis;

– differences in emotional, behavioral or social functioning between the genders may contribute to differences in development during the preschool period: boys have more behavioral and social problems and neurodevelopmental disorders (autism spectrum disorder, attention deficit/hyperactivity disorder, intellectual disability, developmental coordination disorder and other specific acquisition and learning disorders). Nevertheless, this remains a hypothesis;

– finally, biological differences may underpin the skill advantage observed in girls over boys during the preschool period, such as the negative effect of testosterone on brain development.

It also remains to be explained why these developmental differences disappear after age 6 and how boys catch up.

6.2. Mathematics, spatial skills and stereotypes

Spatial skills (spatial visualization, mechanical and abstract reasoning) during adolescence are better in boys. Therefore, it is important to determine when this gender gap emerges and begins to be related to achievement in areas such as mathematics, as well as the underlying factors. One potential factor could be the endorsement of the common gender stereotype that men are more talented than women in the spatial and mathematical domains, which could lead to "stereotype threat", the fear of underachieving due to a negative and approved stereotype.

Knowing the age at which gender differences in performance begin to emerge and at which gender stereotypes are endorsed could lead to a better understanding of this gender cognition gap and its implications, including ways to combat the effects of stereotype threat. In addition, it could help in the design of intervention programs to foster the development of girls' spatial skills, which, in turn, could either promote math performance or reduce gender-stereotype beliefs.

The magnitude of the gender difference in mathematics achievement overall is very small when measured using a standardized test, and in favor of girls when assessed using grades (Moé 2018). However, even though it is small, it differs between countries, which is contrary to the assumption of a "natural" difference.

Although there is little or no gender difference in math achievement, boys are more confident than girls in math and report more positive math attitudes and affects than girls (Moé 2018).

By age 14–16, there is a stereotype favoring boys who actually rate math as more important than girls. These gender stereotypes relating to mathematical and spatial ability appear from ages 8 to 10.

These beliefs could lead to lower self-confidence in girls, less practice on spatial tasks, higher levels of anxiety and, consequently, reduced performance, to the point of confirming the stereotype, through stereotype threat effects.

However, this is not always the case. In fact, recent meta-analyses have shown that the overall effects of induced stereotyping are low to non-existent and that some important mediators can make a difference. The extent to which stereotypes are endorsed, how they are emphasized (explicitly or implicitly) and the perceived difficulty of the task are important elements (Moé 2018).

6.3. Risk taking, risk perception and stereotypes

As we will see in the next chapter on causes of death, there is a significant over-involvement of boys in all types of accidents compared with girls (Assailly 2019), and this very early in life, for example, accidental deaths from choking and asphyxiation in baby carriages between 0 and 3 months, or child pedestrian accidents at ages 2 or 3, ages where we would not expect to find significant gender differences and where, normally, boys and girls would be equally under parental supervision, with very little autonomy in their behavior.

From early life, therefore, boys have more frequent accidents than girls and more severe accidents when they do occur. We have proposed the hypothesis that this stems from three main dimensions: they take more risks than girls, perceive risks less well and accept risks more (Assailly 2019).

Similarly, sensation seeking and its influence on risk taking are classically addressed in adolescence, but studies of children show that, from an early age, boys are more sensation-seeking and risk-taking than girls (Morrongiello *et al.* 2004) and that, within a given type of activity, boys take more risks than girls (Granié 2011).

Differences in risk perception also appear early: by the age of 6, children already have differentiated beliefs about the vulnerability of each sex to accidents. Thus, children of both sexes believe that boys are less likely to have accidents than girls, even if they do the same activities (Morrongiello *et al.* 2000); boys believe they are less likely to be injured, perceive them as less serious, attribute their accidents to bad luck and express more comparative optimism[1] than girls (Morrongiello and Rennie 1998). Conversely, preschool girls identify more dangerous situations on the street than boys, feel more vulnerable and express more apprehension about the risk of accidents (Granié 2013).

Involvement in accidents also follows the same trend and in this area, too, from an early age, boys are less compliant than girls to the demands and requirements of parents, teachers and other authority figures (Granié 2013). Similarly, preschool girls show a greater knowledge of, and compliance with, the pedestrian code of conduct than boys of the same age (Granié 2007). Finally, 9–12-year-old girls demonstrate greater internalization of the behavioral rules for cyclists and tend to show a lower propensity for risk taking while cycling (Granié 2011).

1 A cognitive bias in the perceptions of risk and of self: thinking that we are more likely than others to escape accidents, thinking that our skills are better than the average person, and so on.

Multiple factors have been invoked to explain gender differences: biological, sociological and anthropological. In this chapter, we will focus on psychological factors, including parenting practices and their conformity to gender stereotypes.

Risk education and, more generally, socialization are not the same for girls and boys. When a child engages in dangerous behavior, for example, parents make more encouraging statements towards boys and issue more warnings, reprimands and physical assistance towards girls (Granié 2011). In general, parents are more supervisory and restrictive with girls than with boys throughout development. This also reflects age-old fears about the dangers girls face.

From the beginning of life, it is therefore more gender than biological sex that explains differences in behavior and attitudes, which is what is expected of masculinity and femininity. Conformity to gender stereotypes influences risk taking from an early age. For example, this has been observed in both boys and girls aged 3–6 years (Granié 2010): being recognized as masculine, in other words, being perceived by our parents as strongly adopting behaviors and personality traits that society attributes to the male sex, predicts risk-taking behaviors in these preschool children, regardless of their sex.

Thus, by age 4, most children begin to avoid activities assumed to be "of the opposite sex" and gradually focus on activities considered appropriate for their gender group. By age 5, children become prototypes of their gender group and parents may believe that gender differences are more biological than sociocultural; then, the rigidity of gender stereotypes is strongest between ages 5 and 7.

The decrease in risky behaviors in girls may also be explained by the gender segregation of children: gender segregation thus provides fewer opportunities for girls to play with boys and, as a result, there is less masculine behavior among girls, as well as less dangerous or risky behavior (Granié 2010).

Conversely, boys are more strongly discouraged by people in their social circle from engaging in activities that go against the stereotype: activities that challenge the stereotype are perceived more negatively by boys than by girls, reinforcing "masculine" activities and inhibiting "feminine" activities among boys.

Thus, parental beliefs impact risk education practices in children: risky behavior in boys will be considered innate and unchangeable by education, whereas risk prevention is the primary goal in girls' education (Granié 2010).

Finally, the stereotype threat that we mentioned in connection with spatial skills is found on the road in the skills of adolescent drivers (Granié 2010): in spite of and against all the statistics, the idea that female subjects would be less able to drive vehicles and take risks with them is instilled.

It is therefore the entirety of risk education and the behavioral associations of masculinity that will have to be modified in the future. Finally, the essential question is: for a boy, what does it mean to become a man? It is obviously his objective. For as long as masculinity is defined by risk taking, aggressiveness and excessive self-confidence, there will be little progress to expect in the excess mortality of men.

Therefore, it will be necessary to change the indicators defining masculinity, but for this and well beforehand, education must be much less differentiated according to gender and boys must be raised much more like girls in order to protect them better, and for this, we have seen that the beliefs of parents are one of the fundamental mechanisms of the influence of stereotypes.

7

Health, Disease and Mortality

7.1. Health behaviors

Paradoxically, there have been few studies specifically relating to health behaviors in children: most of the literature focuses on the influences of family environment (such as attachments, educational styles and living conditions) in this area. Consequently, it is the parents who have always been questioned, on the basis that children do not understand health issues, and it is only from adolescence onwards that we study health-related representations and values. However, children can also make decisions about their health and are not only dependent on their parents' influences.

Differences have been observed between Russian and American adolescents on the representations associated with health values, which shows the influence of cultural factors.

7.2. The issue of vaccination

This topic is back in the news because the whole planet has been waiting for a vaccine against Covid-19, but not without ambivalence.

Indeed, vaccines have eradicated whole diseases (smallpox, 40 years ago), and the WHO has just announced that poliomyelitis has officially been eradicated in Africa. It is important to know that on this continent in the last century, each year, 75,000 children were paralyzed for life because of this disease.

Since 1996, intensive vaccination campaigns have prevented 2 million paralysis cases and 180,000 deaths in Africa; 90% of the world's population is now protected, with only a few cases remaining in Pakistan and Afghanistan. This progress has been made possible thanks to highly significant investment from public/private partnerships (such as the Bill Gates Foundation).

Vaccines have also reduced the severity of many infections, especially in children. Furthermore, when a disease has been completely eradicated, populations are then "rid" of both the disease and the need to be vaccinated.

However, removing the need for vaccination is the most difficult goal to achieve, as the vaccination effort must be pursued everywhere and over a long period of time. Indeed, as we have seen with Covid-19, viruses spread with the worldwide movement of people; also, when a few cases remain in conditions of poor hygiene, side effects are always possible, which hampers the social acceptability of vaccination.

The use of vaccines is nevertheless threatened by unfounded fears, misinformation and antivaccination propaganda. These fears and attitudes have accompanied vaccination since its inception at the end of the 18th century and are particularly virulent in France and in Italy.

This has resulted in the re-emergence of mumps, whooping cough, measles and chickenpox epidemics around the world. With globalization, we have seen with Covid-19 how this can take on dramatic proportions.

7.2.1. *Why is there a refusal to vaccinate?*

Many people do not recognize the effectiveness of vaccination and fear the side effects.

The 2016 Health Barometer showed that, among 65–75-year-olds, while three out of four people are in favor of vaccination, 47% believe that flu vaccines can cause serious side effects. The credibility of institutions seems to carry more weight than the content of the information itself. Particular events, such as pandemics, can exacerbate attitudes by altering trust in institutions. Lack of time to discuss with health professionals probably also plays a role. Finally, in some rural French departments, vaccination refusal is part of a confused mix of ecology and conspiracy theory.

In any case, the economic management of vaccination faces paradoxes: coverage must be global, which implies a very low price for vaccines and therefore low profits. Furthermore, eradication of an epidemic due to vaccination signals the end of profits for pharmaceutical laboratories, since people no longer need a vaccination.

This paradoxical relationship between the economy and public health can be observed in various fields. For example, once we have completely eliminated road traffic accidents, this will have a negative impact on economies such as emergency services, rehabilitation centers, car repairs and insurance companies.

7.3. The age 4 health check

For more than 25 years, the departmental services of the French Maternal and Child Protection agency (*Protection Maternelle et Infantile*, PMI) have been responsible for organizing a pre-school health check-up (*Bilan de Santé en École Maternelle*, BSEM) for all children aged four years.

The ELFE cohort coordinating team conducted a "BSEM ELFE-PMI" survey for all children born in 2011 and enrolled in kindergarten in 2014–2016.

It was observed that 40% of children had at least one vaccination outstanding (including hepatitis B), more than 10% were overweight, 35% received health guidance and 13% were receiving developmental, language or psychological guidance.

7.4. Laterality

Left-handed people make up around 13% of the population, and lateralization in children is acquired between the ages of 3 and 3.5 years. If it occurs much earlier, this may be a sign of brain damage.

A genetic etiology of left-handedness is likely, without neglecting environmental factors (cultural pressures): a particular variant in the PCSK6 gene seems to play a role in the determination between right and left.

Left-handedness has long been considered a vulnerability: a reduction in life expectancy by nine years has often been put forward, one of the reasons being that left-handed people have more accidents in a world where objects are made for right-handed people. It has also been assumed that left-handed people are more susceptible to immune or neurological problems.

However, multiple biases and confounding factors have since been found in these studies, particularly since left-handed children are "thwarted" less now than they were in the past. In any case, upsetting a left-handed child to force them to use their right hand is clearly a source of various pathologies.

7.5. Child size

The association between height and social background has been noted in the academic literature for centuries. Child height is positively related to education and income. Taller children perform better in academic tests than smaller children. The relationship between family income, height and school maladjustment is due to the fact that height is associated with greater intelligence.

However, the relationship between child height and family income may be due to environmental factors such as nutrition. Indeed, there are associations between early (postnatal) nutrition and child height and between nutrition and cognitive and social development. For example, iron deficiency in infants and children is associated with poorer cognitive, motor and social–emotional skills and iron supplementation has a positive effect on height.

What are the psychological processes by which a child's size can influence their future? Taller subjects would be more competitive, more socially dominant and would have a better self-esteem.

Possession of certain characteristics, such as being tall, may produce expectations from others (such as peers or teachers) that may influence their behavior towards the subject, which in turn affects behavior and often confirms those expectations.

This self-fulfilling prophecy is also referred to as the "expectancy effect": taller subjects are perceived as more attractive, and attractiveness can in turn influence teacher behavior and evaluation.

Furthermore, it is often thought that short children have negative social experiences, including bullying, less social acceptance and fewer friends, although being tall in girls also has negative psychological effects. Having problematic social relationships can, in turn, affect self-esteem, social adjustment, behavior and school performance.

Another aspect of this problem is that peers, parents, teachers and medical staff treat children in a "size-appropriate", rather than an "age-appropriate" way: tall children are generally perceived as older (and are treated as such), while smaller children are treated as younger.

7.6. Vision and myopia

There will be a significant increase in the rate of prevalence of myopia in the world population in the coming years (estimated at 50% of the world population) and in the associated economic (cost of equipment) and medical (ocular complications from myopia) consequences.

The prevalence of myopia increased from the 1920s to the 1980s. Near visual activity is one of the main factors in the increase in this prevalence, with the development of more intensive schooling.

7.7. Physical activity

Despite compelling evidence suggesting that physical activity plays an important role in overall health, a substantial proportion of young people do not meet recommended levels of physical activity.

Only one-quarter of French children aged 3–10 engage in physical activity five days a week or use active mobility (pedestrian, cyclist) to get to school (see the section on children's road safety below).

Only one-third of adolescents engage in physical activity for at least one hour a day (WHO recommendation).

Physical activity and sedentary behavior are the two independent behaviors that occupy all waking hours of a day. Physical activity, which is defined as any bodily movement that increases energy expenditure (such as active travel, outdoor play or participation in sports), has historically been linked to physical and mental health benefits throughout a person's life. In contrast, sedentary behavior, defined as any waking behavior characterized by energy expenditure less than or equal to 1.5 metabolic equivalents, while sitting, lying or reclining, has become a central component of children's daily lives.

As a result, the debate about whether sedentary behavior, particularly recreational screen time, has a negative impact on children's mental health is becoming increasingly important (see the chapter on the screen issue below). For example, physical activity is moderately associated with white matter microstructure in children's brains, so it may promote healthy white matter development.

7.8. Eating behavior

It is estimated that about half of all parents have difficulty feeding their children at some point, with problems ranging from relatively minor eating issues to major eating disorders and even anorexia.

Since many parents view feeding as a fundamental component of parenting, perceived problems in this area – even at non-clinical levels – can cause considerable concern and negatively impact self-efficacy, perceptions of parenting and subsequent parenting behaviors.

Concerns about feeding have been associated with the use of maladaptive parenting strategies, such as coercion, persuasion, bribery and rewards, and with deficits in optimal problem-solving skills; these factors have been associated with the maintenance and exacerbation of feeding problems in children.

Thus, from the beginning of life, infants develop an innate skill, a "capacity for self-regulation", adjusting their consumption according to hunger and satiety. Unfortunately, this ability diminishes with age from one year onwards, particularly due to parental injunctions ("Finish your plate!").

Thus, parental perceptions of problematic eating behaviors in children, and of their own ability to cope with these behaviors, can have a significant impact on subsequent parental approaches and interactions and on children's future eating problems. Therefore, it is important to try to understand feeding issues, as well as the key correlates of these problems from parents' perspectives.

7.8.1. *Eating behavior problems*

We often confuse two problems:

– *food neophobia* is defined as a rejection and/or reluctance to eat unfamiliar or unknown foods (this has an adaptive and protective value, a refusal prior to the incorporation of the food);

– *food selectivity* (or *pickiness eating*) is defined as a reluctance to eat familiar foods (this is linked to pleasure, the refusal is at the sensory level, post incorporation).

The two are often confused in the literature:

– because a familiar food can become new for the child when it is prepared differently, with a new recipe, a new presentation;

– as both result in a reduction of the food repertoire.

Food neophobia is particularly common between the ages of four and eight (Rubio and Rigal 2008). From a phylogenetic perspective, it could be considered an effective behavioral strategy, to prevent the individual from ingesting toxic substances. However, the highest levels of food neophobia in children are problematic for both public health and education, as they lead to a reduction in the quality and quantity of foods consumed, particularly fruits and vegetables, which are known to prevent obesity and certain types of cancer (Rubio and Rigal 2008).

Cultural factors also have an important influence: Swedes are less food neophobic than Americans; the range of foods offered from early childhood is probably wider in France than in other western countries; also, early diversity is negatively correlated with food neophobia (Rubio and Rigal 2008).

Despite being a normal stage of early development, the persistence of food neophobia beyond a certain age is associated with problematic eating due to inadequate food intake.

Food selectivity (or picky eating) is defined as the consumption of an inadequate variety of foods due to rejecting a substantial number of foods that are both familiar and unfamiliar. The prevalence of children identified as picky eaters in early childhood varies across studies: between 4 and 24 months of age, the percentage of picky eaters increases from 19% to 50% and between 24 and 36 months of age, from 13% to 17% (Rubio *et al.* 2017).

Thus, food sensitivity appears before the second year of life and seems to be one of the main sources of concern around food for a majority of parents. It leads to a limitation of the food repertoire, particularly with regard to the consumption of fruits and vegetables, and studies have highlighted the stress and conflicts of parents during family meals.

Parents attribute the fear of food primarily to a display of opposition and assertiveness on the part of their child. Some strategies that are known to be effective can be applied by parents (such as repeated exposure, modeling, joint meal preparation and using a flavor-based approach), but some counterproductive strategies can also be observed (such as rewards for eating). Parents need to be better informed about food choices and strategies to overcome them. Understanding parental beliefs can help pediatricians offer appropriate counseling tailored to parents' experiences and feelings (Rubio *et al.* 2017).

Furthermore, and as discussed in the first chapter on parenting, parenting styles influence child behaviors. For example, harsh control (coercive measures to obtain child feeding behavior) and gentle control (supportive measures to guide child feeding behavior) have been compared (Rigal and Rubio 2016).

Additionally, and beyond the effect of parental feeding strategies on food avoidance in children, some basic characteristics of children have been considered, such as temperament (Rigal and Rubio 2016); an important aspect of this is "inhibition control" (the ability to maintain, moderate or refrain from behaving as instructed).

After the familiarization phase, consumption of the target food increased in all groups, but with a greater increase in children with high inhibition control and gentle instructions than in children with low inhibition control and harsh instructions, with the other two groups falling between the two.

Thus, we end up with a cumulative effect model, where both parental control strategies and the high inhibition control trait in children contribute to the regulation of refusals and dislikes in eating behavior contexts.

7.8.2. *Risk factors for eating disorders*

The most common non-medical correlates of problematic eating behaviors in children are: difficulties related to temperament, general conduct and coping problems, sensory information processing and food phobia.

In addition, children learn much about what, when and how to eat through social interactions, so difficulties in this area can significantly impede the development and adaptation of eating behavior.

Externalizing disorders and temperament issues may also be more directly associated with the frequency of eating problems if these affect eating and mealtimes (e.g. poor appetite regulation, restlessness at mealtimes and rigidity about new foods and routines).

Thus, children's eating problems appear to be externalized and interactive rather than innately driven or internalizing. The association with externalized disorders suggests that feeding problems may fit a broader profile of challenging behaviors. Problematic eating behaviors can be a challenge for parents, but only when the child's social interactions are also considered impaired.

What about messages aimed at "instrumentalizing" food in order to influence children, such as "eat spinach, you'll be as strong as Popeye", or "eating carrots makes you likeable", or even towards adults, "eat five fruits and vegetables a day"?

In fact, these messages are counterproductive: the more a food is praised to the child, the less they are willing to eat it. This ultimately creates a form of suspicion in the child. Even if the messages have a laudable public health objective, it is better to accompany food with as few types of messages as possible and leave the child with the simple pleasure of eating.

7.9. Anorexia

Anorexia nervosa has been of increasing interest over the past few decades. It is a serious and life-threatening condition with the highest mortality rate of all mental disorders (Albinhac and Bouvard 2019).

It mainly affects adolescent girls with a sex ratio of 9/10; the prevalence can be as high as 2.2%. There is significant psychiatric comorbidity (depression, anxiety). This disease seems to be increasingly frequent with a growing incidence in the 15–19-year-old risk group.

It is a multifactorial pathology, with family dysfunction represented by family discord, high parental demands and insecure attachment, among others (Albinhac and Bouvard 2019). It can be considered a disorder of interpersonal relationships, a "bonds pathology".

Studies have found less caring and nurturing parents, a significant association between parental dysfunction and symptom severity and between attachment insecurity and chronicization (Albinhac and Bouvard 2019).

There is maternal and paternal overprotection in pubertal patients with anorexia nervosa compared to peripubertal patients, hence the hypothesis of a dysfunctional need for separation–individuation in connection with structural failures. Parental deficiencies in primary care would not enable the early internalization during infancy necessary for individuation at the time of adolescence. The sexualization of the body thus reactivates "same body as the mother" fantasies. In this context, the anorexic adolescent who is as one with her mother would not be able to perceive the dysfunctions in the bond (Albinhac and Bouvard 2019).

7.10. Obesity

Obesity is responsible for 5% of deaths worldwide; it is estimated that, by 2030, 30% of the world's population will be overweight; even emerging countries with problems of malnutrition are seeing increases in the prevalence of obesity among children.

Childhood obesity continues to be one of the most challenging public health issues of this century. The prevalence of overweight among children under five years of age increased from 31 million worldwide in 1990 to 41 million in 2014. It is projected that, by 2025, 70 million infants and preschoolers (0–5 years) worldwide will be affected by overweight and obesity.

In an average of 6% of girls and 8% of boys today, it is associated with cardiovascular risks. The caloric value of the food consumed is obviously one of the factors in the development of overweight and it is noted that children may prefer high-calorie foods at a very early age. However, it has not been possible to statistically correlate the preference for high-calorie foods with the body mass index (BMI) of children. Similarly, it has not been possible to statistically correlate parents' preferences for high-calorie foods with their children's BMI. Social desirability factors may be at play here.

Importantly, obesity-related behaviors are established in early childhood and are followed into adulthood: children with obesity have a twofold increased risk of being affected by obesity as adults.

Obese children are more likely to be hospitalized and incur 60% higher health care costs than children of normal weight. The implications of early childhood overweight and obesity extend beyond physical health.

Therefore, understanding the early risk factors of obesity is crucial in informing prevention strategies. The causes of childhood obesity are complex, ranging from genetic to non-genetic influences, including family and community/societal factors.

Genetic factors are now well established:

– a defect in the leptin gene can lead to obesity (leptin is a hormone that informs the brain about our body fat in order to keep it stable. Fortunately, treatment can counteract the disorder);

– in another example, the FTO gene must be in duplicate (father and mother) to promote overweight in India, while only one copy is needed in France for obesity to appear. It is the lifestyle that creates this difference, a genotype/environment interaction;

– similarly, the MC4R gene promotes excess weight but has no effect in cases of high physical activity, an epigenetic effect;

– adoption studies clearly show the existence of genetic factors, since the weights of adopted children are closer to those of their biological parents than to those of their adoptive parents. The same conclusions are reached in twin studies since monozygotic children are more similar than dizygotic ones;

– population genetics studies clearly show interactions. For example, the majority of Pima Indians living in the United States are diabetic and obese, while Pima Indians living in Mexico are not, the difference stems from the fact that the latter have a different diet and physical activity.

Therefore, the existence of genetic factors is now well established, in interaction with other factors, but genetics is mostly used to explain individual differences: at the global level, the contemporary obesity "epidemic" on the planet is mostly related to changes in diet, compared with our ancestors.

Next are the prenatal environment factors, the importance of which we saw in the second chapter: exposure to pollutants and the mother's diet influence the child's weight.

Delivery may then have its influences: currently, 20% of deliveries are performed by cesarean section in France (in some countries, this can be as high as 50%). It has been found that the subsequent weight of children born by cesarean section is significantly higher, from the age of 3–4 years to at least 15–20 years. This risk of overweight and obesity may be related to the loss of transmission of maternal microbiota and its protective effects against obesity during cesarean delivery[1]. Similarly, breastfeeding is less frequent in the case of scheduled cesarean section, as well as in the case of maternal obesity, yet breast milk provides a microbiota that reduces the risk of obesity in the child. There are therefore interaction effects: the risk of subsequent obesity after cesarean section is much higher when the mother is overweight or obese.

With regard to family influences, obesity researchers have used ecological systems theory (Bronfenbrenner 1977) to summarize the complex interplay between these multidimensional contributors to the development of excessive child weight and to inform research and prevention strategies relating to childhood obesity.

Ecological systems theory places parent–child factors as the most proximal influences on the development of overweight and obesity in early childhood. These child feeding factors include child self-regulation, parental feeding practices and family mealtime climate: child development is influenced by individual and dyadic parent–child factors, whereby parent and child behaviors and responses influence each other and contribute to the quality of interactions.

Despite the recognized importance of investigating dyadic parent–child interactions with respect to feeding, the vast majority of research assessing parental and child influences on childhood overweight and obesity has taken a unidirectional perspective, primarily assessing the influence of the parent on the child and largely neglecting the influence that the child may have on parent–child feeding interactions. Parental child feeding practices may be a response to, rather than an influence on, child feeding and weight.

---

1 We now try to correct this in maternity wards with a gauze on the mucous membranes.

A conceptual model of early mother–child dyadic pathways influencing childhood obesity risk has recently been proposed (Bergmeier and Paxton 2020): it places parent–child relationships in a central role for understanding trajectories leading to eating problems and interactions with child BMI. Important elements of the model are attachment security, child temperament and maternal mental health.

The model therefore focuses primarily on the interrelationships between psychosocial factors that are modifiable in early childhood and thus potentially responsive to intervention. It focuses on mother–child factors because mothers are typically the primary providers of child nutrition during the preschool years; however, other caregivers also play an important role.

7.10.1. *Attachment security*

We now have emerging evidence revealing the important role that parent–child attachment relationships play in the development of childhood obesity, through longitudinal studies showing that insecure attachment is associated with a higher risk of obesity during preschool years and predicts obesity in adolescence.

Child self-regulation, resulting from problematic parent–child dyadic interactions, has been proposed as a potential mechanism linking associations between attachment insecurity and obesity risk.

7.10.2. *Temperament*

Child temperament perceived as "difficult", combined with poor parenting ability (which is more likely in mothers with mental health problems), may lead to dysfunctional parent–child interactions. In addition, dimensions of child temperament are associated with specific eating behaviors.

It is possible that parenting behaviors contribute to the development of food reinforcement in children, with certain temperaments through parent–child feeding interactions involving the use of food to comfort infants who are perceived to be more difficult to soothe, such as those with higher negative reactivity.

7.10.3. *The mother's mental health*

Maternal mental health is also linked to problematic feeding practices, including excessive use of control, ignoring child cues and expressing more negative emotions and conflict with their child in feeding-related situations.

For example, maternal depression has been positively associated with applying pressure to encourage girls to eat, as well as with food restriction in the preschool period. Maternal anxiety has been associated with food restriction in toddlers and preschoolers.

It is possible that mothers' individual experiences with mental health symptoms (such as low mood and agitation) may influence the type of control over feeding practices.

7.10.4. *Self-regulation*

Children with weaker self-regulation are considered less sensitive to internal hunger and satiety cues and less able to regulate intake if external cues (in other words, highly palatable foods) are present.

7.10.5. *Other directions and implications for obesity prevention*

On the other hand, ecological systems theory postulates that the family context is embedded in broader sociocultural factors (Bronfenbrenner 1977). For example, parental eating practices and styles vary according to ethnic and socioeconomic factors. Furthermore, parental attitudes about how they perceive children's body sizes (which therefore potentially influence feeding practices) appear to be culturally defined.

7.11. Sleep

7.11.1. *During childhood*

From birth to three months, parents will testify to the fact that the sleep–wake cycle is linked to the hunger–satiety cycle, regardless of the time of night. Then, gradually, from the fifth month, the sleep cycle locks in with the day–night cycle due to the secretion of melatonin. Thus, 90% of one-year-old infants sleep through the night without interruption.

Up to two months of age, a child's sleep has only two phases, reversed from that of adults: REM sleep, followed by slow wave sleep; between two and nine months of age, it has three phases: REM sleep, followed by slow wave sleep, then deep slow wave sleep (Dugas 2019).

From the age of one, the structure of a child's sleep is identical to that of an adult, with a five-phase structure: very light slow wave sleep, followed by light slow wave sleep, then deep slow wave sleep, very deep slow wave sleep and finally REM sleep.

Sleep influences the whole development of the body as well as the brain: height increases during deep sleep through the growth hormone and the quantity of sleep influences cerebral plasticity. Sleep strongly influences cognitive processes and learning; slow wave sleep plays an important role in memory consolidation (learning multiplication tables or the alphabet), through a dialog between the hippocampus and the neocortex. For this reason, an afternoon nap, which improves emotional balance, short-term memory and even the prevention of overweight, is increasingly recommended for children aged three to five years.

Babies who sleep well do not need to be rocked and can fall back asleep on their own, possibly with the aid of a transitional object, as mentioned above. Ease of falling asleep is linked to the security of the attachment, because falling asleep implies being confident.

Sleep disorders (either falling asleep or waking up) are frequent in early childhood and affect about one-third of children. In the vast majority of cases, there is an environmental cause, such as bad sleeping habits or night eating.

Sleep quantity and patterns dramatically change during childhood. Occasional nighttime waking in preschoolers is part of a normal process of sleep development and maturation. At this age, a frequency of night waking exceeding three times a week is considered abnormally high.

Since occasional night waking is common in early life, the effects of sleep disruption may go undetected. During routine examinations, around 20% of pediatricians do not ask any questions about sleep. However, night waking is one of the main complaints that parents raise with pediatricians and recent results have suggested that this is associated with aggressive behavior, hyperactivity, attention problems and impaired reasoning.

Most studies have used a cross-sectional design and have considered sleep disturbances in out-of-school children. Risk factors specifically associated with nighttime awakening in preschoolers include maternal depression, child sleep patterns and atopic dermatitis.

Only the Weinraub *et al.* study and the EDEN study analyzed night waking using a longitudinal approach.

The study by Weinraub *et al.* included 1,200 children (aged between 3 and 36 months) and identified two trajectories using the mixed growth modeling method.

The first represented children who rarely woke during the night during the study period, and the second represented children with frequent night waking between 6 and 18 months of age, but who became similar to the other children thereafter. Analyses of associated factors principally focused on socioeconomic and demographic factors, as well as on maternal and child psychological and behavioral states. Less attention was paid to postnatal exposures such as sleep patterns, passive smoking or television, which are also associated with sleep quality in children.

The EDEN study sought to identify nighttime wakefulness trajectories of children aged from two to five to six years in the mother–child cohort, using the group trajectory modeling method to best characterize sleep evolution before children start school. The second objective was to identify risk factors from birth to age three associated with the identified trajectories.

Night waking trajectories were obtained for 1,346 children. Two distinct developmental patterns were identified: the "2-5 rare night-waking" pattern (77% of children) and the "2-5 common night-waking" pattern. Logistic regressions were performed to identify factors associated with trajectories. Risk factors for belonging to the "common night-waking" trajectory were exposure to passive smoking at home, group daycare, watching television for long periods, bottle feeding at night, high emotionality and low shyness. This approach identified risk factors associated with night waking during a critical age window and laid the foundation for identifying children at higher risk of deleterious sleep patterns. These risk factors are primarily lifestyle habits, indicating that prevention and intervention programs can be highly beneficial for this population.

Sleep deprivation (also called sleep debt) exists in children and has consequences: less than 10 hours of sleep between the ages of two and six years is associated with poor school performance, hyperactivity, impulsivity and, in boys, with verbal abuse and risk of injury.

7.11.1.1. *The internal clock*

The internal clock represented by the suprachiasmatic nuclei of the hypothalamus is controlled by light, the main synchronizer of our clock. The clock is out of sync when there is no longer a phase relationship between biological time (the internal clock) and astronomical time (the watch). An increasing number of children and adolescents experience desynchronization due to excessive use of electronic media, including late night use. We then observe a phase shift in circadian rhythms (a phase delay during night exposure to light) leading to disturbances in, for example, sleep which is shortened and delayed, mood, fatigue and school performance. This risky behavior in children and adolescents is a public health problem.

7.11.1.2. *To sleep in the parents' bed or not?*

It has been observed that 70% of African American children in the United States sleep with their parents, compared with 35% of Caucasian children. So, standards are different. In Europe, infants typically sleep in the parents' room until three months of age, when they are moved to another room with a transitional object. These norms also reveal parents' own attitudes about separation.

7.11.1.3. *To let the child cry during bedtime or not?*

Hearing a child cry is a very stressful situation for parents, especially at bedtime, as parents often feel helpless if children are constantly crying and unable to fall asleep on their own. This helplessness or uncertainty can often be exacerbated by conflicting advice from friends, family members and pediatricians, which can leave parents confused about whether to act instinctively or follow recommended practices.

These sleep struggles in children are the main reasons for seeking help and new solutions in parenting books. An effective way to reduce these symptoms is through behavioral sleep intervention, such as "graduated extinction", also known as "controlled crying" and "sleep training".

Graduated extinction requires parents to partially ignore a baby that is crying while trying to fall asleep and to check on the child's well-being from time to time according to a set schedule. These interventions have been criticized by infant mental health experts, but are very popular among parents, probably because of their frequently reported effectiveness.

Traditions passed down from one generation to the next may be more relevant to child sleep management, especially when previous child-rearing recommendations have encouraged parents not to soothe their baby's crying while they are falling asleep, or at night.

The infant's persistent crying at first explains why many parents report difficulty in implementing the graduated extinction method, or even why parents stop after the first attempt. Biological instinct activates hormones such as dopamine and oxytocin, leading parents to quickly respond to infants' needs in order to reduce the risk of ignoring their demands.

In addition to these parental factors that can influence sleep management, we should not underestimate the role that each child's temperament can play: a child with a "difficult" temperament, with hyperactivity and poor adaptability, has more frequent sleep disturbances.

It does seem that parents with low sensitivity, or parents of children with difficult temperaments, are more likely to use graduated extinction.

7.11.2. *In adolescence*

This is one of the major problems in adolescence, reconciling studies and leisure, or work and leisure: sleep deteriorates, the subject stays up very late and is in sleep debt, in "social jet lag", which is a source of multiple symptoms, such as academic failure and accidents.

The causes of this phenomenon lie in emotional and social pressures, which points to courses of action, including:

– delaying daily school start times;

– intervening as early as 9–11-year-olds to control sleep patterns before they become established and fixed in adolescence (if an adolescent is not exposed to artificial light from screens at night, or does not participate in virtual social activities, they may fall asleep earlier).

Pubertal sleep changes may also be linked to internalized disorders such as anxiety or depression; the causality is two-way: sleep debt may produce anxiety or depression, but anxiety or depression may also produce sleep problems.

A family environment influence has also been observed: the sleep problems of parents and their children are correlated. Sleep routines (bedtimes, wake-up times and sleep duration) are very similar between parents and children. This can even be shown using electroencephalographic measurements and it can be said that the sleep of the parents shapes that of their children, on a behavioral as well as biological level.

In fact, sleep concordance is a particular aspect of a more general phenomenon, a neurobiological marker, neural concordance, which can be observed using brain imaging. A strong concordance between parents and children is also associated with a better quality of sleep in adolescents.

7.11.2.1. *Sleep in childhood and fatigue in adolescence*

Using data from the Avon Longitudinal Study of Parents and Children (ALSPAC) birth cohort, followed from 6 months to 11 years of age, children with chronic fatigue disorders in adolescence were found to have had shorter nighttime sleep (Collin 2018). The probability of chronic fatigue at age 13 was 39% lower for each additional hour of nighttime sleep at age 9, and the probability at age 16 was 51% lower for each additional hour of nighttime sleep at age 11. The average duration of nighttime sleep at age 9 was 13.9 minutes shorter in children who developed chronic fatigue at age 13 and 18.7 minutes shorter in children who developed it at age 16 (compared with children who did not at ages 13 and 16, respectively).

Children who have shorter nighttime sleep durations throughout infancy, primarily because they are put to bed later, therefore develop chronic disabling fatigue in adolescence, suggesting that sleep abnormalities may have a causal role in chronic disabling fatigue.

These children have shorter sleep durations because of an "evening preference" chronotype. Thus, their bedtime is much later and their morning wake-up time would also be much later if not restricted by school start time. Circadian rhythm and sleep homeostasis are increasingly well understood and have genetic determinants. Different polymorphisms in the PER3 gene of the biological clock are associated with morning or evening individual preferences. These polymorphisms also confer different abilities to cope with sleep deprivation in relation to cognitive performance and vulnerability to negative psychological effects, including mood and anxiety in the evening preference group. At the population level, there are numerous genetic associations between these polymorphisms in body clock genes and psychiatric disorders (including major depressive disorder, bipolar disorder and seasonal affective disorder).

Another hypothesis is that sleep abnormalities and chronic disabling fatigue are associated with a common pathophysiological cause (based on the HPA axis, as manifested by differences in cortisol, corticotropic hormone and melatonin, and autonomic nervous system function, in the form of differences in heart rate variations).

7.12. Dreaming

The proportion of REM sleep, and therefore of dreaming, decreases progressively over the course of life: preponderant during intrauterine life, it is 80% in premature infants, 60% in full-term infants and then stabilizes at 20% at around age 10 (Dugas 2019). In contrast, in learning situations, REM sleep can increase by up to 50%.

It is during REM sleep phases that the child reprocesses raw information stored during the day; this is prior to language and takes place from the beginning of life, not from the age two, as had been thought (Dugas 2019). During dreaming, the brain replays the scenes experienced in order to consolidate or develop the new neural circuits necessary in order to integrate the learnings of the day before.

The content of dreams is obviously only accessible when the child is able to speak and monsters and happy or stressful events of daily life can be reported. Nightmares and night terrors are to be taken seriously, because they allow us to understand what disturbs the child's sleep, especially when they translate the anguish of separation from the mother. In a nightmare, a monster can symbolize the emotions felt during the day.

The genetic developments presented below were described by Dugas (2019):

– around the age of three, the child does not distinguish between daytime and nighttime reverie, but both reveal his/her imagination;

– around the age of four, with the beginning of differentiation of the imaginary and the real, the child begins to wonder how the adult could have been present in one of his/her dreams if he/she did not have this dream himself/herself;

– around the age of five to six, the child can talk more about the feeling of the dream and the more active role he/she played in it; themes and places diversify and the child can even modify the narrative of the dream;

– at around 10 years old, the child begins to reflect and question the meaning of dreams.

During these 10 years, the origin of dreams for children evolves in three stages: at the beginning, they believe that dreams originate outside of them and remain there; then, they realize that dreams originate from within, but they believe them projected outside, in the room; finally, they become aware that dreams start from within and remain there.

7.13. Consumption of psychoactive products

These behaviors are now well known thanks to the two major international school surveys, Health Behaviour in School-aged Children (HBSC) and the European School Project on Alcohol and Other Drugs (ESPAD); mention should also be made of the National Survey in Middle- and High-School for Adolescents on Health and Substances (*Enquête Nationale en Collège et en Lycée chez les Adolescents sur la Santé et les Substances*, EnCLASS) and ESCAPAD, a study conducted on a regular basis at age 17.

In 2018, the two international surveys were, for the first time in France, simultaneously conducted according to a unified methodological framework. More than 20,000 middle and high school students, representative of adolescents schooled in metropolitan France aged 11–18, were asked to answer an online questionnaire in class about their well-being and health behaviors, including substance use (OFDT 2019).

Product	Total	Total		Boys		Girls
	2014	2018		2018		2018
Alcohol	64.4	60.0	*	63.6	>	56.3
Drunkenness	13.4	9.3	↘	10.5	>	8.0
Tobacco	27.8	21.2	↘	23.5	>	18.8
Cannabis	9.8	6.7	↘	7.8	>	5.5

= : Statistically insignificant difference between boys and girls; > : boys consume more than girls ;
➔: Statistically insignificant difference between 2015 and 2018; ↘: usages decreased or ↗ increased between 2014 and 2018.
(*) : Following the harmonization of questions in the HBSC and ESPAD 2018 surveys, the comparability of this indicator was not sufficient between 2014 and 2018 to statistically conclude a potential change.

Sources: HSBC 2014 and EnCLASS 2018

Table 7.1. *Experimentation with tobacco, alcohol and cannabis and first drunkenness, by gender, among secondary school students in 2014 and 2018 (%) (HBSC 2014 and EnCLASS 2018/OFDT exploitation)*

Alcohol is predictably the most widely experimented with, and while 44% of *Sixième* (sixth grade) children report having already used it, this indicates that for some, usage may have begun as early as elementary school. Fortunately, drunkenness is more rare, as is experimentation with cannabis, but it nevertheless concerns a significant number of subjects.

For all products, there has been a decline in experimentation in recent years; prevalences are predictably higher among boys for all products, but we note that the gender gaps are now no longer significant. This is one of the strong epidemiological trends of our time: the catching up of female subjects in terms of consumption, risk taking and violation; the gaps were previously much greater between their parents and between their grandparents.

From high school alcohol remains the product the most experimented with by students, more so than tobacco; in particular, drunkenness sharply increases between middle school and high school, from less than 1 in 10 middle school students to half of high school students, which is a sign of the passage into adolescence.

Regular usage and heavy binge drinking are also becoming more common in high school.

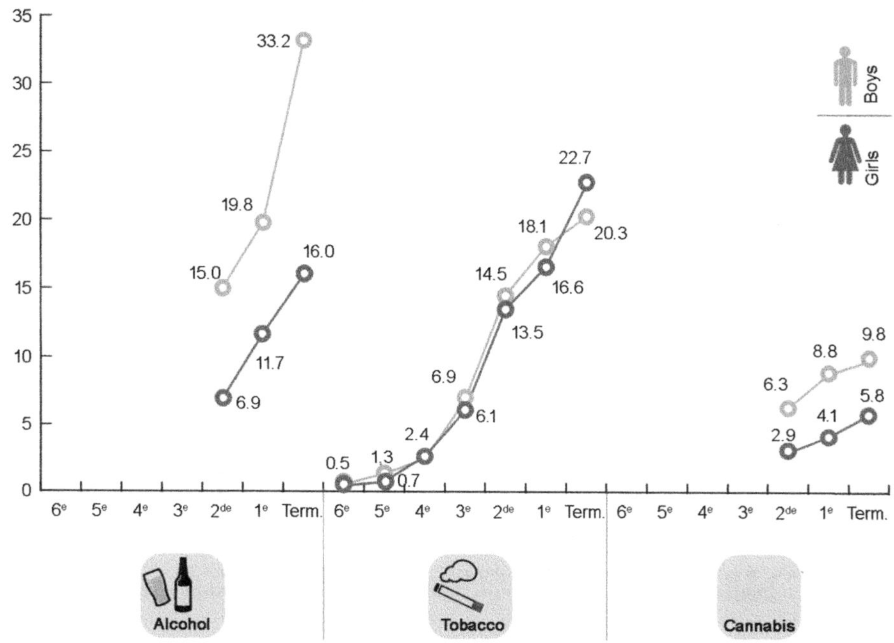

Figure 7.1. *Regular usage of alcohol, tobacco and cannabis by French school level and gender in 2018 (%) (EnCLASS 2018/OFDT exploitation). The terms on the x axis are specific to the French school system, 6eme is 11 years-old up to Terminale which is 17 years-old. For a color version of this figure, see www.iste.co.uk/assailly/psychology.zip*

From high school onwards, alcohol remains the product most often experimented

Tobacco usage is also on the rise in high school, with daily smoking increasing from 6% in *Troisième* (ninth grade) to 21% in *Terminale* (senior year).

Cannabis experimentation also becomes very frequent in high school, reaching almost half of the students in their senior year. Regular cannabis usage relatively remains limited compared with alcohol.

The differences observed between boys and girls in junior high school disappear among high school students, apart from regular use of alcohol or cannabis, which remains more frequent among boys. This means that there is a catching up, as well as the relationship to male risk that we discussed in the previous chapter.

Product	Usage	Total	Total		Boys		Girls
		2015	2018		2018		2018
Tobacco	Experimentation with cigarettes	60.9	53.0	↘	52.7	=	53.2
	Cigarette use in a month	32.8	27.3	↘	27.0	=	27.7
	Daily use of cigarettes	23.2	17.5	↘	17.5	=	17.4
	Shisha experimentation	47.8	41,7	↘	47,4	>	36,2
E-cigarette	Experimentation	35.1	52.1	↗	57.2	>	47.1
	Use in a month	10.0	16.6	↗	20.1	>	13.2
Alcohol	Experimentation	86.6	85.0	➔	85.4	=	84.5
	Use in a year	79.2	77.3	➔	77.9	=	76.8
	Use in a month	63.9	62.1	➔	64.5	>	59.8
	Regular (at least 1 occurrence of use in a month)	14.8	16.7	➔	22.3	>	11.3
Drunkenness	Experimentation	50.5	49.5	➔	53.4	>	45.8
Binge drinking	In a month	41.5	43.2	➔	48.1	>	38.3
	Repeated (at least 3 times a month)	16.0	16.8	➔	21.0	>	12.7
	Regular (at least 10 times a month)	2.7	3.7	➔	5.2	>	2.2
Cannabis	Experimentation	44.0	33.1	↘	36.3	>	30.0
	Use in a year	35,9	26,5	↘	29,1	>	24.0
	Use in a month	22.6	17.3	↘	19.7	>	14.9
	Regular (at least 10 uses in a month)	7.7	6.2	➔	8.2	>	4.2
Other illicit drugs	Experimentation	9.3	8.1	➔	8.4	=	7.8

= : Statistically insignificant difference between boys and girls; > : boys consume more than girls.
➔: Statistically insignificant difference between 2015 and 2018; ↘: uses decreased or ↗ increased between 2015 and 2018.
Sources: ESPAD 2015 and EnCLASS 2018

Table 7.2. *Usage of psychoactive products among high school students in 2018 and comparison between 2015 and 2018 (%) (ESPAD 2015 and EnCLASS 2018/OFDT exploitation)*

In recent years, tobacco and cannabis usage has decreased among high school students, but alcohol usage has remained stable, especially excessive use, which is a source of biological, psychological and social damage; however, alcohol usage among 17-year-olds has decreased slightly.

With regard to the sharp decline in tobacco usage, we should mention two factors: the pricing policy, where increases are known to always reduce consumption among young people, as well as a change in representations and social norms relating to this product, especially since its ban in public places and media prevention campaigns (Obradovic 2017).

On the other hand, vaping is clearly increasing in popularity among adolescents who do not smoke or have never smoked tobacco. This development shows that the motivations for its use by adolescents do not seem to result from a desire to quit smoking, as is generally the case in the adult population (Andler *et al.* 2019).

At age 17, alcohol is consumed in a friendly, sometimes family setting. Thus, in 89% of cases, the latest major alcoholic binge was said to have occurred during a weekend party with friends and alone in only 1% of cases. In 1 case out of 10, it took place in the presence of parents.

Alcohol is used by some young people in a poly-consumption context and 5% of young people smoke and drink regularly, the combination of alcohol and tobacco being more prevalent than the combination of alcohol and cannabis. Only 8% have never used alcohol, tobacco or cannabis.

In terms of how adolescents obtain these products (it should be noted that the sale of alcohol and tobacco to minors has been prohibited since 2009), it can be noted that when high school students go to a tobacco store to buy cigarettes, 55% say they have never had to show their ID and 41% say they are "rarely" or "sometimes" asked for it. Similarly, 51% of high school students who purchased alcohol in the month prior to the survey reported never having to show their ID in a store and 38% "rarely" or "sometimes". Two classic examples of psycho-sociological observation: it is not the law that matters but the degree to which it is enforced.

As for e-cigarettes, the EnCLASS results show a clear increase in their usage, as with adults, affecting nearly one-third of *Quatrième* and *Troisième* pupils (8th and 9th graders) in 2018, and over half of high school students (57% of boys and 47% of girls). Experimentation in high school students has increased by 17% since 2015.

Among high school students, 10% have experimented with e-cigarettes having never smoked a cigarette before, compared with only 4% in 2015; the practice of electronic cigarettes could therefore gradually be dissociated from tobacco use among adolescents.

Usage of other illicit drugs (amphetamines, cocaine, crack cocaine and ecstasy, mushrooms, LSD, heroin and GHB) is clearly much rarer; nonetheless, 8% of high school students reported using at least one of these substances in their lifetime, a level that was stable compared to 2015.

7.13.1. *Predicting addiction to alcohol or cannabis*

In the field of addictions, a genotype/environment interaction has been well demonstrated by the work of Shuckit (1998) on the heritability of the sensitivity to the effects of alcohol in sons of alcohol-dependent fathers, concerning "resistance to the effects of the sensations produced by alcohol". These young people, for whom alcohol has little effect, precisely because they feel a few of the effects of the stimuli, gradually increase their doses in order to feel "something" and in order to be "in tune" and "in sync" with their friends for whom alcohol produces many more sensations. This will be a factor in the evolution towards alcohol dependence.

Thus, what was initially a genetic vulnerability revealed by behavioral genetics is gradually being combined with an environmental effect: Saturday night socialization. The great novelty of this type of investigation should encourage us to be cautious in our interpretations; these results will obviously have to be duplicated, but they can already be associated with the more numerous observations on the genetic epidemiology of alcoholism.

Siblings therefore show an increased tolerance to the initial effects of alcohol, and this initial tolerance is one of the most predictive markers of alcohol dependence (heritability of 60%); it is therefore quite remarkable that the marker identified in these siblings, "alpha5-alpha3-beta4", is the first susceptibility gene that has been clearly discovered in relation to addictive pathologies, in particular tobacco dependence (Gorwood 2009). It is in fact a cluster of genes coding for cholinergic receptor subunits in the ventral striatum and nucleus accumbens, the latter structure playing an essential role in the analysis of the rewards produced by stimuli.

One could imagine that this resistance to the effects of the sensations produced by alcohol exists in other fields, such as sports and driving. Indeed, *the same stimulation does not cause the same sensation in each of us*: you put someone on a carousel and he screams; you take someone else on the most "sensational" attractions at Disneyland and they come down saying they felt nothing. We could therefore imagine future studies on behavioral genetics on this theme.

In addition, the Adolescent Brain Cognitive Development (ABCD) study has proposed a method for identifying children at high risk of early alcohol and other substance use. In this context, risk in childhood refers to characteristic data identified at age 9 or 10 that predicts adverse outcomes in adolescence and a "high risk" classification for alcohol and other drugs.

Historically, studies into mental disorders, such as schizophrenia, alcohol usage disorders and depression have used family history as a risk marker. Family history has been used to identify children at high risk for later alcohol and other substance disorders in many prospective studies.

However, a detailed family history may involve asking one or both of the parents to disclose socially undesirable, embarrassing or, in some cases, illegal behavior. There are other strategies for obtaining this information, such as using public records of DUI or other drug offenses, or using hospital records to establish the parental diagnosis.

Few longitudinal studies have formulated or tested measures to identify children at high risk of early cannabis use. One measure of risk developed to identify high-risk children is the Transmissible Liability Index (TLI), developed by Vanyukov.

Based on the ABCD study, cannabis addiction in adolescence is predicted by a combination of externalized childhood disorders (reported by the parent). Four items stood out: destruction of family or other people's belongings, disobedience, lying or cheating at school, stealing away from home and parental smoking. The addition of the child's internalized disorders does not improve prediction. These markers may also predict alcohol and tobacco use between ages 15 and 18.

7.14. Children's road safety

7.14.1. *Changes in their mobility and security*

The mortality of child pedestrians doubled from the 1950s to its historic peak in 1972 and that of child car passengers almost quintupled; in contrast, the mortality of child pedestrians has decreased much more since 1972 than that of child car passengers: while the overall number of children killed has been divided by 12 (which is the greatest reduction in road deaths that has been observed in France), the mortality of pedestrians has been divided by 30 and that of car passengers by only 5.

In 1955, child pedestrians accounted for 57% of child fatalities. Today, they account for only 26% of fatalities and passengers 56%.

These observations can be linked to the country's motorization phenomenon and its influence on parental attitudes. At the beginning of the 20th century, the street was a living space like any other for children. In the 1950s, almost all children walked to school and the number of road deaths reflected this exposure to risk: the vast majority of children killed were pedestrians, with a small minority being passengers in vehicles. Today, this ratio has been reversed.

The mobility of French children has therefore profoundly changed: a study of a representative sample of 744 French families in 2005 showed that only 12% of 6–11 years old go to school alone and on foot; 70% are accompanied by car. On the other hand, by the time they enter secondary school, only 38% are accompanied by car (hence the secondary peak of accidents at this time). Today, according to a survey of 1,000 parents in 2011, 80% of children go to school accompanied by an adult through the end of elementary school, whereas, in the 1970s, 80% of children in third grade went to school alone. It is not only road safety that motivates parents: for 40% of them, going to school alone is "too difficult or too complicated for their child's age". Next comes the fear of aggression and, finally, accidents (46%). However, apart from abductions by relatives linked to failed divorces, child kidnappings have not increased, which is sometimes the justification given by parents.

Year	All users killed 0–14 years	Pedestrians	Passengers
1955	511	280	
1965	964	480	301
1972	1,248		
1973	1,232		
1980	834		
1985	616		
1990	501	153	273
1995	414	91	234
1999	333	83	182
2000	343	78	196
2001	284	56	184
2011	128	30	76
2012	115	36	65
2013	97	24	60
2014	112	20	69
2016	108	28	60

Table 7.3. *Historical trends in child road deaths by mode of road use*

The most likely hypothesis is therefore that of a transfer of road use modes from pedestrian to automobile travel: in view of what has happened to traffic in cities today, leaving children in the streets, as in the past, would quickly lead to carnage; so, instead of removing the danger from children, we have removed the children away from the danger and instead of adapting cities to children, we have adapted the children's mobility to what cities have become. To put it plainly, they are constantly "carpooled" for the shortest trips, parents organize carpooling between each other, and so on.

The British have higher child pedestrian and cyclist crash rates than we do only for one exposure factor: they are more reluctant to have children carpooling all the time and they try harder to maintain children's pedestrian and cycling mobility, hence a higher exposure.

This favorable trend in child pedestrian mortality has not been without perverse effects; firstly, an accident effect, as we have seen: a lack of learning about urban travel and therefore inexperience in pedestrian mobility, which creates spikes in pedestrian accidents later, at age 11–12, when children have to travel alone.

Another perverse effect is passivity, with children "glued" to the television, computer or games console after school; their absence of physical exercise and the proportional increase in obesity and respiratory insufficiency when going to the institutional medical visits, for instance. What we "gain" in pedestrian mortality, we risk "losing" later on in cardiovascular mortality. If only from a simple physical health point of view, walking is generally considered to be a beneficial exercise. Also, the decrease in its frequency among children, who are increasingly becoming backseat passengers, should be considered a negative factor.

Another perverse effect of this permanent carpooling of children is the increase in urban car trips and air pollution from traffic, which is now reaching critical levels.

Finally, this problem is not without impact on the employment and types of jobs of parents (most often, the mother, parity between parents does not quite apply here yet) who have to "juggle" schedules to pick up their child at the end of school and devote a significant amount of time to this accompanying activity. The "time budget" devoted to this activity has increased sharply in modern times and is a significant factor in differences in salaries, types of employment and status (proportions of part-time work between women and men within companies).

Finally, there is a high level of ambivalence towards this problem: notably, when a child suffers a fatal accident, the population of the district revolts; in some cities, people have gone so far as to build their own signs, others barricades. However, human beings are never coherent for very long: the first demand of parents in terms of safety in a city is the area around schools, but, as soon as they pick up their child, they park anywhere in front of the school. This is one of the examples that best illustrates the ambivalence of the citizen towards road safety in terms of the conflict between personal and collective interests. The Americans call this NIMBY: *not in my back yard.*

Moreover, complaints from parents about safety outside school gates are all the more absurd since it is often not there that children are killed as pedestrians, since speeds are rather low, but actually in the last crossings before the family home in residential areas, since the child is the victim of a "nest syndrome" (feeling safe near home and in a hurry to get back). Finally, the topic of child mobility is bound to strongly evolve in the future, because the environmental protection stakes have become so critical, especially in cities, that radical changes in travel behavior are to be expected soon.

7.14.2. *Intergenerational transmission of accidents, offences and driving styles*

Children "model" their behavior on that of their parents, through simple exposure to the manifestation of risky behavior, by simple observation of what their parents do and allow to be seen. In reality, transmission corresponds to various mechanisms:

– direct observation and imitation of what parents are doing;

– cognitive mediation modeling: the child's perception of parental behavior, what the child believes the adult is doing (which does not always correspond to reality);

– the influence of factors common to the behaviors of young people and their parents. For example, adherence to gender stereotypes and the "gender schema" are transmitted from parent to child. We know how important this masculinity/femininity dimension is for the various forms of self-endangerment.

Long before they start driving, children are therefore a "formidable video recorder" of 18 years of experience of what their parents do at the wheel. Their driving style reflects their motivations, attitudes, representations and values. In this, the back seat is the front row of the cinema.

Parents have a significant impact on their children's behavior and road risk, through three processes:

– the general process of socialization that the family carries out, namely the transmission of values, such as the respect for rules or of others;

– the imitation models that they offer, which is the objective of this chapter;

– managing the dangerous phase from age 15 to 25.

The way in which the interactions and filiations between these three dimensions operate seems to be a fundamental question, yet very little work has been carried out on this topic. In France, only one study has been carried out, by Credoc, in 2005, on 745 families. This study demonstrated the transmission of road behaviors:

– accelerating at a yellow light: 52% of young people do so if their parents do, compared with 39% if their parents do not;

– not drinking at parties: 55% of young people do so if their parents do, compared with 42% if their parents do not;

– running a red light: 40% of young people do so if their parents do, compared with 29% if their parents do not.

To summarize, 65% of parents have a positive influence: young people generally copy safe behaviors; 15% have a neutral influence: positive and negative influences offset each other; 21% of parents have a negative influence: young people generally copy dangerous behaviors.

There is only one father/mother difference: the father's positive influence is more important to boys (70% father/son concordance compared with 58% father/daughter concordance).

Positive influence is more pronounced among managers. It is also stronger among parents who do not change their behavior in the presence of the child. They do not need to change. There are no differences in this respect between young people who have practiced accompanied driving and those who have not. When young people were asked who had helped them the most in terms of their behavior on the road, one or other of their parents was cited as the main influence, while the influence of driving instructors seemed negligible.

Thus, research (Assailly 2007) has shown strong intergenerational reproduction of traffic violations and crash involvement; parents' crashes are more predictive of the child's crashes when they become drivers than their parents' violations; meanwhile, parents' violations are more predictive of the child's future violations than parents' crashes. Thus, two transmission channels exist.

On the other hand, accidents are, by their very nature, rare events, but more permanently, an entire driving style is transmitted to the child, regardless of exposure factors. This relationship is strongest for mistakes and ordinary traffic violations. With regard to aggression, it is more the family ties that are in question, which confirms that it is the ties that enable the containment of violence in the child.

The anxious, unsafe or cautious driving styles of fathers are thus directly reflected in their sons' driving styles. No associations have been found between the driving styles of mothers and sons. Conversely, anxious, unsafe or cautious driving styles of mothers are directly reflected in the driving styles of their daughters.

Thus, each parent's own driving career contributes to the construction of their child's driving career. In addition, multiplicative and synergistic effects have been noted when both parents share the same negative trait. We might ask whether a study conducted on the sharing of a positive trait would also observe multiplicative and synergistic effects. In any case, we can hypothesize that a "low-risk" parent is a "resiliency" factor, which compensates for the vulnerability created by the "high-risk" parent. When both parents are at risk, the child lacks this protective influence.

Traffic education programs in schools or driving schools will only be effective if they can change inadequate family traffic socialization, which is still far from being the case.

In addition, we have noted an evolution of the parental model that is given to the child to observe: In the past, during family trips, only the father was at the wheel, so he was able to influence both the boy and the girl; then, when women arrived at the wheel, the well-known identification with the parent of the same sex came into play (boys tending to identify with their father, girls with their mother); finally, today, with the rise in divorce, custody awards and accompanied driving, we will, in the future, have young men who will have had their mother as their main role models. This will be a positive factor for road safety, since women commit far fewer offenses and have far fewer accidents than men. The reduction in road insecurity sometimes takes unexpected paths.

Finally, we should mention the transmission mechanisms suggested by road safety research: social modeling and more indirect influences, such as parents with a bad accident or offense record who may also have other "bad habits" (such as substance use and non-compliance with laws and standards). These various "symptoms" would reveal the existence of a more general trait transmitted to the child.

It should be noted, however, that these studies are epidemiological: they indicate to us the robustness of the relationship, but not the explanation of its existence. For that, focus groups, interviews, observations and so on would be needed to disentangle what is genetic or cultural, road-related or otherwise. This intergenerational transmission of road behaviors needs to be better understood in its mechanisms.

When it comes to the genetic transmission of traits such as sensation seeking or resistance to the effects of sensation, our room for maneuver is limited, unless we enter into early detection strategies. In contrast, when it is a learning process, modeling the young person's behavior on that of the parent, we can make a greater attempt to direct the transmission: gradual access to driving, in particular, gives the parents back responsibility and a greater role in supervising the young person's driving behavior.

Whether in the context of accompanied driving in France or gradual access to driving in the United States, these educational innovations should be like "second chances" given to parents, so that they can use them as an opportunity to improve their driving behavior, and so that they truly protect the child, not only by verbal messages that lead to "do as I say, not as I do", but by offering more positive modeling to the child.

In conclusion, parents should be given more information about their responsibilities as role models and should be told that their bad driving habits will be imitated as much as their good ones. By behaving dangerously behind the wheel with their children in the back seat, they are contributing to a lack of road safety in future generations.

7.15. Emotions, emotional development and emotional intelligence

Since Darwin, then Damasio (1994) and Goleman (1997), we have become aware of the role of emotion in behavior and decision-making.

There are six primary, universal emotions, also present in animals, and very closely linked to bodily sensations (recalling William James' famous quote: "The more rational statement is that we feel sorry because we cry, angry because we strike, afraid because we tremble, and not that we cry, strike, or tremble, because we are sorry, angry, or fearful, as the case may be"):

- joy is used to share with others;
- fear serves as a warning against threats;
- sadness allows for the acceptance of loss;
- anger allows for things to be changed;
- disgust enables us to avoid intoxication;
- surprise enables us to stay awake.

Each has a positive or negative valence, except for surprise, which can have both.

To these primary emotions, we can add secondary emotions which are mixtures of primary emotions, but which have a more cognitive aspect: shame, guilt, jealousy, contempt, pride, indignation, admiration, rage and nostalgia.

While these emotions are universal, genetic (temperament) and environmental (social learning through imitation and attachment security) factors play an equal role in their development and individual characteristics (e.g. not all children are afraid of spiders).

We have devoted a particular study to fear and anxiety (Assailly 1988), which we present in the following section.

7.15.1. *Fear and anxiety*

Our work on fear is based on the following question: how is fear and anxiety expressed in children and adolescents? How can we explain the observed evolutions?

Two successive approaches were taken: first, a study of the general psychology of fear; second, a study of the differential psychology of fear regarding the level of fear feeling.

7.15.1.1. *General psychology of fear*

Three hundred and ten children and teens between the ages of 9 and 16 were surveyed on the following: What scares you (the topics)? Why does it scare you (the issues)? The cross-sectional evolutionary experimental device was used, with each subject questioned again one year later. In addition to this study of the universes of fear, we asked a question about identity references ("Who am I?").

The psychogenetic evolution of fears between childhood and adolescence is described by the difference proposed by Freud between "phobia" and "expectancy anxiety".

In children, the predominant type of fear is phobia. In this case, this concept, used here without pathological connotation, describes a fear where the stake is symbolized by an agent, an object or a situation. The most frequent fears concern the "bestiary of fear" (devouring and then prickly animals[2]), fantastic creatures ("traditional" creatures, such as ghosts, witches and more recent creatures, such as the characters from cinema, horror and science fiction films, video and the Internet), aggressors (such as thieves and kidnappers) and obscurity ("being in the dark").

In adolescents, the predominant type of fear is expectancy anxiety, a category that brings together fears whose content is more abstract or where the danger is more

2 This psychogenetic evolution is interpreted from an evolution of the stakes: devouring animals refers to engulfment, the destruction of the body; with prickly animals, it is the violation of its cutaneous envelope and thus of the protection which it confers. The latter remains more in adolescence, and is associated with other emotions, such as repulsion or disgust, and refers to Didier Anzieu's Skin-Ego concept (first differentiation of ego within the psychic apparatus, the body envelope being the first border between ego and non-ego).

uncertain or distant in time (such as war, terrorism, death, the future, disability, illness, old age and loneliness).

Within this transformation, we have made the hypothesis that certain fears have a transition function, they are "pivot fears". For example, the situation of darkness/loneliness ("being alone in the dark") which does not describe an object, but a container likely to receive different contents at ages 9 and 16 (children and adolescents are not afraid of the same things in the dark); furthermore, this situation also announces the time of the day when reality gives way to the imaginary, to dreams and nightmares.

Other themes ensure a transition. For example, the fears linked to school life, which introduce issues relating to failure, inferiority and the future, the school constituting a microcosm of society for the child. We should also mention the fear of falling and vertigo, because this theme maintains symbolic relations with destruction, separation and culpability. Finally, the fantastic world, a source of fears and wonder since the dawn of humanity, can also ensure transition, because it expresses multiple categories of anguish: it associates intermediate forms between animals, human and nature, but announces adolescent fear themes relating to the social and political world; it is also associated with darkness (in the cinema room), dream life (the night thereafter), ambivalence (taking pleasure in being frightened) and with identification (fear for the hero).

The main tendency of the phobia/anxiety evolution reached within the universes of fears is thus that the recourse to a symbolic expression of anxiety decreases between childhood and adolescence; the significance of this tendency can be linked to the evolution of the child's imagination. A symbolism of abandonment in the first years of life (Spitz, Bowlby) is, in school-age children, followed by a symbolism of aggression by various animal or human agents. In adolescence, these themes of abandonment and aggression do not disappear completely, but the object of anguish becomes, rather, existence itself and the dimension in which it takes place: time (in a way, it becomes "Kierkegaardian").

We can also interpret this tendency as being one aspect of a general factor of development, which includes everything that "growing up" means: cognitive, psychosocial and identity development, in short that of a "being in the world".

Thus, we can suggest a parallelism, a correspondence between the evolution of fears with age and that of identity, as two registers of development that are joint and reverberate with each other: in the referential structure of the self in 9–10-year-olds, bodily references (body, adornment, orality) can correspond to the threats to bodily integrity that constitute the issue of phobias; references to activities of 11–12-year-olds can correspond to school fears expressing guilt, inferiority and failure; finally, the description of self through personality traits in 13–16-year-olds can correspond to fears of self.

In the background of these transformations, there is thus a clear continuity; in childish fears, we can see the roots of adolescent and adult anxieties: within certain situations like darkness/loneliness, the external danger to the self gives way to the internal danger to the self. This continuity is also observed at the level of the categories of anguish expressed by fears: fear of the unknown and the unfamiliar remains a constant; the anguish of separation is symbolically expressed by the child, then more abstractly by the adolescent; the anguish of guilt is transformed by the internalization of the danger.

7.15.1.2. *Differential psychology of fear about the level of feeling fear*

By asking ourselves whether some subjects are more fearful than others, we ended up paradoxically considering that the subjects most at risk are those who are "not afraid enough" or "not afraid at all" with regard to issues such as risk taking, addiction or transgression.

We recall that while fear has negative connotations for most of us, and is sometimes likely to lead to a request for care ("this child is phobic"), it is also a fundamental adaptation mechanism in all animal species, including our own: an individual who would never be afraid in a natural environment would have an extremely short life.

Similarly, our work on risk taking, addiction and transgression (Assailly 2007, 2014) has led us to believe that children "at risk" of accidents or delinquent acts are those who are not afraid enough. The risk taken is often, in fact, inversely proportional to the level of perceived fear. An important mechanism here may be a *lack of sensitivity to loss*, produced by *the epigenetic effects of early emotional stresses*, such as insecure attachments or various forms of abuse.

These epigenetic effects are located where biological and emotional history intersect. Remember that an environmental epigenetic effect does not modify genes, does not change the cellular DNA structure, but does influence "gene expression". We keep the genes received from our parents all our life, but it is not because our genes are always there that they always express their influence with the same intensity: some genes play a more important role during childhood, others during adolescence and others in adulthood.

If we consider, for example, the genes that control responses to fear and stress, the emotional environment will gradually shape the child's HPA axis. Let us briefly recall what the HPA axis is and what its function is: when we feel fear or stress, the hypothalamus is stimulated and secretes CRF (corticotropin releasing factor).

This hormone then stimulates the pituitary gland, releasing another hormone, ACTH (adrenocorticotropic hormone), which, in turn, stimulates the adrenal glands, which releases the two main stress response hormones: adrenaline and cortisol.

A circular feedback then takes place: when cortisol reaches a certain threshold, this information is transmitted to the control center of the hypothalamus in order to block the process, since even though these substances are essential for adaptation, they can also have harmful effects on the body.

Several studies on the neuropsychology of dangerous behaviors have been carried out on the somatic marker framework (Ouimet and Brown 2007), which is composed of frontal alterations, amygdala hyperactivity, hippocampal hypoactivity, HPA axis hypoactivity and cortisol secretion.

CRF and cortisol will therefore act on the gene expression that regulates the HPA axis: emotional stress in early life causes a weakening or destruction of neurons in the hippocampus, the area of the brain that encodes "emotional memories" and thus a lack of sensitivity to loss. A byproduct of the emotional history and insecure attachments of childhood, alexithymia, may also be linked to this lack of feelings.

The hippocampus is therefore in charge of the biological memory of emotional stress. This is understandable when we look at clinical populations that present hippocampal damage, such as Vietnam war veterans, suicide victims, abused children and traffic offenders.

While early childhood "drenching" of the hippocampus with CRF and cortisol damages neurons, only later does more extensive damage result in the weakening or disappearance of classes of neurons in adolescence, when the adolescent brain undergoes extensive neuronal branching. This neural damage caused by emotional stress is associated in adolescence with risk taking, impulsivity and addiction.

An epigenetic effect may also be linked to intergenerational transmission: insecure attachment may be the product of childhood history and stresses of the mother.

An epigenetic effect also suggests that resilience is possible (through psychotherapy and selective life skill interventions, for instance). Is a return to normal hippocampal volume possible? In theory, hippocampal neurons can regenerate, but under what conditions will this be stable? Although reversibility of the epigenetic imprint is possible, it could be a "marker" that would quantify the effectiveness of treatments and therapies.

7.15.2. *Emotional intelligence*

Emotional intelligence is a constellation of emotional perceptions assessed through the use of questionnaires and rating scales. It is associated with health status, school performance, job satisfaction, life satisfaction and subjective happiness, stress management and so on.

Since the 1990s, we have understood that emotional intelligence represents a potential that influences the child's future (Goleman 1997).

The first opportunity to develop elements of emotional intelligence occurs in the early years of a child's life and this ability continues to develop throughout the schooling period. Emotional abilities that are acquired later depend on those that are formed during the early years of life and, predictably, the child's emotional intelligence is correlated with those of their parents.

For example, academic performance is influenced by emotional intelligence and its components, such as: whether the child knows what type of behavior is expected and how to control bad impulses; whether the child is able to wait, follow instructions and ask for support from the teacher; whether the child is able to express their needs when around other children.

Low-achieving students lack one or more of these elements of emotional intelligence, whether or not they have cognitive difficulties.

7.15.3. *Anxiety and depression*

Anxiety disorders affect about 7% of children, begin on average around age 11, often persist into adulthood and increase the risk of developing other pathologies.

The same mechanisms are evoked as those of adult anxiety disorders (such as negative thoughts and interpretation biases, deficient self-efficacy, emotional overactivation and avoidance of anxious situations), but they are not found in all anxious children; there could therefore be subgroups of children for whom these mechanisms are present to a greater or lesser degree. Three such groups have been identified: "typically" anxious children (generalized anxiety disorder); children with social communication difficulties (more often boys); children who avoid anxiety-provoking situations.

The frequency of depression increases during adolescence, but increases twice as much in girls as in boys. This statistical difference between the sexes clearly raises the problem of the difference between the detected and the real, under the influence of gender stereotypes: we generally expect depression, like other psychopathological disorders, to be rather "feminine". In this case, boys and men who suffer from a depressive state may very well see this state denied by themselves, their parents and their doctors (e.g. "a man doesn't cry… he takes it in his stride"). This is evidenced by a threefold rate of suicides among boys, which is a paradox if they really are less depressed than girls.

7.15.4. *Stress and burnout at school*

School stress is steadily increasing in France when comparing French children to those in other industrialized countries. A significant number of bullying incidents are reported by young French students, as well as an overall negative perception of school (in this context, France is ranked 22nd out of 25 countries), with regard to various criteria explored relating to unease in the school environment (physical and psychological bullying, passive exclusion of the victim, subjective assessment of the school).

This unease among young French people is obviously similar to that observed in Japan, a country well known for its academic elitism. In France, only one teenager out of five declares that they like going to school. Moreover, nearly 40% of them say they are stressed by having to go to school, as shown by the strong anxious apprehensions they report, which are sometimes even associated with various somatic symptoms.

Academic stress, like all stresses, corresponds to the concept of perceived stress: the perceived gap between the demands of a stressful situation and the resources of the individual, when the stakes of academic success exceed the resources and skills of the student. When it becomes chronic, school stress can lead to a state of exhaustion that we call "burnout". School burnout is therefore the equivalent for adolescents of professional burnout for adults and consists of the same three dimensions: emotional exhaustion induced by the demands of school, chronic fatigue and low achievement as a student. School absenteeism can become an avoidance strategy for this situation.

School burnout can have various negative consequences for health (somatization, depression, consumption of psychoactive products and so on) and obviously for schooling (academic failure, absenteeism). However, these various aspects can be both causes and consequences.

Among the risk factors, we note gender: girls are more affected than boys, which may seem paradoxical since today they perform better at school, but they are also more sensitive to school problems, hence their vulnerability.

School stress also increases with age in adolescence, which is logical since the demands of schooling increase with the age of the students. In addition, certain personality traits can predispose to these problems, such as perfectionism, narcissism and low self-esteem.

As we have just mentioned, product addictions can be causes or consequences of burnout, but so can non-product addictions: adolescents with problematic Facebook use (inappropriate cognition and behaviors related to the use of this network) are more likely to suffer from school burnout (we will return to this point in the chapter on screens).

Apart from individual factors, contextual factors can also promote school burnout. The main stressors at school can include revisions, exams, grades, workload increasing with age, conflicts in the classroom and sanctions, as well as the choices to be made in terms of school orientation. For example, at the end of the second year of high school, students have to choose between three main courses of study: literary, economic and social sciences, or science. This is a decisive school year, a potential source of stress, as it greatly conditions access to higher education, even the immediate professional future.

More generally, periods of transitions are critical moments in the occurrence or development of school burnout, as they are for all life transitions (such as house moving and divorce).

In addition, relationships with teachers may also play an important role. French adolescents generally report that their stress has more to do with academic pressure from teachers than with parental pressure.

Finally, sport/study streams are more at risk, which can be understood through the phenomenon of doping: the pressure to succeed is greater for these students.

Among the contextual factors, there are also family factors. Parental support is obviously a protective factor against school burnout; conversely, family pressure to succeed can encourage it. An intergenerational transmission is possible: the level of school burnout is higher among adolescents whose parents are suffering from professional burnout than among adolescents whose parents are not.

7.16. Hyperactivity

Children with attention deficit hyperactivity disorder (ADHD) exhibit a pattern of disruptive behavior in which inattention and/or hyperactivity and impulsivity predominate. The prevalence of this disorder in France is of the order of 2–5% up to age six, then 7% thereafter; Inserm's collective expertise has mentioned that this prevalence varies from 0.4% to 17% depending on the country, according to the diagnostic methods, definitions and measurement criteria used.

This diagnosis depends on the country as well as on the era: during the age of nomadic hunter-gatherers, ADHD would have been adaptive. Sedentary lifestyles and urbanism put modern-day children at a disadvantage; in fact, hyperactive children control their behavior better when they play outdoors than indoors. Similarly, the disorder is associated with school failure, or at least with difficulties, but, here again, we could ask whether an activity as sedentary as sitting for eight hours a day is well adapted to their profile. Thus, even without previous academic success, hyperactive subjects can be very successful later on in acting, speaking, training and expert roles, because always being alert, dynamic, independent, innovative and non-conforming can become an asset.

ADHD is diagnosed more frequently in childhood and more often in boys than in girls.

As shown by the work in developmental psychopathology, this disorder is very heterogeneous. There are many different behaviors, comorbidity (in 65% of ADHD cases, there is another associated diagnosis), trajectories (remission or not) and therapies. Several etiological hypotheses have been proposed:

– Genetic factors, however, the diversity of profiles and the frequency of associated disorders do not support this view.

– Environmental factors, either in a psychoanalytical approach (psychopathology of the parents), or in that of the attachment theory (hyperactivation of insecure attachment signals) or psychosocial factors (influence of screens and social networks; see the chapter on screens below).

– Cognitive factors, for example, in Barkley's self-regulation theory (deficits in response inhibition and self-regulation), Rapport's working memory model (working memory disorders), Sonuga-Barke's dual pathway model (deficits in executive function and reward/motivation) or finally in Nigg's multiple pathway model (deficits in executive function, approach motivation/retroactivation and the risk of failure).

Thus, the function of working memory is the temporary storage and maintenance of information in order to direct behavior towards a goal. Hyperactivity is associated with a significant deficit in visuospatial and verbal working memory. Other cognitive functions have also been suggested, such as prefrontal control of anticipation, receipt and delay of rewards. ADHD is associated with a preference for small, immediate rewards over large, delayed rewards.

7.16.1. *The consequences of ADHD*

7.16.1.1. *Social skills*

Social skills are among the important aspects to consider during the course and management of hyperactive children. They are significantly impacted: there are difficulties in recognizing emotions, in particular a more difficult recognition of fear compared with other emotions and alterations in theory of mind and empathy skills (Léger 2020). Children with combined type ADHD are generally more socially challenged than those with a purely inattentive type.

When comparing hyperactive children to control participants and subjects with autism spectrum disorder (ASD), there is a significant impairment in social skills in the ADHD group compared with that in the control group, with intermediate scores between the control and ASD groups; the symptom profile of ADHD is therefore qualitatively similar to that of ASD, but of lesser intensity (Léger 2020).

7.16.1.2. *Aggression*

One study analyzed the joint influence of positive and negative parenting behaviors and ADHD symptomatology on aggressive behaviors in three- to six-year-olds (Meyer 2020).

DHD symptomatology and negative parenting behaviors are associated with aggressive behaviors. Multiple regression analyses show that there would be a partial mediation: the presence of aggressive behaviors in children seems to be partly explained by parental behaviors, but it is even more so when the child has symptoms of hyperactivity and inattention.

7.16.1.3. *Overweight*

Numerous studies now highlight the links between obesity, overweight and ADHD in adults, adolescents and children, both in clinical and general populations, and controlling for multiple confounding factors. The disorder is therefore a risk factor for obesity.

In children, the dual diagnosis of ADHD and obesity has significant psychological consequences: social stigmatization, lowered self-esteem and academic difficulties.

Impulsivity and in particular response inhibition deficit and difficulty in tolerating delays are linked to abnormal eating behaviors that lead to obesity. Brain dysfunctions in the reward system have been described in both ADHD and obesity.

Indeed, functional neuroimaging studies support the involvement of prefrontal, striatal and cerebellar regions in ADHD. In particular, the frontal area (superior frontal gyrus, precentral and inferior frontal gyrus), parietal area (postcentral gyrus, angular gyrus, subparietal sulcus), temporal (superior temporal gyrus) and occipital (medial occipital gyrus) cortex, insula and basal ganglia are involved in children.

Studies of subgroups of children with ADHD and binge eating disorders show abnormalities common to both disorders, specifically related to reward circuitry (basal ganglia, amygdala, orbitofrontal and prefrontal cortex), response inhibition (frontostriatal and frontocerebellar circuitry) and emotion regulation and processing (amygdala, insula, striatum, anterior cingulate cortex, prefrontal cortex).

7.17. Suicide

Children are not considered a particularly high-risk population for suicide deaths. However, this phenomenon exists in children under 12 years of age, but it is probably underestimated because it is a taboo subject, an "unimaginable" and the differential diagnosis with accidents or abuse can be difficult.

We recall that, in terms of suicide, we distinguish between people who think about committing suicide, those who attempt suicide and those who die.

Suicide deaths are the tip of the iceberg: surveys have shown that there are 20 times more attempts (200,000) than deaths (11,000) in the general population[3].

In 1997, general population surveys showed that 7% of 11–19-year-olds had attempted suicide (7% in France, with the figure varying from 7% to 12% depending on the country), which is far from negligible. Today, according to the survey on health and consumption during the call to prepare for defense (ESCAPAD), conducted by the French Observatory of Drugs and Drug Addiction (*Observatoire Français des Drogues et des Toxicomanies,* OFDT) in 2011, 2.2% of the 27,400 adolescents surveyed reported having made at least one attempt in their lifetime requiring hospitalization, and, of those, one adolescent in four reported having made more than one attempt. These attempts were three times more common among girls (3.2% compared with 1.1% among boys). The average age of the first attempt was 14.4 years (14.5 years for girls compared with 14.2 years for boys). In addition, 10.7% of adolescents (13.7% of girls compared with 7.8% of boys) had had suicidal thoughts in the past year. The prevalences are lower today, as the phenomenon is decreasing, as we will see later.

3 We would be tempted to say, "fortunately".

In these populations, suicidal ideation seems to be a good predictor of attempts, alongside physical violence, family discord and solitude. Moreover, only one quarter of attempts led to hospitalization; we can therefore see that working on suicide from hospital statistics leads to a strong under-reporting. Adolescent attempts, themselves, are predictive of adult suicides (half of the "successful" suicides were preceded by one or more attempts).

7.17.1. *Modes of suicide*

The use of firearms is more frequent among young people than in the rest of the population; the same is true for jumping from a high place. Hanging and firearm use are more frequent among boys. While hanging remains the leading cause of death among girls, poisoning (essentially drug overdoses) is the second-most frequent cause of death among girls and is therefore much more frequent than among boys.

Thus, we can better understand the discrepancy between twice as many attempts and half as many deaths among girls: girls engage in less "expeditious" modes which undoubtedly correspond more to "calls for help" than to a real desire to end it all. The maximum frequency of overdoses among girls is observed in the Provence–Côte d'Azur region (36%).

	Rate per million		
	2000	2005	2010
1–14 years-of-age	4	3	4
15–25 years-of-age	81	72	64
25–54 years-of-age	229	222	208
55–74 years-of-age	253	240	223
75 years-of-age and above	545	461	407
All ages	210	195	180

Table 7.4. *Historical trends in suicide*

From the 1960s to 1985, suicide mortality among young people in France rose sharply (at a time when mortality from traffic accidents had sharply decreased, raising questions about possible substitution); this trend then stabilized and, from 1985 to the early 1990s, the rate remained more or less the same.

Since 2000, this cause of death has decreased more among young people (by 20%) than in the general population (14%).

Children are more likely to have suicidal thoughts, while adolescents are more likely to present suicidal gestures.

For the main risk factors, children under 12 years of age are more likely to have a family history of depression and to have been bullied than adolescents. Regarding bullying, cyberstalking is strongly associated with suicidal ideation in both children and adolescents (cyberstalking will be discussed later in the book).

Certain life events are also risk factors, such as divorce or separation, the death of a loved one, difficulties at school or conflicts with peers.

Victims of abuse, neglect or sexual violence need to be specifically monitored as these are major risk factors, as is the presence of mental health disorders.

In this context, early detection of suicidal ideation is essential to prevent suicide, given that the presence of suicidal thoughts is a major risk factor for a future suicide attempt. Furthermore, suicidal ideation and behavior in children are warning signs to seek help for emotional distress (psychological suffering) caused by different risk factors.

7.17.2. *Geographic disparities*

In 1997, the suicide rates of young people (as well as adults) were highest in Brittany and in the north and lowest in the south and around the Mediterranean, a reversed cartography compared with road accidents. In addition, people did not commit suicide in the same way in the four corners of France: in the west, hanging was the most frequent method (50% of suicides by boys in Brittany); in the south, firearms were used (56% in the Midi-Pyrénées, 41% in Aquitaine). The more frequent use of firearms in the south could be linked to the more general phenomenon of antisociality.

7.17.3. *The sociological paradox of suicide*

As international comparisons show, young people commit suicide more in rich countries than in poor countries. We are therefore faced with a paradox: the quality of life of young people is improving and is today without comparison with the conditions their grandparents experienced when they were young; if the quality of life is improving, then it should be perceived as being more worth living, but we are observing the opposite.

In fact, when an environment becomes very dangerous and the quality of life deteriorates (due to wars and economic crisis, for instance), there is a decrease in the frequency of suicides and road accidents, because people are able to direct their anger and locate the origin of their problems outside of themselves, or perceive problems differently. On the other hand, when the environment improves, people are no longer able to blame the environment and resentment can turn inward, depression and self-blame, leading to suicidal thoughts.

Consequently, we arrive at a symmetrical conclusion: a better quality of life leads to high suicide rates and low homicide rates, a worse one to low suicide rates and high homicide rates. In rich countries, the ideology of success, abundantly transmitted by the media, weakens young people because it reinforces narcissism; the spectacle of success is constantly displayed to those who fail, who can only blame themselves.

These symmetrical evolutions do not only concern young people, they also apply to adults and can be explained by Durkheim's theoretical model (when the economy deteriorates for the whole of society, the living conditions of the working class become less "anomic"), or Ehrenberg's model (the "uncertain" individual, tired of being ourselves in the heart of a France in crisis, manages his/her depression with pharmacopeia).

7.18. Autism

7.18.1. *Warning signs*

A large body of work has examined the early signs of autism spectrum disorder (ASD), particularly with respect to its core symptoms: impaired social and communication skills and repetitive and inflexible behaviors or interests.

In retrospective interviews, parents of children with ASD often reported that they became concerned about their child's development at 13–19 months old, and 15–30% of parents were concerned even before the child's first birthday.

In general, the main developmental areas of concern in the early years of life are the ability to self-regulate emotions and basic functions, such as feeding and sleeping.

Additionally, children later diagnosed with ASD had more infant visits to primary care centers than others, particularly for crying, feeding and sleep problems.

Various studies have found no difference in breastfeeding rates when children with ASD were compared to their unaffected siblings and other typically developing children. Some mothers reported problems with their child's feeding from birth and a late transition to solid foods.

In addition, based on data from parents, the frequency of sleep disorders is high in children with ASD, ranging from 50% to 80%.

Other dysfunctions in emotion regulation have also been observed in the early years of life in children later diagnosed with ASD, but the extent to which parents perceive these early signs of pathology is unknown, as they may be common to many other disorders, such as debility.

7.18.2. *Comorbidity*

Emotional problems, symptoms of hyperactivity or attention deficit and learning problems are the most common problems associated with ASD; these symptoms are perceived as less damaging in girls by parents and teachers.

7.19. Mortality

In 1740, in France, when life expectancy was 25 years compared with 80 years in 2015, nearly one in three newborns died before the age of one, compared to 3.8 deaths per thousand births in 2018. Thus, while it used to be common and was therefore more commonly accepted as possible to lose a child young, it has now become a very rare event and, as such, particularly impactful for parents and those around them.

Due to its rarity, the death of a child is experienced as an unbearable injustice in contemporary French society that is pessimistic, individualistic, utilitarian and productivist, in which a child is the object of the narcissistic projections of its parents.

7.19.1. *Children under one year of age*

Among the deaths in this age group, we distinguish:

– perinatal mortality (fetal deaths and deaths between zero and six days): anoxia, respiratory distress of perinatal origin and congenital anomalies;

– neonatal mortality (between 7 and 28 days);

– post-neonatal mortality (between 28 days and 1 year): sudden infant death syndrome and congenital anomalies.

All of the above make up infant mortality. The latest available data provided by Inserm is for the year 2016.

Year	All	Male	Female
1997		5,358	4,166
2000	4,340	4,954	3,693
2005	3,549	3,959	3,120
2010	3,428	3,769	3,071
2013	3,443	3,748	3,123
2016	3,700	4,120	3,212

Table 7.5. *Children under one year, deaths per million, all causes (source: Inserm-CépiDc, Epidemiology Centre on Medical Causes of Death)*

Mortality between 0 and 1 year of age is extremely high, as many people are killed between 0 and 1 years of age as between 1 and 19 years of age for both boys and girls. In terms of deaths per million of the population, mortality rates do not become higher than those for zero to one-year-olds until after age 50. This is as true today as it was in the past, although we have made progress on this target: around 3,700 deaths per million in 2016 compared with around 5,000 in 1997[4].

However, for the past decade, the infant mortality situation has not improved in France unlike other countries (Branger and Picherot 2019). Until the 1990s, we were

4 And we can only imagine what the situation is in developing countries. Infant mortality in France has, of course, significantly decreased over the last century, with notable increases during the two world wars and the Spanish flu; the progress is attributable to a combination of factors (hygiene and education in the first half of the century, then vaccinations).

among the best countries in the world on this indicator, now we are ranked 25th in the world, while countries such as Japan, Iceland, Slovenia and Finland have continued to reduce their infant mortality rates.

After one year, it is tempting to say that death is far away. Two causes are mainly responsible for this significant mortality: perinatal mortality (half of the deaths) and congenital anomalies (one-fifth).

Although their frequency has decreased, congenital malformations are still an important cause and there are no more differences between boys and girls today than before.

Sudden infant death syndrome (SIDS) is most common between the second and third months of life, during the winter months and among boys. Its frequency declined sharply from the 1970s to 2000 and has continued to fall by half ever since, both in the rate per million children and as a percentage of total deaths (indicating that this cause has declined more than others). Progress has been mainly attributed to putting babies to sleep on their backs, as well as to limiting room temperature to 20°C (the etiology of sudden death was considered to be multifactorial).

Mortality due to infectious diseases has also strongly decreased, as the health of infants has evolved like that of their parents in the face of AIDS-type epidemics. Accidents are also decreasing, and we can see that there is an excess of accidental deaths among men from the beginning of their lives. At this age, these are essentially domestic accidents, there are very few road accidents and, curiously, they already concern more boys.

We should also mention two important reports on the subject of infant mortality: one on suspicious deaths of infants under one year of age (Tursz *et al.* 2005), the other on abuse (Tursz 2014b), which question some of the statistics presented here, particularly relating to sudden infant deaths, accidents and the high number of deaths classified as "unknown or unspecified causes", "ill-defined symptoms and morbid conditions", with child abuse still an under-recorded taboo in France.

There are multiple reasons for this analysis of the reliability of the data at this age: as we have seen, in childhood, the first year of life is marked by the highest mortality; diagnostic uncertainties, even in the case of an event as apparently circumscribed and clear as a death, are great and the occurrence of an "unexpected" death in an infant, free of any known pathology or malformation, notably labeled as "sudden infant death syndrome", poses delicate problems of interpretation; we have mentioned the high proportions of deaths "of unknown or unreported causes", the very high rate of so-called accidental deaths, particularly deaths through non-traffic-related accidents, at an age when the child has little capacity to be an actor in his/her accident, a rate much higher than those in northern European countries and, conversely, a very low rate of reported and recorded homicides.

The report of the study by the public prosecutors' office on suspicious deaths of infants under one year of age (Tursz 2014a) concludes that official French mortality data greatly underestimates the number of infant homicides, in particular because the Inserm coders cannot decide from their documents on the intentionality of the acts. More intense epidemiological surveillance of abuse, homicide and children at risk would therefore be essential in France.

There are significant departmental disparities relating to this mortality: it is high in the overseas departments, in Île-de-France (the suburban departments, not Paris intra-muros) and is lowest in Pays-de-la-Loire and Auvergne.

These disparities are understandable when we consider that infant mortality is correlated with the unemployment rate, the poverty rate and the schooling rate of women. Similarly, the United States ranks only 46th in the world for this mortality, which clearly shows that in a rich and ultra-medically equipped country, it is social inequalities in health that will weigh on this mortality.

The stagnation of the infant mortality rate in France over the past decade can therefore be explained by three types of factors (Branger and Picherot 2019):

– declarative practices, voluntary interruption of pregnancy and euthanasia differ from one country to another, but these differences alone cannot explain the stagnation in France;

– similarly, medical causes, such as a lower quality of obstetric care in France, seem unlikely; it is true that vaccination coverage (measles, meningitis) is lower than in other countries, but this can only play a small role (a few dozen cases per year); on the other hand, very premature births and their consequences can be a factor; they are more significant in France and it is the monitoring of very premature births that may be deficient;

– finally, social causes seem to play an important role, in particular precariousness: it is associated with unemployment, poverty, poor access to health care, unhealthy housing, addictions and illnesses of the parents and, therefore, an increased risk of prematurity and malformations.

It is on this last factor that we understand the departmental disparities: these correlates of precariousness are more frequent in the overseas territories and in the Paris suburbs. Our health system (which is said to be "the best in the world") tries to "catch up", to compensate for the consequences of precariousness on the poor health of women and children, but cannot succeed completely; as precariousness is currently increasing, the infant mortality situation cannot improve.

Cause of death	Deaths per million
Boys, less than one year old	
Certain conditions originating in the perinatal period	2,024
Congenital malformations and chromosomal abnormalities	699
Ill-defined symptoms and morbid conditions	512
Sudden infant death syndrome	241
Unknown or unspecified causes	214
Other ill-defined symptoms and morbid conditions	57
External causes of morbidity and mortality	90
Accidents	69
Transport accidents	8
Accidental falls	3
Accidental drowning and submersion	8
Other accidents	50
Homicides	16
Girls, less than one year old	
Certain conditions originating in the perinatal period	1,629
Congenital malformations and chromosomal abnormalities	631
Ill-defined symptoms and morbid conditions	340
Sudden infant death syndrome	170
Unknown or unspecified causes	142
Other ill-defined symptoms and morbid conditions	28
External causes of morbidity and mortality	65
Accidents	54
Accidental falls	3
Other accidents	48
Homicides	11

Table 7.6. *Latest mortality data (year 2016)*

7.19.2. *Children aged one to four years*

From age one, causes of death become more diverse. Rates drop sharply, with mortality between ages 1 and 14 being the lowest across all age groups.

	All	Male	Female
Year	Deaths per million		
1997		301	256
2000	242	262	220
2005	194	207	180
2010	165	171	158
2013	165	178	152
2016		231	192

Table 7.7. *Historical trends in mortality among children aged one to four years (source: Inserm-CépiDc, Epidemiology Centre on Medical Causes of Death)*

Among boys, accidents are the leading cause of death; at this age, these are essentially domestic accidents, followed by cancers (essentially leukemia) and then road accidents, which account for only one-fifth of the total.

In girls, domestic accidents are also the primary cause of death, followed by congenital anomalies, most often cardiac, and then cancers.

Children's domestic accidents occur in the home or in its immediate surroundings (such as the garden, yard or garage). Of the total number of accidents, 84% occur in children under one year of age, 75% between one and two years of age, are still very frequent (more than 50%) up to five years of age and decrease in older children in favor of outdoor accidents (school, sports). These are intoxications, burns, suffocation by foreign bodies, falls, drownings and defenestrations.

From the beginning of life, accidents are less prevalent among girls. We can also see how accidents reflect life: at this age, we are most often at home and less rarely on the road, which is reflected in the proportions. It also reflects development: when the child cannot yet lift its head, suffocations are frequent (and there is already an excess of male mortality for this cause, whereas it is often difficult to distinguish male and female babies and we do not expect significant behavioral differences at this age); as soon as the baby can walk, falls and defenestrations predominate.

Mortality of children within this age group halved from the 1970s to 2000, due to reductions in household accidents and leukemia, and has since sharply fallen again, demonstrating the significance of the progress we continue to make in these areas. Accidental mortality has decreased both in prevalence (rates halved) and proportion to all causes. While there has been some progress in tumors, it is not as great as for accidents, particularly among boys. At this age, prevention is certainly more applicable to accidents than to tumors.

7.19.3. *Children aged five to nine years*

	All	Male	Female
Year	**Deaths per million**		
1997		167	113
2000	122	138	105
2005	95	107	83
2010	84	96	71
2013	86	94	77
2016		114	65

Table 7.8. *Historical trends in mortality of children aged five to nine years*

Among boys, cancer was previously the leading cause of death (27%) for this age group, followed by motor vehicle accidents (21%) and domestic accidents (17%). For girls, the ranking was identical (27%, 20% and 11%, respectively). We concluded at the time[5] "that from the age of 5 the child 'arrives' on the road as a pedestrian, and especially as a car passenger, and the traffic accident takes precedence over the domestic accident". Today, this is no longer true; road accidents are less frequent than domestic accidents (35% compared with 43%). Is this a sign that prevention (or other factors?) has been more effective on the road?

Mortality in this age group is therefore greatly decreased in both boys and girls, with the excess male mortality being maintained over the years.

5 Assailly, J.-P. (2016). *La mortalité des jeunes*. Codes Rousseau.

Overall, the prevalence of accidents has sharply declined as has their proportion of the total number of deaths. Is this a sign that accidental mortality lends itself better to prevention than other causes at this age? For cancers, it would be more appropriate to speak of stagnation, with their relative share of deaths increasing over this period.

7.19.4. *Children aged 10–14 years*

Previously, road traffic accidents were the leading cause of death among boys (24%), followed by cancers (19%) and domestic accidents (18%). Among girls, cancer remained the leading cause of death (22%), with road traffic accidents second (20%) and domestic accidents third (8%).

	All	**Male**	**Female**
Year	**Deaths per million**		
1997		183	131
2000	154	182	124
2005	104	121	86
2010	93	104	80
2013	85	94	76
2016		119	95

Table 7.9. *Historical trends in mortality among children aged 10–14 years (source: Inserm-CépiDc, Epidemiology Centre on Medical Causes of Death)*

Today, while general mortality has sharply declined, road accidents have declined more than other causes; they are now only the fifth-most frequent cause, with suicides becoming as frequent in this population (which is not in itself a very reassuring sign for our society).

7.19.5. *Children between 15 and 19 years of age*

Previously, among boys, road traffic accidents were the leading cause of death, accounting for almost one in two deaths (43%). Other types of accidents were the second-most frequent (13%), followed by suicides (11%). Among girls, the trend was the same, but with a less marked increase in violent mortality (cancers still weighed heavily, compared with accidents and suicides).

Overall, these statements all remain true today in a context of a halving of the mortality rate since the 1997 data; moreover, we note a "law" that we will often find in relation to the differences between boys and girls: both sexes are benefitting equally from historical progress, but, in the end, the gap between the sexes remains: 70% of those killed on the road are boys and the rates per million are double for boys.

	All	**Male**	**Female**
Year	**Deaths per million**		
1997		643	272
2000	477	664	283
2005	370	526	207
2010	304	440	161
2013	236	321	146

Table 7.10. *Historical trends in mortality among 15–19-year-olds (source: Inserm-CépiDc, Epidemiology Centre on Medical Causes of Death)*

What will change is the respective significance of the different causes, as some have declined more than others. From the age of 14, two phenomena (the beginning of puberty for boys on the development side and access to mopeds on the road safety side) will triple the mortality rate and install road accidents as the primary cause, today as in the past, and more generally sharply increase the rate of violent mortality (accidents in everyday life, suicides, homicides).

However, because road safety in this population has improved more than other causes, traffic accidents now only account for 29% of male deaths compared with 43% in 1997.

Although the prevalence of all causes has decreased over this period, suicides have not decreased in the same proportion and are becoming more frequent than accidents in everyday life, among both girls and boys. For girls, cancers still carry a significant weight compared to accidents and suicides.

8

Socialization and Antisociality

8.1. Lying

Although lying is considered morally reprehensible, all individuals lie, and this from early childhood. Indeed, by the age of 3 or 4 years, children are capable of lying, whether for their own benefit (antisocial lying) or for the benefit of others (prosocial lying); in fact, by the age of 2 years, some lying is already possible in 30% of subjects (Demedardi *et al.* 2021).

Everyone lies at times, because lying all the time or never lying would be counterproductive, the first resulting in loss of trust of others, and the second in the inevitable conflicts that would result.

Therefore, all children lie and yet their parents tell them never to lie, to always tell the truth. How does this learning take place? In fact, children very quickly learn the role of lies in communication and social relations.

Lying assumes a theory of mind, knowing that we know something that others do not know that we know. The executive functions of inhibition (resisting not telling the truth) and planning also play a role in the skill of lying. Another executive function, working memory, will be associated so that the child can maintain a lie over the long-term (not cleaning his mouth in front of the adult while he claims not to have eaten the cake). In short, lying assumes intelligence.

Thus, from the age of 4 years, the child knows that he cannot lie to everyone in the same way, that some will unravel more than others.

It is not known whether compulsively lying children become compulsively lying adults, as we do not have longitudinal studies for this, but retrospective studies have been conducted on offenders, and it appears that they were great liars as children.

A lie can thus be defined as a statement contrary to the truth, made with the intent to manipulate the thoughts or behaviors of others. Two broad categories of lies are generally distinguished in literature: prosocial and antisocial lies (Demedardi *et al.* 2021). The latter, sometimes referred to as selfish lies, are intended to deceive others for the benefit of the person who produces them. For example, they are told to avoid punishment after a transgression or to obtain an undeserved reward.

Prosocial lies, sometimes called white lies, are intended to benefit others rather than the person who produces them. They may be told to please, comfort, protect or even help others at the person's own expense. Unlike antisocial lies, prosocial lies are socially encouraged, since they help establish or maintain positive and harmonious interpersonal relationships. For example, by the age of 3 years, most children will answer "no" to the question of whether they think an overweight person is fat. The same is true when a child is given a gift that they do not really like (although the Internet now makes it possible to resell this gift on December 26, a practice that is becoming more widespread).

The first research on lying in children focused on the conceptual and moral understanding of lying from a Piagetian perspective, then later on the development of lying behavior.

Interest in the scientific study of lying is growing rapidly, for at least two reasons. On the one hand, studying lying behavior in children allows us to advance our understanding of the development of abilities, such as theory of mind, inhibition or emotional regulation.

On the other hand, identifying the determinants of prosocial lying is essential from a societal point of view, more specifically in the judicial context. A child may indeed be led to lie in court in order to protect or help an accused adult, with all the dramatic consequences that this behavior may entail. It is therefore essential to identify the motives that may lead a child to lie in court. However, it appears that the proportion of children likely to lie from as early as 3 or 4 years old varies according to the type of prosocial lying we are interested in.

Thus, at preschool age, producing a lie for the benefit of another and at one's own expense may be more difficult than stating a lie to be polite. Regarding the development of this type of lying, the vast majority of research shows that children tend to lie more as they grow older (Demedardi *et al.* 2021). This increase in lying behavior with age is observed as much for lies expressed to avoid harm or to comfort others as for lies intended to cover up a collective transgression. The same is true for lies told to cover up the transgression of a loved one.

In addition to the fact that as they grow older, children seem to engage more in prosocial lying behaviors, the lies they develop become increasingly convincing. Thus, when it comes to lying to avoid hurting others, as they grow older, children are able to maintain the consistency of their lie in the face of questioning.

This relationship between prosocial lying behaviors and the development of executive functions has been demonstrated from as early as 4 years of age for altruistic lying, and also for lying to cover up the transgression of others.

Thus, prosocial lying also appears to be related to emotional development. In order for the polite lie to seem plausible, the child will not only have to regulate their emotions (such as not getting angry when receiving the last gift on their list), but also learn how to express an emotion of joy when feeling anger.

8.2. Lying in parents

Parents often emphasize the importance of honesty when socializing their children, yet parents around the world lie to their children in order to gain obedience.

The role that parenting through lying plays in children's social and moral development is not entirely clear, namely, what are the links between parenting through lying, children's lying behavior and children's subsequent psychosocial outcomes?

Within this framework of social learning, of parental socialization, education through lying can promote lying behavior in children because parents model lying behaviors that their children can imitate.

Similarly, when unrelated adults model dishonesty to children, adult dishonesty can affect children's moral behavior. For example, 5- to 7-year-olds are more likely to lie about their cheating behavior in a game if an experimenter has lied to them before the game.

Thus, it is possible that repeated exposure to parental lying erodes trust in interpersonal relationships. If children learn that their parents are untrustworthy, they may have less confidence in their relationships. As a result, children may experience the development and maintenance of difficult relationships with loved ones, which may lead to the development of internalized disorders, such as social withdrawal and depression.

Furthermore, children who observe parenting by lying inadvertently learn ineffective ways of handling difficult situations and managing conflicting interpersonal relationships. By observing parental lying, children may become aware of its effectiveness in inducing behavioral adherence from others. Ultimately, children may imitate their parents and turn to pathological lying to achieve compliance, which is an example of an externalized disorder.

To date, only one study has examined these associations (Setoha and Zhoa 2020), which examined a sample of young Singaporean adults who reported exposure as children to parenting through lying.

The research involved 379 young adults who reported their childhood exposure to deceptive parenting, their current deceptive behaviors towards parents and their psychosocial adjustment. Results revealed that adults who recalled childhood exposure to higher levels of parenting by lying exhibited higher levels of deception towards their parents and higher levels of psychosocial maladjustment; thus, lying may negatively impact children's psychosocial functioning later in life.

8.3. Antisociality

8.3.1. *Phylogeny and ontogeny of equality, hierarchy and dominance*

The distribution of resources, territory, partners and priority decision-making rights is a central issue in all animal species. Children must also discover how their social environment is structured: who is friend or foe, superior or inferior and so on, and how this will determine each other's behavior.

Social hierarchies are ubiquitous across species and cultures, allowing some individuals to have better access to certain resources, partners, living conditions or influence than others.

Because of the existence of so much possible information and cues in a given social situation, this learning capacity requires that the child already knows, in some way, what is driving social relationships and what data is relevant to recognize them. This suggests that innate representations and motivations have evolved to recognize the types of social relationships that have critical adaptive value.

Early ethological and naturalistic observations (Thomsen 2019) have shown that preschoolers form dominance hierarchies at times that resemble those of other species, for example, more formidable, agonistic individuals who systematically dominate others in conflicts over certain resources (such as toys).

Representations and even motivations regarding principles of equality and hierarchy emerge early in childhood, suggesting that they are part of the set of innate socio-cognitive mechanisms with which all humans are endowed. Preverbal infants appear to be egalitarian, predicting and preferring outcomes to be distributed equally in the absence of other information, approaching equality rather than unequal distribution. However, if one agent has previously dominated another, the child expects third parties to distribute most resources to the more dominant agent (Sheehy-Skeffington and Thomsen 2020).

Children also use formal indices of relative body size (Thomsen 2019), coalition size and histories of winning and losing, gains and losses to predict who will dominate whom in a zero-sum conflict[1], because others defer to them to motivate selective affiliation behavior (Sheehy-Skeffington and Thomsen 2020).

Although, in principle, egalitarian expectations do not necessarily imply altruistic sharing of personal resources, the systematic individual differences that functionally link the two seem to emerge in infancy: a large majority of children who expect an equal distribution of resources also share their favorite toy with an unknown experimenter, whereas most children who expect an unequal distribution keep their favorite toy to themselves. It is important to note that this link between egalitarianism and altruism is already "parochial" (or "in-group" to use a more scientific concept), with children's desire to ensure equal outcomes being limited to in-group members, once group identity is made evident (Sheehy-Skeffington and Thomsen 2020).

Egalitarianism or social dominance orientation is partly heritable: the largest twin study to date found that egalitarianism or dominance orientation is substantially hereditary (24% and 37%, respectively). Importantly, the joint variance between social dominance orientation and political attitudes primarily reflects the same genetic, rather than environmental underpinnings (average genetic correlation of 0.51).

As a result, adolescents resemble their parents in general anti-equality, as captured by social orientation towards dominance, which in turn mediates the similarity of parents and children in general prejudice.

It is also worth mentioning the influences on egalitarianism processes at the societal level, which is the most relevant socioecological context for deciding on the distribution of resources between groups. Differences between countries in the average levels of egalitarianism are observed from childhood. Using economic

1 In game theory, a zero-sum conflict is one in which the sum of the gains and losses of all players is equal to 0. This means that the gain of one player is necessarily a loss for the other.

games, we observe that the tendency of children to oppose inequalities among others, or unequal situations that benefit them, appears earlier and more reliably in individualistic western cultures.

Indeed, information about social rank motivates how preschoolers behave and coordinate with others: whereas dominant individuals are avoided in many species, so as not to provoke aggression, in highly social species they may offer coalitional strength, as well as access to resources and influence, so that approaching and affiliating with other high-ranking individuals may be adaptive.

This relationship between rank and resources is well understood: children expect third-party resource distributions to benefit a physically dominant agent rather than a subordinate agent; 3- and 4-year-olds will themselves favor a dominant individual in third-party resource distributions and explicitly expect those who give or deny access to use resources to be accountable.

Like other primates, young human children therefore also seek affiliation with high-ranking lineages, but unlike bonobos, they will pay significant attention to whether others voluntarily defy their priority, reflecting the importance of consenting authority in cooperative human society.

8.3.2. *The construction of the notion of transgression*

Participation in social groups exposes children to various domains of social knowledge, including the moral and conventional domains. As children become familiar with these domains, they begin to distinguish between the transgressions that characterize them: moral transgressions, actions that lead to injustice or harm (such as stealing, hitting and kicking), are considered as distinct from conventional transgressions, actions that defy normative behavior or do not follow social rules (such as sneaking into a line).

Children distinguish transgressions in these areas across a variety of dimensions, including the severity of transgressions, their degree of punishment, their generalizability and their conditioning to rules or authority; thus, moral transgressions are judged more negatively than conventional transgressions.

However, some factors may influence children's judgments, for example, social group membership: children have a more nuanced moral compass, in which social transgressions are judged not only on the characteristics of the act but also on the characteristics of the person committing it.

Indeed, children are very sensitive to social groups, quickly recognizing similarities and differences between group members and themselves, as outsiders, as well as with strangers or opponents. They not only distinguish between members of different social groups, but also exhibit a positive bias in judging more favorably for members of their group.

Finally, children behave like adults.

8.3.3. *The Lacanian vision of antisociality: the child between the real, the imaginary and the symbolic*

Lacanian psychoanalysis proposes some notions that apply particularly well to the question of transgressions in children and adolescents. At its heart, we have the Freudian distinction between the reality principle, which corresponds to the constraints that reality imposes on us, and the pleasure principle, reinforced by all the repressed impulses in our unconscious. Every child is born in a position of omnipotence, due to their lack of viability and their total dependence ("for me to survive, the world must obey me").

In Lacanian theory, the symbolic is what defines, constrains and limits and is manifested in the social view of self and the fear of sanctions. In the family universe, this superego is represented by the father figure.

When there is no father (as in the growing proportion of single-mother households), or when the father does not fulfill his function, but prefers to remain a "buddy daddy", the symbolic law[2] is not transmitted to the child; from then on, the child is confronted with the absence of limits and we speak of "lack of paternal authority" or "foreclosure". In the absence of this law, and faced with the impulses of the imaginary (omnipotence, desire, symbolic violence), the child will need to go and look for limits to his omnipotence in the real world, with all of its risks and dangers.

If we talk about delinquency, reality will be prison: we need prisons to understand what we are not allowed to do in a society. In a sports context, reality is represented by the red card: we need red cards to understand what we are not allowed to do on a soccer field. Finally, when we talk about road safety, reality will be the accident, so that we understand what we are not allowed to do on the road.

In these three areas, we see how it is indeed male father figures (police officers, referees, driving instructors) that young people – and all those who remain immature

2 Also called "castration" by Lacan.

– come to challenge, sometimes violently, in order to find the limits that have not been transmitted to them at home. They are looking for the father figure.

8.3.4. *Self-control*

Self-control theory, or the general theory of crime (Gottfredson and Hirschi 1990), is one of the most documented and influential theories of deviance, delinquency and crime, not only in the field of criminology, but also in the social and behavioral sciences, more specifically developmental science.

The central tenet of the theory is that low self-control, characterized by a strong tendency towards impulsivity and risk taking, plays a crucial role in the inability to refrain from deviant and criminal behavior when the opportunity arises.

It is therefore interesting to examine the developmental trajectories of self-control and deviance, as well as the relationships between them.

One of the most important tenets of Gottfredson and Hirschi's theory is that self-control develops primarily during the first decade of life. Once self-control stabilizes between the ages of 8 and 10 years, its relative level (or rank) is expected to remain unchanged.

Thus, although the average level of self-control differs between subjects, this level remains largely stable between ages 8 and 16 years.

If we distinguish between two facets of self-control, impulsivity and sensation seeking, we note that each dimension follows different developmental trajectories over time, with levels of self-control possibly changing for some, but remaining stable for others.

In the NICHD longitudinal Study of Early Child Care and Youth Development, children were assessed six times, from ages 4.5 to 15 years. The results show that children's self-control increased significantly during childhood, but sometimes leveled off between ages 8.5 and 10.5 years. Deviance also changed in parallel, but in the opposite direction; there was a steady change in deviance in early adolescence. Finally, self-control and deviance were bidirectionally and longitudinally linked across all assessments through childhood only. These results support theoretical predictions that self-control develops primarily during childhood (up to age 10) and remains stable thereafter. They also support longitudinal and bidirectional links between self-control and deviance, which are largely identical in scale before age 10.

Recent behavioral genetic data actually shows that a high proportion of the observed heritability may actually underpin the shared variance between self-control and deviance. In fact, factors such as difficulty in delaying gratification and impulsivity that are characteristic of low self-control also constitute a propensity for delinquent behavior, and since these characteristics are heritable, self-control and deviance may simply share some common underlying genetic factors.

8.3.5. *Antisocial behavior and its determinants*

Antisociality is a heterogeneous concept that includes a variety of behaviors, such as fighting, vandalism, concealment, disobedience and irritability.

Among the determinants, we have seen, above, the influence of the quality of the mother–child attachment or the lack of paternal authority.

Although a few long-term studies are available, as this issue requires follow-up over very long periods, we must mention the Danish longitudinal study of over 1.3 million people, which shows that unstable family structures are associated with a higher risk of subsequent violent criminal offenses by children compared with those who lived continuously with both parents throughout their upbringing. This association is attenuated, but persists after adjusting for parental socioeconomic status.

Absolute risks were higher in men than in women, whereas relative risks were higher in women. Relative risks were also greater for paternal compared with maternal separation, at least until mid-childhood and increased with the number of separations.

Elevated risks were observed for all separation scenarios studied, except when the child was separated from both parents at birth and remained separated throughout childhood. Separation from a father for the first time at a young age was associated with higher risks than if the paternal separation had occurred later in life, but there was little variation in the age-associated risk at the first maternal separation.

Another well-known finding is that antisociality is correlated with family socioeconomic status, with differences not just between rich and poor families, but across the socioeconomic spectrum.

Is the effect of family socioeconomic status on antisocial behavior indirect (passing through various mediating variables: for example, low status may produce poor parenting that then leads to antisociality) or, conversely, can status have a direct effect on behavior?

Disadvantaged status may be associated with emotional problems in parents, lack of warmth, coercive discipline and a degraded home environment, all of which can result in behavioral problems.

Family stress is a concept that suggests that economic hardship exacerbates child problems primarily through parental psychological distress and poor parenting, both of which interact with a variety of risk factors or protective factors, such as social support.

Recent research does point to the influence of mediators, such as poor parenting, literacy difficulties, stressful life events and neighborhood problems. These mediators are observed for all the various manifestations of antisociality.

These mediators should therefore be the targets of interventions aimed at reducing antisocial behavior problems in children.

However, no observational or correlational study can assume or infer causality. Family adversities are often correlated with each other, and multiple family transitions may not only represent broken parental relationships, and also a myriad of other household dysfunctions. Furthermore, aggression and violence are known to "run" in families through presumed genetic and environmental pathways. Parental antisocial traits could influence the quality of the parent–child relationship, and also the environment in which children are raised, and thus their likelihood of reoffending.

The only scenario in which no high risk was observed was for children who had never lived with a parent from birth to age 15. It is possible that children placed in the care of social services from birth are particularly well cared for and are thus protected from family disruption and other adversities in the family environment during childhood. We will revisit this point in the section on foster care.

8.4. Abuse

8.4.1. *Introduction*

Child abuse (trauma perpetrated by another human being, such as sexual abuse, physical abuse or witnessing domestic violence) occurs with alarming frequency. It is estimated that, worldwide, 1 billion children are abused each year.

In Canada, 32% of the overall adult population reports having been abused as a child, including 26% for physical abuse, 10% for sexual abuse and 8% for exposure to domestic violence; data from the United States is similar (18% for physical abuse and 11% for sexual abuse).

These stats seem enormous. However, we mentioned in the chapter on mortality how this phenomenon is largely underestimated in France, a taboo hidden behind accidents and sudden deaths or "unknown causes" in childhood.

Remarkably, only a small minority of cases is known to child welfare agencies and this is particularly true for physical abuse. Therefore, screening needs to be greatly improved in the future if children are to be better protected.

As numerous research studies have shown, victims of child abuse are at risk of numerous aftereffects, both in childhood and adulthood, such as poor physical health, depression, suicidal tendencies, post-traumatic stress disorder, academic difficulties, sleep problems in adolescence, delinquency, addiction and revictimization and domestic violence. Early exposure to violence and adversity in children is even associated with accelerated aging, chronic inflammation and early mortality. These effects are independent of country, society and culture.

8.4.2. *Cultural factors*

As early as 1981, Leon Eisenberg suggested that the first task in preventing child abuse was to identify the sociocultural factors that contribute to the problem. Understanding how human groups and cultural contexts define what abuse is, and what it is not, is necessary for standards to change; we can then ask what prevention programs are transferable.

Childhood abuse thus increases the risk of depression later in life; however, the influence of cultural factors on this relationship is less well understood. To this end, baseline data from the multiethnic HELIUS study (Amsterdam, The Netherlands) was analyzed and included 22,551 participants aged 18 to 70 years of Dutch, Surinamese African, South Asian Surinamese, Turkish, Moroccan and Ghanaian nationality.

Ghanaians who reported physical violence in childhood were the only ethnic group with significantly increased odds of depression, as were Moroccans who experienced sexual abuse in childhood. No gender differences were found in the relationships between abuse and depressed mood. Thus, the association between various types of abuse and depressive symptoms is not always consistent across ethnic groups.

For example, in Cambodia, individuals believe that sexual or physical abuse of children is due to "cultural attractors", including poor character from a very young age, astrological vulnerability to abuse, a pre-established entanglement between the child and the abuser (they are "destined" to meet), a sexual need and a moral blindness that portrays the abuser as blameless.

Although these traits are similar to those identified in explanations of violence against women, there are notable differences, such as the role of the *tiracchāna* in explaining sexual abuse, including incest. Thus, we might identify a cultural epigenesis of sexual abuse in children in order to develop a culturally appropriate plan to prevent child abuse.

8.4.3. *Meta-analyses*

Attempts to conduct meta-analyses on the association between different forms of child abuse and depressive symptomatology in adulthood have been limited by the wide range of definitions of child abuse in literature.

One work (Humphreys 2020) therefore sought to meta-analyze a single, widely used dimensional measure of child abuse, the Childhood Trauma Questionnaire, with respect to diagnosis and symptoms of depression in 192 unique samples covering 68,830 individuals.

The association between total scores and scores of specific forms of child abuse (emotional, physical and sexual abuse, and emotional and physical neglect) and depression was assessed using a secondary effects meta-analysis.

Higher child abuse scores were associated with a diagnosis of depression and higher depressive symptom scores.

Emotional abuse and emotional neglect showed the strongest associations.

8.4.4. *Very long-term effects*

One study (Degli Espostia 2020) examined the associations between child abuse and antisocial behavior through life. This study used 50 years of longitudinal data from the 1958 British birth cohort (8,088 subjects) to measure child neglect (prospective) and abuse (retrospective), as well as antisocial behavior from childhood to adulthood.

Child abuse was associated with higher levels of antisocial behavior at seven different time points in life (from ages 7 to 50 years). Antisocial behavior was significant during childhood and adulthood among those who were abused, independent of confounding factors. Individuals who experienced multiple types of abuse were at the greatest risk for antisocial behavior, with each additional type of abuse associated with increased risk during childhood.

Thus, child abuse is associated with an increased risk of antisocial behavior, with a stable and consistent association through age 50. This emphasizes the burden of child abuse and the importance of providing long-term support to those who experience it.

8.4.5. *Historical developments*

With regard to abuse, as for any other aspect of life, researchers are always asked to answer the question, "Are abuse trends decreasing, increasing, or remaining stable?"

This immediately raises the question of the validity of the measurement of the phenomenon: is it really increasing, or is it just that we are detecting it more? Is it really decreasing, or is it just that we are not paying attention to it anymore?

For example, looking at sustained changes over time and long-term trends, studies have shown that violent deaths of children have declined since the 1970s, which may suggest an actual reduction in child abuse.

Regarding historical trends in abuse towards children, we have English data (Degli Espostia 2019): there was a 90% decrease in infant mortality from 1858 to 2016, an 83% decrease in those guilty of child cruelty or neglect from 1893 to 2016, but a 182% increase in child protection registrations from 1988 to 2016.

Specifically, over the period 2000–2016, the number of crimes against children, child welfare registrations and children in foster care increased significantly. Age and type of child abuse emerged as significant factors for both long-term trends and 2016 estimates. In 2016, adolescents (ages 15–19 years) were twice as likely to die from homicide or assault as infants (<1 year) and six times as likely as children (ages 1–14 years).

The consistent finding of sustained declines across indicators is a compelling indication of downward long-term trends in abuse towards children.

Between 1858 and 2016, there was a significant 96% reduction in child deaths, but a 1% increase in adolescent deaths. The same trend was observed for sex crimes against children, with a 55% decrease in those guilty of sexual relations with children under the age of 13 years, but a 32% increase in those guilty of sexual relations with adolescents aged 13–16 years.

In 2016, more adolescents died by homicide or assault than any other age group. However, fewer adolescents were placed on the child protection register than any other age group. These findings are consistent with the hypothesis that certain developmental ages are more vulnerable to abuse, with adolescents being at greater risk than younger age groups.

In 1988, physical abuse was the most common reason for placing on the child welfare register. In 2016, neglect was the most common reason and was about five times more common than physical abuse. This change was due to a large increase in registrations for neglect and emotional abuse, as well as a decrease in registrations for physical and sexual abuse. US studies have also found that physical and sexual abuse (but not neglect) have declined significantly since the 1990s.

Multiple sources to measure the incidence of abuse over time (child welfare statistics, abuse-related hospital admissions and violent child deaths) would be desirable to examine trends in abuse.

Research on child abuse prevention has suffered from a lack of copyright-free, multidimensional, validated measurement instruments to assess changes in victimization or behavior.

In order to reduce victimization, we need to evaluate interventions through rigorous, randomized or quasi-experimental studies that measure whether or not victimization actually decreases.

Multidimensional, validated instruments exist, such as the Parent-Child Conflict Tactics Scale or the Childhood Trauma Questionnaire, but these are protected by copyright and are expensive for emerging countries.

The ISPCAN (International Society for the Prevention of Child Abuse and Neglect) Child Abuse Screening Tool (ICAST) is a validated, multidimensional, copyright-free questionnaire. It assesses the past-year and lifetime prevalence of physical, emotional and sexual abuse of children, using either parent (ICAST-P) or adolescent (ICAST-C) testimony. It has been used in numerous studies around the world and is available in 20 languages.

8.4.6. *Mistreatment, sexual abuse and traffic accidents*

The pediatrician Jacqueline Cornet (Cornet 1977) studied a population of 300 young accident victims (all types of accidents) admitted to Malakoff[3] emergency services. The author observed that a very large proportion had been beaten during childhood. Contrary to stereotypes, the most injured were not those left to themselves, but those who had received a very (too?) severe upbringing.

She interpreted this correlation causally by suggesting that there was a form of reproduction, an “internalization” of violence, and that the young people beaten were in a process of repetition by then “taking hits” on the road.

Psychiatrist Marc Shelly has worked on young people, consulting at the Fernand Widal Hospital screening center, and CIDJs (802 young women aged 18 to 22 years, 631 young men aged 19 to 25 years). According to his observations, young women who had been sexually abused as children, but who had not been able to disclose this secret, had eight times more traffic accidents than those who had not been abused. When they were able to disclose their secret, they “only” had two and a half times more accidents. Sexual abuse after puberty, however, was not associated with the frequency of traffic accidents. Finally, sexually abused boys do not have this excess accident rate, regardless of their age at time of the trauma.

This work completes a series of studies on the link between sexual abuse and risky behaviors (such as risky sexual behavior, repeated abortions, substance abuse, suicide attempts and self-mutilation). By analogy with the concept of psychosomatic disease, this work considers accidents as a socio-somatic disease, a hypothesis close to that of Jacqueline Cornet: young women who have been abused report an “unconscious” desire to expose themselves to socially acceptable suffering, to be able to complain, which was not the case with sexual abuse.

The effects of abuse would be different for boys: they would externalize the violence outside themselves, in fighting and delinquent acts, whereas girls would rather turn the violence against themselves. We have developed this question of the meaning of violence in relation to sexual differences in the chapter on mortality. Moreover, this work takes us back to the heart of Alice Miller’s hypotheses: what Freud did not want to see and categorized as fantasy was very often, on the contrary, a very real mistreatment or abuse.

Violence in adults is born from the violence they have experienced in the family (“it’s for your own good”) setting. This opposition between reality and fantasy is also found at the heart of attachment and psychoanalytic theory; thus, Freud passed

3 In the Paris suburbs.

from the theory of seduction to that of Oedipus. According to Bowlby or Anna Freud, "real" separations cause trauma, which Melanie Klein refuted.

Finally, we know, with regard to substance abuse, the fundamental role of the protective factor played by the disclosure of the trauma, this particular form of social support: having someone to talk to, putting words to the trauma to give it meaning.

Nevertheless, we must note two methodological remarks about this research. On the one hand, it will be necessary to verify that confounding factors do not underpin the fact of having been beaten or abused and to explain the correlation with the accident, which was done in the Shelly study. On the other hand, both of these studies are retrospective and also allow for hypotheses, but not conclusions.

Finally, as always, there is the question of interactions between genetic and environmental factors: in the Dunedin (New Zealand) longitudinal study, among children who had been sexually abused, those with a variant of the MAOMA gene were twice as likely to develop aggressive behavior and three times more likely to be convicted of violent acts than children who had been sexually abused but did not have a variant of the MAOMA gene. In contrast, the presence of this gene is not associated with problems among children who have not been abused.

8.5. Sexual abuse

Sexual abuse towards children is a prevalent and worrisome social phenomenon, especially among girls.

The prevalence of sexual abuse can vary greatly from country to country. For example, in the United States, it is 1.6 per 1,000 and in Turkey, it is 1.4 per 100. However, this prevalence is certainly highly underestimated in most countries because of the taboo that this situation represents.

Sexual abuse and mistreatment of children in institutional and religious settings are now recognized phenomena. Public attention to this problem has followed two interconnected streams: media exposure and victim organization and activism. Beyond a certain threshold, this problem has re-entered the public debate.

Numerous studies have shown that sexual abuse is a risk factor for the development of a series of aftereffects that may develop during childhood, adolescence or adulthood. The most commonly identified effects in adulthood in women who have been sexually abused are post-traumatic stress disorder, depression and suicidal ideation and behavior.

However, a significant proportion of victims of sexual abuse do not present clinical problems during adolescence or adulthood. The proportion of adolescents who do not present aftereffects ranged from 10% to 53% depending on the aftereffects considered, whereas, in adult samples, this proportion would be from 15% to 47%.

The aftereffects of sexual abuse vary greatly from one victim to another, so we might think that sexual abuse is not a risk factor predicting a specific disorder, but rather a general risk factor for the development of psychological aftereffects, although a proportion of victims will not develop aftereffects (either through resilience or because of less severe abuse, for instance) or they will diminish over time.

While the impact of sexual abuse is increasingly well-documented, the mechanisms by which it may or may not lead to the development of various aftereffects are less well understood. Although a considerable number of models have been proposed to try to explain the development of aftereffects following sexual abuse, very few have been empirically validated.

However, existing models have the advantage of suggesting different factors that can be studied. Among these, several models emphasize the role of sexual abuse characteristics, the role of disclosure and support characteristics and the influence of other forms of mistreatment during childhood.

The support received following the disclosure of the sexual abuse is therefore a factor that can influence the development of aftereffects, as we saw earlier in relation to accidents. In fact, when the reactions following the disclosure are perceived as helpful by the victim, the risk of developing aftereffects decreases. This factor could even be further associated with the development of aftereffects than the characteristics of the abuse.

In addition, the potential role of intergenerational continuity of childhood sexual victimization as a factor that may increase the risk of aftereffects in adulthood has been explored. This continuity refers to the presence of sexual abuse in the childhoods of both parent and child, without the parent being the abuser.

Thus, women involved in intergenerational continuity (in other words, having a mother or child who also experienced sexual abuse), compared with sexually abused women who are not involved in intergenerational continuity, have a greater frequency or severity of psychological difficulties in adulthood, including symptoms associated with post-traumatic stress and depression.

Another category of factors that may explain the development of certain aftereffects in victims of sexual abuse concerns the presence of other forms of abuse. There is indeed a significant co-occurrence of mistreatments in childhood: between 13% and 43% of adults report having experienced two or more forms of abuse.

Specifically, sexually abused children are more likely to experience other forms of mistreatment than children who have not been victims of this type of abuse, and the various forms of childhood abuse, including sexual, physical and psychological abuse and neglect, cumulatively increase the risk of mental health problems in adulthood, including post-traumatic stress disorder and depression.

8.6. Exposure to domestic violence

According to UNICEF, 275 million children worldwide are exposed to domestic violence each year. In France, data from the national survey on violence against women shows that, in 2001, 10% of French women were victims of domestic violence and that, in more than half of the cases, children were present during the violence, except in cases of sexual violence. Domestic violence is therefore a phenomenon that affects many children.

The socioemotional development of the child exposed to domestic violence is disrupted and the socioemotional profile varies according to whether the mother has left the violent partner or not, and also according to her stress. The child's socioemotional difficulties are more significant when the mother is still living at home with the violent partner than when she has left him. The higher the maternal stress, the more the child's socioemotional adjustment is threatened (Savard 2014).

Domestic violence is therefore a major social problem known to cause many difficulties for the child exposed to it, but not all children are affected by domestic violence in the same way and may present different adjustment profiles: some children may present many difficulties while others may present few or no problems. To date, a few studies are available to understand this heterogeneity in children's adjustment difficulties.

The most common indices used to identify these profiles are externalizing and internalizing disorders, but self-esteem or post-traumatic stress symptoms have also been considered.

The characteristics of violent events have often been related to the extent of the difficulties of the children exposed to them. Thus, the frequency and intensity of the domestic violence to which the child is exposed are positively correlated with the extent of the child's externalized and internalized disorders; the occurrence of externalized disorders is consistent with social learning theory (Bandura 1977): the child exposed to domestic violence may come to consider violence as a satisfactory mode of problem solving, particularly if it is associated with benefits for the abuser, who may thus be led to reproduce their parent's aggressive behaviors.

Similarly, the manifestation of internalizing disorders is consistent with the stress sensitization hypothesis, which states that repeated exposure to a conflicted and violent family environment heightens the child's reactivity to these events, amplifying the effect of the violence on the child's anxiety and depressive symptoms.

Rates of concomitance between exposure to domestic violence and parental violence are high. Children exposed to domestic violence are approximately twice as likely to be directly victimized by physical or other forms of emotional abuse. Research on this dual victimization shows the cumulative effect of both types of abuse on children's adjustment.

Among the factors retained to explain the difficulties of children exposed to domestic violence, the mother–child relationship is one of the most important and most studied: domestic violence, and the physical and psychological health problems it generates in the mother, contribute to diminishing the quality of her relationship with her child and, consequently, the child's ability to adapt; the more negative parenting behaviors, such as coercive and inconsistent disciplinary practices, the more externalized or internalized problems the child exhibits. In contrast, some mothers are able to maintain positive maternal behaviors despite the adversity of domestic violence; warm, supportive and consistent maternal behaviors towards the child are associated with fewer externalizing or internalizing problems in the child.

Violence can also negatively affect a child's attitude towards their mother by causing them to perceive her as a helpless and fragile victim on whom they can hardly rely for comfort. Such perception may exacerbate the externalized and internalized difficulties of the child exposed to domestic violence, for whom the mother is often the main source of support.

The child's analysis of the violence also helps to explain their adaptation difficulties. When the child is active in dealing with the abuse, they attempt to assess their role in causing or stopping the abuse and to judge the level of threat the abuse poses to their safety and that of the family. The more the child blames themselves for the violence or feels threatened by it, the more difficulties they will have in coping. Shouldering the blame for the violence or feeling a strong sense of threat would more specifically lead the child to experience feelings of hopelessness, anxiety and depression, but blame could also be associated with externalizing disorders.

Domestic violence may also lead to "parentification" of the child, reflecting the diffusion of intergenerational boundaries in the family and referring to a role reversal between parent and child that leads the child to take care of the parent emotionally or instrumentally. Parentification is likely to be detrimental to the child's development, as it involves the child putting aside their own needs in order to meet the needs of the parent. Several studies have shown that parentification is associated with externalizing and internalizing disorders. In the context of domestic violence, the more severe the child's exposure to violence, the more they will be "parentified", which in turn predicts the extent of internalizing disorders.

8.6.1. *Consequences for the physical health of children and adolescents*

Children often suffer from illnesses such as respiratory infections, insomnia, allergies, gastrointestinal problems and visual or auditory problems, such as ear infections; the higher the level of domestic violence between the couple, the more health problems are manifested in the child .

8.6.2. *Consequences for the cognitive and academic development of children and adolescents*

These children tend to have more learning and concentration difficulties. Cognitive and academic problems are most often manifested by intellectual, verbal or mental impairment.

8.6.3. *Consequences for child development according to the environmental context*

Beyond the effect of domestic violence, environmental factors can cause difficulty and influence the child's development; thus, they are important elements to consider. The results of studies that take into account the environmental context confirm the existence of significant links between maternal risk factors and child development. Parental alcoholism in relation to uncaring maternal conduct, maternal mental health problems, socioeconomic problems associated with maternal stress, environmental violence, lifestyle changes associated with avoidance behaviors and maternal support-seeking are all variables that influence child development in situations of domestic violence.

8.7. Foster care

At the end of 2016, 145,000 children aged 0–17 years, which represented 1% of the children in the French population, were placed with the child welfare system (*Aide Sociale à l'Enfance*, ASE). Placement of a child can be administrative, in the form of temporary arrangement (*Accueil Provisoire*, AP), contractualized by an agreement between the departmental council and the child's parents, or a judicial arrangement, ruled by a juvenile court, as in 89% of cases. Of these judicial placements, 30% are motivated by a proven "danger" to the child in the parents' home (Even and Sutter-Dallay 2019).

Wards of the state, known as *Pupilles de l'État*, minors who are abandoned or orphaned, represent only 1.5% of the children entrusted to the ASE, hence the difficulties of adoption today; factors such as contraception, voluntary interruption of pregnancy and the policy of maintaining links with the biological family have contributed to the virtual disappearance of the permanent abandonment of children.

In 2016, 52% of children were in foster homes and 38% were in institutions, primarily children's social welfare homes (*Maison d'Enfants à Caractère Social*, MECS) (Even and Sutter-Dallay 2019).

In France in 2016, 57% of children in care were boys. More than half (52%) were adolescents aged 11–17 years, 21% were children aged 6–11 years and 14% were children aged 0–5 years. Finally, 13% were of legal age in 2016; however, placement was continued after reaching legal age.

Obviously, problematic characteristics can be found in the family history and environment, including: various neonatal complications, absence of paternal filiation and separation of the parents, psychiatric pathologies and addictions in the parents and abuse.

Among the parents of children in care, 40% had themselves been placed as children, many of whom had been subjected to physical and sexual violence. However, this retrospective view, which is typical of clinicians, only allows us to see the phenomenon of reproduction and intergenerational transmission, which is favored by psychoanalytically inspired experts around the concept of repetition. This view does not allow us to see the opposite phenomenon, that of resilience, that only longitudinal studies enable us to understand, that is, adults who, having previously been placed in foster care as children, will not place their own children: these subjects disappear from the social gaze and are of no interest to anyone.

8.7.1. *Longitudinal/retrospective approach*

When establishing a relationship between a characteristic of an individual or their family and what happens to them over their lifetime, there are two possible approaches:

– *Retrospectively*, we start from the individual's present, we observe a fact (a characteristic, symptom or crime, for instance) that we will call "effect"; then, we examine their past and observe another fact that we will call "cause": the young person drinks, his father drank, the young person commits a crime, their mother abandoned them, and so on. Lawyers often use these kinds of arguments as "extenuating circumstances" in courts of law to try to clear their client: "My client had a difficult childhood". Clinical approaches (including those of psychotherapists, doctors and social workers) can only work retrospectively because of their function. They often only lead to the emergence of the phenomena of intergenerational continuity and repetition.

– *Longitudinally*, we follow the subject in the future in order to try to find relationships between their present as a "cause" and his future as an "effect". This longitudinal follow-up implies setting up a long and costly experimental device, but it is the only one that is truly demonstrative, since in this way it is possible to see, among a population of subjects who have undergone the same cause, how many will manifest the effect and how many will not. Longitudinal approaches highlight more the phenomena of intergenerational breaks or cessations, children who do not do as their parents do. The retrospective approaches of lawyers or clinicians always only perceive the sons of delinquents who become delinquents, the sons of alcoholics who become alcoholics and so on, but never those who do not become delinquents or alcoholics, because these subjects disappear from the social gaze. We will give here an example from our own work.

When we began working on the adult outcome of children placed in foster care by the ASE (Assailly *et al.* 1989), the retrospective view of practitioners on their parental fate was very bleak. These children would not, as adults, be capable of raising their own children and would abandon them, because their own mother had been an "old" child from the service, which would indicate the fatality of intergenerational repetition. However, when we found a population of these subjects in adulthood, what did we see? While a significant proportion had no children, and therefore there was no risk of abandonment (this "biological non-reproduction" could be analyzed, certainly, as a form of intergenerational transmission), the vast majority (95%) of those who did have children had not reproduced what they themselves had experienced in childhood and raised their children well.

To illustrate, we can cite other examples. Delinquent adolescents almost always start as aggressive children; however, the majority of aggressive children do not become delinquent adolescents. Similarly, battered children have often had parents who have experienced this type of abuse; in contrast, when battered children are followed through to parenthood, they mostly become loving parents.

One of the most important goals of developmental psychology is therefore the prediction of behavior from the knowledge of previous conditions. The ideal path for this prediction is the longitudinal study, which is the only method in order to lay the foundation for this knowledge: knowing by whom, when and how a given behavior will develop (and/or disappear). It is this information that can make preventive action more effective by indicating where and when to act.

It is true that during childhood, various vulnerabilities of emotional regulation can obviously be observed among young people in foster care, particularly among young victims of abuse: post-traumatic stress, internalized disorders (such as anxiety and depression), externalized disorders (provocation and attention deficit hyperactivity disorder), addiction, suicidal ideation and attempted suicide.

Children in care therefore seem to suffer more from developmental and/or psychiatric disorders than children in control groups who are not in care. The identification of risk factors that promote the emergence of these disorders in this population, and of potential protective factors, is therefore a major public health issue, given the size of the population concerned, and with a view to considering prevention and screening strategies.

Having a history of abuse before or during placement is logically an important risk factor for emotional vulnerability. Another factor has emerged that raises complex theoretical, practical and policy issues: that of repeated separation during development.

In fact, since the 1980s, an ideological change has occurred, brought about by psychoanalytically inspired experts and practitioners, which is influencing the practices and policies of the ASE: the doctrine of maintaining links with the biological family.

This doctrine is based on questions around the concept of filiation; we are not unaware of the importance of this theme for children in care and adopted children during adolescence, the main "developmental task" of adolescence being precisely the construction of identity, answering questions such as "Who am I?"

1) The problem is that this doctrine has had perverse effects: as soon as a biological parent demands the return of the child, the foster care placement is interrupted; then, if the deficiencies of the biological family environment do not improve, social workers are forced to replace the child, producing an incessant "ping pong" of the child during its development. These children are not "without family" to use the title of a book by Hector Malot, but experience "a hundred families". Sometimes, during periods of transition, even institutional care is necessary.

2) This question also has legal implications, the balance between the rights of the child and the rights of the parent arises for confidentiality of origins as well as for the management of care by the ASE, but this is beyond our competence.

3) However, what longitudinal studies do demonstrate is that stability of placement is a protection factor for child development. In our longitudinal study (Assailly *et al.* 1989), we observed a range of outcomes from the most to least favorable: adopted children, children with stable family placements (for at least 10 or 15 years), children with unstable family placements, children with multiple institutional and unstable family placements.

4) In fact, the doctrine of maintaining ties with the biological family is countered by the fact that it will produce a collateral effect: the continued exposure of the child to the sometimes very serious deficiencies and stresses of the family environment.

Children with stable placements are therefore much less likely to develop internalized and externalized disorders and, for the same reasons, early placement is also a protective factor.

These determinants also explain why foster care is much better for the child than institutional care: one of the best demonstrations was that of the *Bucharest Early Intervention Project*, a randomized, blinded, controlled study conducted in Romania on 136 children aged 0–31 months of age in institutional care (Clément 2019). Within this population, two groups of children were formed. The children in the first group remained in institutions, with those in the second group placed in foster families specially created for the study, because, at the time the study began, this placement mode did not exist in Romania. The results of this study showed that the foster children showed more secure attachments at age 1 and less internalizing disorders as they grew up. Moreover, they had higher developmental and intelligence quotients.

To conclude on the evolution of children in care, we see that they are at the heart of the problems of vulnerability and resilience; helping with this resilience will imply freeing ourselves from ideological prejudices in order to better organize the prevention and treatment of their psychological problems.

8.8. Parental usage of psychoactive substances

Maternal use of psychoactive substances is considered a significant risk factor for abuse and neglect, due to the consequences of intoxication, withdrawal or associated psychiatric comorbidity: poor parenting skills, instability and economic hardship are typically associated with maternal use.

In addition, family history of psychoactive substance use is a robust risk factor for increased use by adolescents and adults. Parental use, in particular, is linked to that of their offspring, with effects appearing as early as adolescence, a developmental period when most people first have access to products such as alcohol and tobacco.

Thus, a family history of tobacco use is associated with early and persistent tobacco use by young people across social groups (e.g. in the United States, this correlation is found among Caucasians, African Americans, Hispanics and Native Americans).

This social modeling takes three forms: neither parent smokes, one parent smokes and the other does not, or both parents smoke. The obvious questions are whether the non-smoking parent counteracts the influence of the smoking parent, whether the fact that both parents smoke instead of one changes the risk already incurred, whether the mother is more important than the father or vice versa, whether the effect is different for boys and girls and so on.

For this purpose, the Hutchinson cohort study (3,000 American children followed from 8 to 18 years of age, with information on parental smoking when the children were 8 years old) has provided the most relevant and reliable answers. There is a progressive gradation of the risk that the child will become a regular smoker at age 18, according to the number of parents who smoke. When only one parent smokes, there is a 64% increase in the risk of addiction for the young person (relative risk of 1.90) compared to homes where both parents do not smoke. When both parents smoke, this adds another 25% increase in risk (relative risk of 1.39) compared with homes where only one parent smokes; overall, having both parents smoking increases the risk of the child becoming addicted by a factor of 2.65. This could almost be called a dose/effect relationship.

Moreover, the transmission was clearly observed over several generations (grandparents, parents and children). Finally, there were no differences according to the sex of the parent, the sex of the child or any matching effects: the father's use does not influence the son any more than the daughter, nor does the mother's use. Interactions with the effects of changes in family structure (such as divorce) remain to be clarified: having two parents who smoke undoubtedly has a greater effect when both live at home and, with recomposition, the influences of the behaviors of four "parents" should be studied, which becomes very complicated. The effects of home rules should also be studied. Some rules (such as no smoking in the home) are protective, even though the parents are smokers, but, on the contrary, some educational practices (such as punishing the adolescent for smoking) are only protective if the parents do not smoke themselves. Logically, there must be a move away from the "do as I say, not as I do" attitude.

It will also be important to study the interaction with genetic factors that predispose to tobacco use and with prenatal exposure. It will also be useful to analyze the part played by all of these factors in behavioral changes in the young, such as when weekly use changes to daily use. Finally, parental smoking is associated with child smoking, but may also be associated with child cannabis use. Thus, there is not always a one-to-one resemblance; however, it is easy to imagine that the parent and child are using two different products for the same reasons.

With regard to cannabis, there is consistent evidence of association of use between family members: between parent and child and between older and younger siblings. For example, children of mothers who use cannabis begin use on average two years earlier than children of mothers who do not use it (Okechukwu and Chen 2018), an earliness associated with cognitive impairment and mental behavior, so it is important to identify young people at risk and offer prevention.

Hospital studies of cannabis-dependent subjects show strong intergenerational reproduction. Twin studies show significant intra-pair correlations in cannabis dependence due to the shared environment (such as between Vietnam veteran twins).

As far as alcohol is concerned, a family history of alcoholism is associated with early and persistent alcohol use in the young. Having an alcoholic parent increases the risk of early alcohol use in the child and we know the detrimental impact of addiction to development in the young. Children of alcoholics are three times more likely to start drinking by the age of 14 years and four times more likely to have experienced drunkenness by the age of 17 years, a combination of genetic and environmental factors obviously underpinning this phenomenon. Longitudinal follow-ups of children of alcoholic parents show that self-control and resilience in the young person play a role in this intergenerational transmission, even when externalized disorders are controlled.

More generally, the child's temperament acts as a moderator of family risk factors, such as parental psychoactive product use. An even more influential factor than parental alcoholism is the family density of alcoholism (family members other than parents); this is more related to alcohol/drug comorbidity and alcohol dependence of the young person than to illicit drug use or alcohol abuse alone.

Family alcoholism can have both specific and general effects. Those specific to family density are related to "the heritability of sensitivity to alcohol effects". "Resistance to the effects of sensation" has been revealed by the work of Schuckit (1998, 2006) on the heritability of sensitivity to the effects of alcohol by the sons of alcohol-dependent fathers: these young people, for whom alcohol has little effect, precisely because they feel little of the effects of the stimuli, progressively increase the doses in order to feel "something", in order to be "in tune", "in sync" with the rest of their friends, for whom alcohol produces many more sensations. Many young people followed between the ages of 15 and 25 years will become alcohol-dependent.

What is initially a genetic vulnerability highlighted by behavioral genetics is gradually combined with an environmental effect, Saturday night socialization. We could imagine that this resistance to the effects of the sensations produced by alcohol exists in other fields, such as sports and driving. Indeed, the same stimulation does not cause the same sensation in each of us: you put someone on a carousel and he screams; you take someone else on the most "sensational" attractions at Disneyland and they come down saying they felt nothing.

The link between the family's history of alcoholism and illicit drug abuse or comorbidity is mediated by the youth's personality (impulsivity and low popularity). It is possible, in fact, that young people with these traits will use substances to regulate negative effect. Thus, children of alcohol-dependent parents who are impulsive will be more likely to fail in school, be rejected by "conventional" peer groups, be affiliated with peer groups that will model their substance use and be less deterred by the negative consequences of substance use.

Other longitudinal follow-ups of young children of alcohol-dependent parents through adolescence emphasize behavioral control and self-resilience (flexibility of control) as factors that mediate the relationship between the father's and child's alcohol use.

The "shared biological vulnerability" hypothesis proposes that the biological factors that predispose individuals to psychoactive product use also predispose them to obesogenic eating behavior. This would occur because the rewarding characteristics of certain foods, namely, processed foods rich in refined carbohydrates and fats (such as chocolate, ice cream and pizza), overlap with those of psychoactive products (such as alcohol and cocaine).

In addition, when individuals attempt to remove processed foods from their diet, this attempt may trigger psychological (depressed mood and irritability) and behavioral (increased craving and inability to concentrate) withdrawal symptoms, similar to psychological and behavioral withdrawal symptoms.

Furthermore, similar neural reward circuits are activated when individuals consume processed foods and when they use psychoactive products. That said, neural reward circuits activate in response to a variety of stimuli (e.g. money, sexual images and music), not just with processed foods.

Thus, adults with a family history of alcoholism have a greater preference for sweet tastes in taste tests of drinking solutions.

In addition, the association between family history of alcoholism and obesity appears in the reinforcement of duration. In these nationally representative samples, the association between family history of alcoholism and obesity among adults was stronger among those interviewed in 2001–2002, compared with those interviewed in 1991–1992.

This may be due to the rapidly changing nature of the food environment over the past few decades, which has become more toxic with greater availability of processed foods high in refined carbohydrates and fats.

8.9. Discord and separation of parents

Conflicts are a part of life, especially in the lives of couples. Properly managed, they can even contribute to strengthening family harmony and children will benefit from parental conflict resolution. Unfortunately, not all conflicts are well-managed and parental discord is a strong predictor of child maladjustment, in general, and externalizing disorders, in particular. Thus, children adjust better after divorce if the relationship between the parents was conflictual before the divorce; children whose parents remain married, but in a high conflict relationship, do worse than children whose parents divorce. This makes sense, as children whose parents divorce are no longer "in the middle of the firing line". Numerous studies show various types of effects of discord on the child, such as sleep, health and behavioral problems.

8.9.1. *Discord between parents*

Among the possible sources of conflict between parents, values and attitudes about child rearing play an important role and are often one of the causes of divorce. This degree of conflict or harmony seems to remain stable over the years: it is a chronic feature of the family and is likely to have effects on the child. More generally, the harmony of the couple concerning their child's education is a form of social support for them both, reducing the risks of conflicts and helping to develop their educational skills.

For the mother, in particular, the congruence of values allows her to adapt to her role. Indeed, a classic, and still majority, sharing of parenting implications is that mothers have the responsibility for care and fathers the responsibility for play. Mothers will place more importance than fathers on congruence of value systems between partners, as they have more child-rearing responsibilities.

8.9.2. *The negative effects of discord*

Various hypotheses have been put forward:

– Children imitate their parents and will reproduce this aggressiveness (social modeling).

– Parental conflict leads to deficient parenting and disciplinary control of the child.

– Discord is a stress for the child, who reacts to this stress.

– Children inherit the genes that drive parents to conflict.

– Children pose behavioral problems to distract parents from their conflict.

– Children are the cause of parental discord.

The associations between parental discord and child behavior problems will reflect a variety of mechanisms, both environmental and genetic, as discord does not occur randomly in all family environments: indeed, some factors (such as poverty, early union and motherhood) are common to parental discord and child maladjustment.

Discord is an "embedded" characteristic within a more general environmental and genetic context. Furthermore, the child's reaction to parental discord can be seen from the perspective of attachment theory: a control system that aims to preserve the child's emotional security, in a way, a replica of the search for initial security in the early days of the mother–child relationship.

The influence of this factor on the relationship between parental discord and child problems is even likely to change with age; in other words, adolescents are more sensitive than children to this phenomenon or, at least, their reactions become more complex and include more space for this issue, which does not mean that the effects of discord are more pronounced in adolescents.

It is also possible to differentiate between the direct effects of discord on the child, as with all stresses, and the indirect effects, when discord disrupts parental behaviors and the relationships of each parent with the child. In the latter case, it is through educational practices that the conflicts have effects on the children.

Conflict creates a situation where parents become increasingly focused on their own problems, become emotionally disengaged, are less available to monitor their children and even resent those who are too much like their partner and become angry or hostile.

Adult discord "rubs off" on the adult–child relationship. Research shows that disharmony between parents often results in a deterioration of parental behavior and parent–child relationships, but this is not always systematic. Sometimes, one of the parents is more involved in the child's education, precisely because of the conflict. In this case, the parent's behavior will act as a moderator of the discord: if it deteriorates, it worsens the effects, if it remains good, it moderates them.

It is also worth mentioning the impact of discord on triadic interactions: reversals of alliances or coalitions, role changes, "scapegoating" phenomena, disruptions of triangulation and so on. Conflict also has an effect in itself, which does not pass through the parent–child relationship: thus, latent conflicts, hidden from the child, have less negative effects than conflicts openly exposed to them, whereas both types of discord would normally be equally likely to deteriorate relationships and behaviors.

Children are not sensitive to all types of conflict. Between the direct effects of discord and the indirect effects on parent–child relationships, we must consider the perceptions and expectations that children, and later adolescents, have of these phenomena. These perceptions will be different between subjects, which is why siblings exposed to the same conflict will react differently, because they will have different expectations about the conflict.

Thus, we know that a tendency to shoulder the blame and the perceived level of threat act as moderators between parental discord and negative developmental outcomes for the child. Child perceptions are not the cause of negative developmental consequences, but they do exacerbate the negative effects produced by parental discord.

8.9.3. *Family (re)composition*

Today, the majority of children are raised by both parents. A large and growing minority of children are being raised by a single parent, due to increases in divorce and births to single mothers. Currently, 2 million children under 18 in France, or 17% of the population, are in this situation, 3 million, or 25%, if we count children of legal age living with their divorced or separated mothers. In 60% of cases, the child lives with a single mother. This large minority can constitute up to half of the children in certain environments (such as inner-city Paris).

The contemporary increase in divorce can be summarized in a few figures: 5% of young people in 1971, 20% in 1993, 23% in 1999 and 25% in 2003. Of course, this question must be considered from a dynamic, diachronic point of view: periods of single parenthood can be transitory and intercalated between periods of two-parenthood. In fact, there is a re-composition in one in two cases of separation.

Work in this area has generally concluded that health, safety and relationship with the law are more impaired among children raised by single parents. For example, the literature on the genesis of delinquency has often pointed to the absence of the father.

This type of result gives rise to two main hypotheses. The first, psychoanalytical and psychodynamic, focuses on the notion of lack of paternal authority and emphasizes the negative effect of the father's absence on the young person's psyche, the search for limits and the need for transgression; symmetrically, it conceives the role of the father as that of a third party, who enables the separation from, and detachment of the symbiotic fusion with, the mother, a factor of autonomy (we saw previously the Lacanian concept of foreclosure, which corresponds to the consequences of this deficiency on the integration of the law).

The other hypothesis, more sociological and psycho-sociological, focuses on the living conditions of the single mother and emphasizes the negative effect of the loss of economic, psychological and social support from the father and the impact of this loss on the mother's stress and her ability to "manage" the child. Currently, divorce is, in fact, one of the major causes of impoverishment of households and women.

The development of single parenthood can have effects on the young person's "social capital": fewer ties with the other parent, the educating parent's work reducing the time spent with the child, less supervision of the child with respect to accidents and so on. In fact, single parenthood is not a risk factor in itself, but a marker of a certain number of adversities. In this context, there is a significant difference in being raised by a single mother, a senior executive or a working mother. A national health survey in Great Britain conducted in 1997 showed that the correlations between psychological morbidity, accidents and single parenthood no longer hold when controlling for the mother's income and socio-educational level. The influences of family structure are thus subject to multiple interactions with other variables such as income, the child's sex and the types of adults present in the home.

With regard to aggression, the differences in aggression classically observed between girls and boys are less in "single mother" households than in two-parent households. This is because single mothers are forced to expand their behavioral repertoire to compensate for the absence of the father. The daughters of single mothers are said to develop more significant "androgyny": more assertiveness and self-confidence in conflicts.

In most social settings, children living with a single mother are judged to be more aggressive than children living with both parents; the degree of "connection" between the child and the biological father is a protective factor against child aggression. In contrast, the single mother–child aggression correlation, compared to "intact" homes, is no longer observed in low-income families. When economic stress becomes too great, neither parent is available to help the young person with self-control.

"Mother and new partner" families, compared to "single mother" families, are associated with more aggression in boys than in girls (which is well understood empirically). In another area, that of illicit drug use, we know that if African American or Hispanic children in the United States lived as much with both parents as Caucasian children, the difference in drug use between the different populations would be very strongly affected. We see how this type of work brings home the complexity of this field.

8.9.4. *Divorce and its effects*

The interest of researchers in divorce has clearly been reinforced by the increasing frequency of this event in the modern times. This rise in divorce does not necessarily indicate a rejection of the institution of marriage, but rather of partners falling out of love. For example, in the United States, 75% of men and 66% of women remarry. That said, the rate of increase in remarriage is not increasing like that of divorce. Moreover, divorces are more frequent in cases of remarriage (10% more than for first unions).

Couples with remarried women divorce twice as frequently as couples with remarried men. This is understandable considering that divorce rates are 50% higher in remarriages with children from a first marriage. However, this last observation depends on the sociocultural background: in the United States, it is true for Caucasians, but not for African Americans. The criteria for marital harmony may thus vary culturally.

One of the trends in the increase of divorce frequency today concerns what has been called "gray divorces". Due to increases in life expectancy and remarriage, the financial autonomy of women and the psychological impact of retirement, divorces are now also increasing among 50–80 year olds, with one third of divorcees over the age of 50 years. This concerns children, because a rather intriguing observation is that couples who have grandchildren divorce less than couples who do not, and even less than couples where only one partner has become a grandparent. The effect is observed even when controlling for social background. Could the birth of a child put the brakes on a "gray divorce"?

The cohorts of children who experienced the large increases in divorce in the 1970s are now adults. Long-term longitudinal follow-ups, such as the National Child Development Study (all English children born in a certain week in 1958), provide a picture of the long-term effects of divorce. The results of the studies depend on the cohort: those for more recent cohorts lead to fewer negative conclusions, because of the contemporary trivialization of divorce.

In the 1950s, psychiatrists who were well-known and published books believed that, like women's work, divorce was an event from which children would not recover; they were supposed to become delinquents, drug addicts and so on. What psychiatrist would talk in such stigmatizing terms today? Beyond the impact of ideology in the human sciences, what is playing out here is simple statistical trivialization: children of divorce were extremely marginal in the 1950s, but they are no longer so today; claiming that they would all become scarred for life can no longer be supported when they make up half of the classrooms at school.

The general conclusion that can be drawn from the meta-analyses is that parental divorce, or certain factors associated with it, have a negative impact on the subject's well-being. That said, the long-term effects appear to be modest, once controlling for confounding factors. Put another way, while there are differences between children of divorce and others, there is even more variability within the children of divorce group itself.

Multiple variables can play a role as confounding factors. Divorce has a greater impact on only children and the higher the number of siblings, the less impact divorce has. Either only children are more sensitive to intra-familial conflict and stress, or their parents detect more problems in them. Of course, the temperament of the child also influences their reaction to divorce.

Moreover, it depends on the number and nature of family characteristics that could be assessed before the divorce, in the (often futile) attempt of "all else being equal", to compare the families of divorced and married couples. Correlations with youth outcomes may be due to the influence of pre-separation factors.

When these factors are taken into account, is there still an association between family breakdown and behavior? Often, this association disappears when the pre-separation period is taken into account. Are there really causal relationships? Would the young person really have behaved differently if the parents had not separated? What behaviors are the result of the break-up of the couple and the specificity of the people affected by these break-ups? For example, we put all separated parents "in the same bag", but the reason why they separated surely has a major influence.

When simply comparing averages, various studies reveal a poorer state of health in young adults who experienced divorce as children, in terms of mortality or illness. Socioeconomic consequences also seem to persist when children of divorce reach adulthood, in terms of unemployment, income and housing (National Child Development Study, 1997, on subjects aged 33 years).

For example, girls from single-mother homes and boys from blended families are more likely to drop out of school at the minimum legal age. Generally speaking, children of divorce are often judged as more "mature" and more "autonomous", accepting responsibilities earlier.

These situational traits are sometimes even viewed positively by parents, especially in the case of girls, as social competence or resilience. Hence, parent–child relationships are less conflictual in divorced families than in intact families. However, they can become a source of maladjustment: if tasks exceed their capabilities and if adolescents perceive them as a burden that handicaps them in relation to their other activities, this will produce anxiety, depression, low self-esteem or even rebellion and resentment.

Early sexual activity (before age 16), early couple formation, abortion or early parenthood have all been associated with separated families for both girls and boys. These early responsibilities may be related to early school leaving; however, the results of studies are not always consistent. There is a difference between boys and girls in this respect: when they marry, both boys and girls marry early. However, there is another consequence frequently associated with parental divorce for boys from disadvantaged social backgrounds: they do not marry at all, sometimes because they have become an indispensable economic support. Logically, this is not observed among boys from privileged social backgrounds and this sociocultural difference is not observed among girls.

What is more surprising is the correlation between parental divorce and an earlier age of first menstruation for their daughters. An early first menstruation age is a risk factor for various problems, such as: depression, eating disorders, self-image dissatisfaction and substance use.

In general, early first menstruation is linked to family stress. Is this a biological factor of conservation of the species? Do girls who feel that they cannot rely on their past to protect them become women sooner so that the future can compensate? Conversely, a harmonious family climate and a father's investment in education are associated with a later onset of menstruation.

It has also been observed that the quality of the father–daughter relationship has a greater influence on the menarche age (age of first menstruation) and, more generally, on the timing of puberty than the mother–daughter relationship. The more the father is absent, the faster this maturation takes place. Similarly, the presence of a stepfather is associated with earlier menarche, even more than the absence of the biological father. The longer the cohabitation with a stepfather, the earlier the menarche. The stronger the conflicts between the daughter and her stepfather, the stronger the correlation. This phenomenon also appears in animals, and involves pheromones. It is called the "male effect" (when an unknown adult male enters the group).

However, is it family stress alone that causes early menarche? Other hypotheses can be considered: genetic factors, since there is a correlation between the menarche ages of the mother and the daughter. This heritability hypothesis is confirmed by studies of monozygotic or dizygotic twins.

Early menarche may itself become a predictor of other problems, such as depression and substance use. It is not simple; therefore, this psychobiological factor of early menarche that can explain early unions and births. Similarly, age at first sexual intercourse is certainly linked to the early formation of a couple and a family, but only partially explains it, especially among boys.

It is possible that one factor in this early age is less strict, more permissive parental control on these issues, probably because the parents are themselves looking for a new sexual partner. Two correlations with these early responsibilities (or exits from the family) are interesting: they are more common both among children raised in a stepfamily and among girls. It remains to be seen what factors contribute to these early exits.

Does the early and/or illegitimate fertility of girls, but not boys, indicate female vulnerability, or is it simply that boys' accounts of it are less reliable? Why does divorce appear to have a greater effect on girls, for example, in terms of depression? Is it because the greater emotional closeness to the mother, both before and after the divorce, will cause the child to react more strongly to later roles as wife and mother? Is it because girls have a greater sensitivity to the mother's behaviors and internal states than boys?

It is no coincidence that this sexual differentiation occurs at the age of role taking and gender identity affirmation. The socialization of boys turns them towards competition and exploration, that of girls towards interpersonal relationships. While this area is dysfunctional, it affects girls more. They may find themselves “trapped” in family problems and be led to “brood” more and more. The question of connection and union is more of a “feminine” issue. Or, in other words, transmission does not happen in the same way for women and men. The psychological difficulties of boys in adolescence have their origins more in early childhood (e.g. in attachment construction), while those of the girls are more during adolescence.

Moreover, the deficiency in parental social control is more important for girls. Parents probably pay more attention to their daughters’ choice of partner than to their sons’. This can be seen as a legacy of the past, when the choice of husband completely determined the social future of the daughter. However, after the parents’ divorce, there is usually only one parent left to control the girl. In the case of boys, the socioeconomic consequences of divorce are more important: it encourages them to drop out of school and an early marriage will be “at risk” of ending in separation. The phenomena of resilience, in particular, should be studied to see whether or not, when the child maintains a good relationship with one of the parents, this emotional security will be sufficient to make them overcome the after-effects of the discord and the separation.

8.9.5. *Children of divorce and children of bereavement*

Children from intact families fare better, children of divorced parents less well and children orphaned of a parent are somewhere in between. However, the death of a parent does not affect all children equally: it is more common in poorer social backgrounds and it more often involves the father, rather than the mother. The reason for the loss is fundamental: loss through death does not result from abandonment of the child, and abandonment can generate fear of future abandonment. Furthermore, conflicts are stronger in divorce situations than in death situations. Finally, extended family support may be more important in death situations than in divorce situations.

The death of a parent does not appear to have the same adverse consequences as the separation of parents in the various developmental domains. Certainly, it should be possible to differentiate between parental death at birth, during adolescence and during adulthood. Only a few behavioral disturbances are observed during adolescence among subjects without a parent (use of psychoactive products, early autonomy); however, it is not certain that they remain in adulthood.

Although remarriage or “recohabitation” appears to have a socioeconomic advantage for the widowed parent, this does not always translate positively to the child. There is a "disadvantage gradient" that positions children living with step-parents after widowhood between children living in intact families and those living in single-parent households. This is particularly true for early home leaving and suggests the negative influence of intra-family conflict.

8.9.6. *Blended families and single-parent households*

If there is one newsworthy subject in the world of family psychology, it is this one. Family recomposition has become a "mass phenomenon". Out of the 10 million French people who have been divorced, 38% have "rebuilt their lives"; one and a half million French children live in blended families, and this number is constantly increasing (7% in 1993, 12% in 1999 and 14% in 2003). Logically, the proportion of children living in single-parent families has decreased over the same period (from 14% to 11% in 1999). Another well-known development is that women are now also involved in recomposition, which was not historically the case, even though the balance has not yet been achieved.

Recomposition has a rather good image in the media, in movies, on TV and so on. After the misfortune of the break-up, a new Prince(ss) Charming arrives, a source of newfound happiness, improved family budget (an express way out of poverty)[4], a masculine presence presumed to be favorable for discipline, for instance. However, what exactly is the situation?

When the stepfamily tries to structure itself along the lines of the nuclear family, problems often arise; the same type of relationship within an intact family and a stepfamily will not necessarily produce the same effects. The factors of adaptation or maladjustment of the child are not the same. The blended family implies more flexible, more open functioning. Recomposition forces the young person to adapt to a stepparent (stepfather or stepmother), and also sometimes to their own children, resulting in many possible conflicts in perspective, which are "squared" when the two parents remarry.

This new family can even become a network of subjects who have no biological ties over three generations (new grandparents, parents and siblings). New siblings, new births, even new adoptions when the stepparent adopts the child: all these developments can produce jealousy, feelings of abandonment, disownment and uprooting. In short, anguish.

---

4 However, because of modern developments in women's employment and better enforcement of maintenance allowance rulings, the situation is improving for women who do not remarry.

Restoring family relationships after remarriage takes longer than after divorce: an estimated two to three years for divorce and five to seven years for remarriage. Moreover, since a quarter of these remarriages lead to a new divorce within five years, and this is most often the case when children are involved, we can conclude that, for these reconstituted families, re-stabilization has never occurred.

For example, we know that in the first year after remarriage, mothers have poorer monitoring and emotional involvement than non-divorced mothers. However, when remarriage is stable, maternal behavior gradually improves and no further differences are observed.

In terms of the relationship between the child and the stepparent, we see an evolution. At the beginning of the story, the stepparent is certainly not as close to the child as a biological parent would be, but wants the marriage to succeed. Stepfathers will behave as polite strangers, not showing negative reactions to the child, but also exercising less control and supervision. Over time, an aloof, disengaged parenting style will remain the rule, but conflict and negative reactions may also increase, especially between stepparents and stepdaughters.

Physical abuse is seven times more common between stepfathers and children than between fathers and biological children, and the rate of infanticide is 100 times higher among stepchildren than among biological children. These differences are most pronounced among infants and young children.

Of course, conflicts can sometimes arise from the fact that it is the child who rejects the stepparent, with the child's persistent hostility overwhelming the stepparent. As for stepmothers, their integration is generally more difficult at first than for stepfathers. Due to expectations, biological fathers will force them to be more involved in the children's education than biological mothers with their new partners, which will be a source of conflict. For these stepmothers, pushed into a less distant, but more active and direct role than stepfathers, the biological father's support for their parenting behavior and the agreement between the two partners will be factors of primary importance.

Thus, negotiated authority (which we have seen is the optimal disciplinary strategy for the child), particularly between stepfathers and stepsons, is not always implemented in stepfamilies if the conditions are not met. More generally, it is the whole question of parental authority that is shaken up by recomposition.

Moreover, recomposition does not only pose problems of relations between the child and their stepparents. There is also the question of the child's relationship with the parent who does not have custody. Moreover, the behaviors of the father and mother are predictably different after divorce and recomposition: non-custodial mothers try much harder (twice as much) to keep in touch with the child than non-custodial fathers. Surprisingly (except from an ethnological/sociological perspective), mothers, and even more so non-custodial fathers, maintain more contact with their sons than with their daughters. Finally, recomposition can also be the cause of conflicts between the siblings. These conflictual relationships will have a knock-on effect on the relationship between parents and children and, in the longer term, on the socialization of the young person.

With regard to the behavior of offspring, smoking in adolescents is more associated with blended families than with single-parent households; the same is true for suicide attempts. The quality of intra-family relationships is the major risk factor in this area. The general conclusion of the work in France, as well as in the United Kingdom, is that children living in stepfamilies fare worse than children in intact families – which was to be expected – and also, on several criteria, that children living in stepfamilies also fare worse than children living in single-parent homes.

For example, children in stepfamilies had more accidents and presented more bedwetting than children in single-parent homes. In stepfamilies with a stepmother, children show more deviant behaviors, lower self-esteem and more distress than in single-parent homes. Moreover, the fact that school boarding is currently on the rise and is more frequent in this type of family is probably not a coincidence and reveals the importance of conflicts.

The gender of the child plays on these influences: boys benefit more than girls from a harmonious relationship with their stepfather, their social behavior is more affected. Girls are more exposed than boys to adjustment problems when they live in a blended family. Social background also plays a role: in the United States, African American children living in stepfamilies fare better than Caucasian children (for whom the stepfather is more "advantageous").

With regard to mental health in adulthood, there were a few differences between subjects from blended families and subjects from single-parent homes. Similarly, there was no difference in alcohol abuse. On the contrary, the use of illicit drugs was seen to be more frequent among the subjects from blended families.

We also see that the age of the child at the time of the family event, particularly the remarriage of the parent in charge, has a strong influence on outcomes. When the child is an adolescent, the outcomes are negative for schooling and family relationships, whereas when the child is younger, there are fewer negative outcomes, probably because adjustment is easier.

To conclude on recomposition, the impression is that the money or the support of the parent does not compensate for the stress on the child. It is the conflict between the stepparent and the child that is relevant, more so than the marital satisfaction.

8.9.7. *The issue of joint custody*

For some time, joint custody has been increasingly seen as a remedy for the negative effects of divorce on children. The absence of the father and living in a single-parent home after divorce are often assumed to have negative consequences for behavioral and emotional adjustment. The importance of continued contact with each parent has often been advocated and legislation promoting joint custody has emerged. Nevertheless, various authors, particularly of psychoanalytic inspiration, have questioned this analysis, notably by invoking the question of the stability of the bond with a primary attachment figure and the question of the stability of the family structure.

What exactly is the situation? Reviewing literature on the subject yields mixed results: a substantial proportion of children in joint custody experience confusion and distress. There are a few differences between joint custody and single-parent homes in terms of children's symptoms. However, there are inconsistencies in the results of work on this topic.

The child's legal situation, what the matrimonial judge has decided and the child's actual situation, that is, what the parents actually do about the child, do not always match. Children in theoretically different situations may in fact be in very similar situations, especially in terms of the time spent with each parent.

The frequency with which the child is "moved" also has an influence, such as disruption of peer relationships and, instability. In fact, there is little difference between children in joint custody and those in single-parent homes in terms of their adjustment. Access to the father is not a panacea.

The psychological functioning of parents after divorce is clearly crucial. Post-divorce parental anxiety and depression affect the child's adjustment by altering the quality of parental behavior. Joint custody does not address the negative effects of parental conflict. The initial phase of divorce, when parents negotiate custody arrangements, is a crucial period for the child's subsequent adjustment.

The post-separation co-parenting relationship influences adjustment for the entire family. For example, a combination of high cooperation and low conflict is associated with positive effects on child adjustment. Specifically, children living in families with cooperative co-parenting styles show significantly fewer behavioral problems and have a closer relationship with their fathers when the father does not have custody of the child.

Conversely, high conflict and low cooperation are associated with adverse effects on child adjustment. In fact, high conflict co-parenting produces a higher risk of triangulation between parents and emotional, behavioral and academic problems. In general, post-separation parental conflict is one of the factors that explain the discrepancy between the outcomes of those who are still married or in a union and those who are separated.

In light of these observations, it is important to better understand the factors that lead to less conflict and more cooperation in post-separation co-parenting. Among the many determining factors, the type of custody of the children (joint or sole) seems to be an important variable to take into account in order to better understand the co-parenting relationship in the context of separation. In fact, custody could be defined as the way parents manage decisions related to the children and the number of interactions they have after separation.

Some studies have shown that joint custody is associated with a cooperative relationship, while other authors have concluded that the custody arrangement is not related to post-separation co-parenting. Finally, some studies have identified joint custody as being associated with aspects of conflictual and less cooperative co-parenting. Meta-analyses were therefore necessary, showing that families with joint custody reported significantly more cooperation than families with sole custody. Furthermore, parents with joint custody reported better relationships with their ex-partners than parents with sole custody.

Current meta-analyses indicate that parents with joint custody show more cooperation than parents with sole custody, regardless of the occurrence of relationship conflict. In order to correctly interpret this finding, it will be important to consider whether joint custody tends to facilitate cooperation between parents or whether parents who choose joint custody are predisposed to cooperative co-parenting.

Parents with joint custody are more likely to have higher levels of education and earnings than those in sole custody. This may suggest that parents with higher socioeconomic status tend to choose joint custody. Greater personal and social resources associated with higher socioeconomic status could explain why parents with joint custody see cooperation as more important than those with sole custody.

However, given that only a limited number of studies have compared families in terms of sociodemographic characteristics, this finding should be treated with caution. In other words, it does not seem possible to clearly determine whether parents with joint custody have a different profile than parents with sole custody, which might explain the greater mutual cooperation they demonstrate.

It can be hypothesized that, regardless of the parents' individual situations, joint custody encourages the development of stronger cooperation; this could be explained by the fact that fathers are more involved in joint custody parenting. The quality of post-separation co-parenting relationships is better when the mother sees her "ex" as a responsible and involved parent. This may explain, in part, why greater cooperation is observed in cases of joint custody.

A second possible explanation for this hypothesis concerns the relief that joint custody gives parents. By its very nature, joint custody could give parents a break from the responsibilities of single parenting when the other parent takes on more responsibility. This relief could be seen as cooperation.

An examination of moderators determined when the custody arrangement influenced cooperation. It appears that the person who valued cooperation moderated the association between custody and cooperation. Mothers reported significantly more cooperation in joint custody than fathers. Men and women are known to have different perceptions of the same relationship; however, it is not clear why women see more cooperation than fathers in joint custody.

It is possible, therefore, that the majority of parents who chose joint custody came to a mutual agreement or negotiation: mothers perceive more cooperation in joint custody because they have agreed to this type of arrangement.

Historical trends also influence the association between custody and cooperation. Specifically, joint-custody families report significantly more cooperation than sole-custody families; however, this is only true for studies from the 1980s and 1990s. In the 2000s, there has been no difference between joint- and sole-custody parents in terms of cooperation.

This could be explained in two complementary ways. First, joint custody was not common during the 1980s and 1990s and this arrangement has gradually become more common since the late 1990s. Thus, in the 1980s and 1990s, the few families with joint custody probably chose this type of arrangement to meet their needs, whereas families in the 2000s may have been influenced by the growing popularity of this type of custody. However, parents who chose their custody arrangement (rather than having it imposed on them) are more likely to be mutually cooperative. In other words, interpreting the link between custody and cooperation requires some caution.

8.9.7.1. *The moderators*

Three main variables emerged. First, this association appears to vary with the length of time since separation. In joint custody, conflict appears to increase with time. However, this finding must be interpreted with caution. This does not mean that the perception of conflict in joint custody increases over time, as there is no longitudinal study of the evolution of conflict. In fact, there is no difference in conflict between custody arrangements when parents have been separated for one to three years, but there is a significant difference when parents have been separated for three years or more, with more conflict in joint custody.

Why is there more conflict in joint custody three years after separation? On the one hand, the type of custody arrangement determines how decisions about the children are made and how much interaction the parents must have. Joint custody involves more interaction between the parents and greater parental involvement on both sides. Joint custody appears to lead to more transitions between residences than sole custody. More frequent transitions are likely to cause more stress for parents and children. On the other hand, there is considerable variability between the initial custody arrangement and actual custody practice. Many families seem to use the initial custody plan as a guideline that provides opportunities for negotiation. Over time, and as the child develops, the custody arrangement will require renegotiation and flexibility on the part of coparents. For example, it is possible that because parents with joint custody will be required to interact more frequently, and will have to adjust to many transitions between residences, they will experience more conflict due to the inevitable changes brought about by the child's development over time.

A second hypothesis that might explain these observations concerns family recomposition, which is an example of a transition leading to a renegotiation of boundaries and roles between parents. Over time, the probability that one of the two parents will form a new union increases. Thus, we can assume that after three or more years following separation, a large number of the families studied are likely to have had at least one recomposition, linked to reduced parental involvement and more conflictual interactions. In other words, it is likely that parents with joint custody face more demanding renegotiations of boundaries and roles as a result of family recomposition than those with sole custody, and that this may lead to more conflict over time.

To conclude on custody, and in relation to all these confounding factors, the legal ruling thus seems to play a minor role. The most important factor remains a family dynamic made up of a combination of interacting factors. More than the time spent with each parent according to a judgment, it is the harmony of the relationship that is preponderant, on the one hand, between the child and each of their parents and, on the other hand, between the parents themselves.

8.9.8. *Conclusion*

While divorce is a life event, separation is not an event, but a process. We have seen that children who have lost a parent fare better than the children of divorcees, that single-parent households fare better than blended families and that regularly maintaining ties with a non-custodial parent is not a guarantee of success.

Loss or absence does not explain everything. It is the issue of conflict (and always the issue of the affective connection) that seems to emerge as the most influential. We need to look at the stress of the divorce, the totality of the resources following the divorce and the interactions between these two factors, not just the presence or absence of one factor *per se*.

For example, the negative economic impact of divorce will be offset by a loving relationship between the child and the custodial parent. Similarly, the positive effects of maintaining a relationship with the non-custodial parent will be negated if there is conflict. Conversely, an initially distant parent will become closer as a result of divorce.

Separation is a marker of many of the components of adversity that exist in both intact and separated families. It is this back and forth between the study of normal development and the study of at-risk groups that advances developmental psychology. Conflicted families may sometimes suffer more harmful effects than families where the divorce was voluntarily chosen to end the conflict. These "children of divorce" sometimes conclude from this that the separation was an effective strategy, not a failure, and as adults they may be more able to cope with conflict situations and demonstrate flexible coping strategies.

Some separating parents are aware that divorce can have an impact on children; however, they lack information and research findings in this area are certainly not available to them. The following findings are especially important to consider:

– Not all children of divorced parents present significant aftereffects.

– Certain factors aggravate or diminish the consequences of separation for the child.

– Boys are not systematically more vulnerable than girls and girls may not emerge unscathed from this event.

As we have seen, remarriage is not a guarantee of success. The divorce rates of these second unions are significant and a follow-up/accompaniment of the impact of these unions on the child would be beneficial, as recomposed families do not function in the same way as "initial" families. The impact of conflicts in particular should be better taken into account. However, the child's desire to maintain contact with both parents must be respected and encouraged, both as a right and because there is no evidence to suggest that this in itself has negative consequences.

8.10. Peer influence

In the context of socialization, peers come to play an important role, second only to family. Childhood friendships foster the development of theory of mind and self-esteem (Mallet 2015). They are important in transitional phases (entry into elementary, junior high and high school). They are also a protective factor against bullying and cyberbullying (see below), as the presence of a friend attending these events lowers cortisol levels. Friends thus come as a second attachment system, a second security base for exploration and autonomy.

One of the most important transitions of adolescence is the increasing importance and influence of peer relationships. While friendship emerges relatively early in childhood, research on peer groups has shown that the influence and importance of peers increases in early adolescence, complementing and perhaps rivaling the role played by parents.

This pattern continues until peer influence peaks in mid-adolescence and begins to gradually decline in late adolescence, these friendship structures can help the adolescent move from a parent-related identity to an identity defined by friends and, finally, to an individualized identity. Thus, this period of adolescence may be an ideal time to study changes in the peer network and their implications for development.

Because the increase in psychopathology or psychoactive product use often runs in parallel with the increase in the influence of peer relationships in early and mid-adolescence, peers may play some part in causing or maintaining psychopathology or use at this age.

For example, having supportive friends may help adolescents avoid depression; conversely, co-rumination among friends (discussing problems, focusing on negative emotions and so on) increases the overall level of depressive thinking; the influence of peer contagion will then extend to both negative behaviors (such as deviance training) and emotions, including emotional distress such as symptoms of depression.

A great deal of research has shown that simply associating or bonding with peers who engage in risky behaviors makes children or adolescents more likely to engage in such behaviors themselves; adolescents who engage in typical age-appropriate risk-taking behaviors (alcohol, tobacco, illicit drugs, aggression) are more likely to have friends who exhibit the same behaviors.

Moreover, it is not necessary to observe a behavior in a peer in order to imitate it; it is enough to think that this behavior is popular within one's group and that risk taking is the "price to pay" to acquire this popularity; one of the many examples is the motivation evoked by young people having their first sexual intercourse at a very early age: these subjects invoke that popularity at school may be dependent on being able to break the rules. That said, the subject's perception of what is normative within their peer group is obviously subject to distortions.

However, there have been criticisms of the findings of works regarding the facilitation of peer risk taking: when attributing similarity in behavior to peer influence, the possible effects of confounding factors are overlooked: for example, measurement error, when peer behavior is elicited by the subject's own account (including self-justifications and possible projections); thus, children and adolescents are not always very accurate in their recollections and evocations of peer behavior.

8.10.1. *The selection phenomenon*

Correlation is not causation and the co-occurrence of a behavior in a young person and one of their peers is not absolute proof of an influence: in fact, this co-occurrence may very well originate from another mechanism that is symmetrical to it: selection ("birds of a feather flock together").

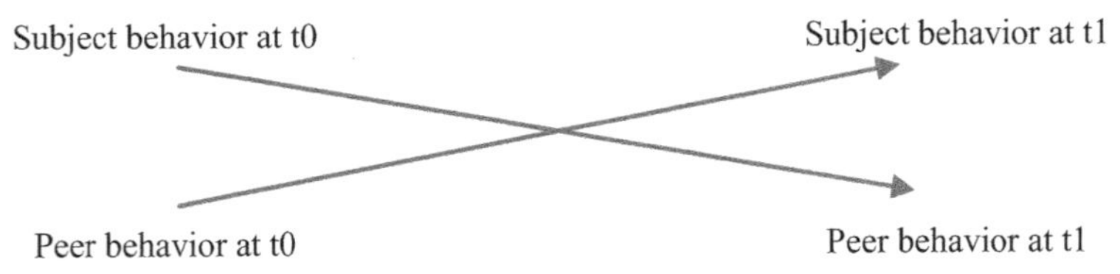

Figure 8.1. *The concept of "flocking". For a color version of this figure, see www.iste.co.uk/assailly/psychology.zip*

Indeed, a child or adolescent may choose to associate and bond only with subjects who exhibit the same types of behaviors as them among the set of available peers; risk taking, transgression or substance use could be the causes and not the consequences of peer selection: each of us tends to seek the company of others who resemble us, mirrors of ourselves, which can be translated by the concept of "flocking". For example, risk-taking subjects will choose risk takers as friends, cannabis-using subjects will choose other cannabis users, delinquent subjects and so on as friends. Then, clearly, this selection can become an influence.

Flocking (or selection) is illustrated by the arrow from subject behavior at t0 to peer behavior at t1; influence is illustrated by the arrow from peer behavior at t0 to subject behavior at t1.

The selection hypothesis is particularly strong during adolescence (gang socialization), and also exists in adults (e.g. the selection effect is strong for the similarity of spouses with regard to risk taking, addictions and transgressions).

In order to separate the two effects of influence and selection, longitudinal and not just cross-sectional studies are needed. These show that the two effects are of equal importance.

Thus, these works on influence and selection do not invalidate the notion of peer influence, but, in fact, specify that the relationship between peers and self-endangerment is bidirectional, whereas, too often, we tend to conceive the relations between the group and the individual as a linear relation, with only one direction ("influencers", who influence the influenced). From a preventive point of view, it is necessary to emphasize this selection effect, because it pinpoints the subject's responsibility and on the type of environment that he creates around him.

Other aspects of the relationship between peers and antisociality have been analyzed, including the influence of sociometric status, from three aspects.

8.10.2. *Peer influence and peer rejection*

Peer rejection is associated with the development of dangerous and/or aggressive behaviors and peer rejection in childhood predicts the development of dangerous and/or aggressive behaviors in adolescence; it is more specifically predictive of conduct disorder in adolescence than is association with antisocial peers.

Thus, juvenile delinquency in adolescence may be a group phenomenon but is predicted by the opposite phenomenon in childhood: peer rejection. Longitudinal sociometric studies of the young person's networks over time would be needed to elucidate this issue. Thus, the evolution towards antisociality follows different developmental pathways in boys and girls and rejection by non-deviant peers during childhood and affiliation with antisocial peers intervene differently.

8.10.3. *Peer influence and identification*

Moreover, not all peers are equally influential: social modeling theory associates influence and identification, because it is mainly through the peer(s) with whom the young person identifies that they are influenced. Therefore, the proximity of behaviors and feelings must be taken into account when assessing influence, as well as the number of friends available.

For example, the influence of the "best friend" may be stronger than others, but its importance should not be exaggerated; it depends on the pre-existing similarity of behaviors and parent–child relationships.

Finally, one factor that moderates the influence of the "best friend" is the fact that teenage friendships, even the best ones, do not always last very long.

8.10.4. *The question of popularity and its two faces*

Popularity (as understood in adolescence by sociometric tools) is often seen as a marker of positive social adjustment. However, popularity could also be seen as a marker of vulnerability to antisocial behavior.

The most popular adolescents are those who have the most self-esteem, secure attachments and appropriate interactions with their mothers and peers. Thus, popularity is positive for socialization: popular adolescents are also those who will show less hostile behaviors, but they are also those who are more likely to show deviant behaviors, because these behaviors are precisely "normative" and appreciated within the peer group.

Thus, aggressive children are not always those who are rejected; they may even be popular among their peers and, indeed, may alternatively employ coercive or prosocial strategies to "get their way". Thus, there is no deficit in social skills, but rather different motivations.

8.10.5. *Parent–peer interactions*

In an ecological logic of human development, environmental influences interact strongly. Thus, parenting strategies, peer relationships and peer behaviors interact. For example, the effects of negative parenting characteristics are mitigated by the effects of positive peer relationships and the effects of negative parenting characteristics are exacerbated by the effects of associating with antisocial peers.

Similarly, adolescents who spend the most time with peers after school and for whom parental supervision is deficient exhibit more risky behaviors. Similarly, and from a longitudinal perspective, parenting style at age 10 for the child has been found to be associated with antisocial peer involvement at age 12, which then predicts the likelihood of later behavior problems.

These interactions clearly reveal the direction of one aspect of social development: family characteristics predict interactions with peers, which in turn predict risk taking in adolescence as a result of growing autonomy. Parental strategies and peer pressures are thus highly intertwined.

In addition, a gender difference was noted: parents and peers play inversely, and differently, for boys and girls; parent orientation reduces risk taking, whereas peer orientation increases it. However, for boys, it is mainly peer influence that produces risk taking, whereas, for girls, it is problems with parents that produce it.

In fact, we can see here the influence of a difference between boys and girls in adolescence: boys see family life as a threat to their autonomy, and are more likely to detach themselves from it and seek the company of peers, which in turn will influence them; due to gender stereotypes, girls remain more oriented towards family life, in parallel with the friendships of adolescence, and will therefore be more sensitive to the influences of the family environment, whether positive or negative.

9

Activities and Leisure

On the seashore of endless worlds children meet. Tempest roams in the pathless sky, ships get wrecked in the trackless water, death is abroad and children play.

Rabindranath Tagore

9.1. Play: from act to thought

Play is "child's work", preparing them for adult life. It is a specific form of manifestation that can be found in every child, regardless of gender, ethnicity, culture or society. Every child needs to play to develop and form their own personality. A playful atmosphere means, above all, freedom and joy, a withdrawal from reality and an entry into the world of the imaginary and the impossible, which can become possible.

Animals also play all sorts of games during their childhood (macaques play rugby, kittens jump high etc.). When they stop playing, it is because they have become adults. Even the notion of "spectators" exists: young animals play less when they are no longer being watched. Play has a Darwinian function, of adaptation: if we prevent a young animal from playing, certain behaviors (such as mating and dominance) cannot be acquired.

The value of play activity for the development of the child is very important. All the higher mental function characteristics of the child's personality are rapidly formed and developed in play, such as voluntary attention and behavior, memory and motivation.

Play has a strong influence on the cognitive development of the young child, as Piaget has shown and as he summarized in his concept "From Act to Thought": the child begins to think through his gestures. When a child does not point his fingers towards an object in order to communicate their intention to the adult who is taking care of them before the emergence of language, this is a worrying sign (language delay, autism). This transfer of the motor act to thought is also at the heart of the Wallon perspective and the models of embodied cognition.

This transfer ensures that the child is thinking about images and representations, developing skills and understanding the point of view of others.

Parental involvement in shared play with the child depends on the child's age. At age 5–7 years, play becomes more independent of the adult. At preschool age, interest in board and computer games steadily increases and interest in outdoor play gradually decreases. This emphasizes the importance of the problem of lack of physical exercise in childhood.

9.2. Sports activities: Homo Ludens... Citius, Altius, Fortius... Bread and games...

Before practicing a sport, children practice motor acts, such as running, jumping and throwing, but with the sole purpose of feeling the pleasure of the gesture, not to be "better", to "beat" others, to play "against". For this, socialization, rules, measures and institutions are needed.

The motor acts that children and then adolescents perform in their sports activities will "sculpt" their brain: different cortical areas develop when running the 100 meters, as opposed to throwing a javelin.

From the very beginning of participation in team sports, children learn not to play alone, but "as a team".

Even so-called "individual" sports require involvement in a collective (trainers, coaches, training partners etc.). Integration into a sports team and the "values of sport" has been seen as an incubator of citizenship and a remedy for antisociality for children and adolescents. It remains to be seen whether this incubator actually works.

In fact, 300 15–25 year olds die every year in sports accidents, with extreme sports contributing the most to this mortality. Without going to extremes, the over-intensive practice of a sport can also be assimilated to a risky behavior, when it is associated with doping, alcohol or drug consumption or acts of violence.

9.2.1. *Sports: health behavior or risk behavior, social or antisocial?*

Young people who participate in competitive sports are less at risk from the point of view of health behaviors, because the vast majority of them do not smoke or drink, they pay attention to their diet and they obviously exercise. Their risk of disease is therefore objectively lower.

However, their accident, injury and disability record is no better than that of young people who do not play sports. Of course, on an epidemiological level, all the accidents they may have in the context of their sport activity come into play, but on a psychological level, there is also a relationship to performance, to sensation, to self-improvement, which does not necessarily protect them from accidents.

A precise approach to this phenomenon has been carried out in France (Choquet and Com-Ruelle 2003) by distinguishing three populations: young people who do not play sports, young people who play sports moderately and young people who play sports intensively. Contrary to expectations, the curve is U-shaped: young people who do not play sports and young people who play sports intensively (and the thresholds of "too intensive" are low) consume more psychoactive substances and display more violence than young people who play sports moderately.

Thus, by studying the answers to a questionnaire of 12,100 young boys and girls aged 14–19 years, we observe that young people practicing sports intensively (more than eight hours of training per week) smoke more, drink more, take more sleeping pills and are more violent than young people who practice moderately. The results are particularly worrying among girls: 15% of those who practice sports intensively had used illicit drugs other than cannabis (compared to 5% of non-athletes), 45% had been in a fight at least once (compared to 35% of non-athletes) and sexual violence was twice as high among athletes.

Should we see the influence of peer pressure (famously "burning the candle at both ends") and of the search for sensations in this excess risk among young athletes, which is also at the root of their investment in sports, the need for performance, the fight against the stress of failure and the ideology of competition? A correlation does not tell us what the causal relationships are: are the intrinsically most violent young people those who turn to intensive sport, or is it the practice itself that generates violence?

In addition, the problem varies depending on the type of sport:

– For both sexes, risky behaviors are associated with surfing, skateboarding, boxing, bodybuilding and weightlifting (sports that could be described as “unconventional”).

– For girls, risky behaviors are associated with soccer, rugby, judo and karate (more “conventional” sports for them).

– For boys, risky behaviors are associated with gymnastics and dance.

– For boys, the sports least associated with risky behavior are cycling, track and field, horseback riding and skiing.

– For girls, the sports least associated with risky behavior are swimming, sailing, tennis and golf.

As we can see, causality is complex because it cannot be reduced to divisions such as between team and individual sports, or sports where there is a high or low suspicion of doping, for instance.

Thus, sports can be considered simultaneously as a resource and as a risk, but they do not emerge “unscathed” from this work; in particular, the myth of sports as, for example, a “magic potion”, a “miracle recipe” or an “outlet for aggressiveness” from the problems of youth is shattered. Risky behaviors do not magically disappear by walking through the doors of stadiums and gyms. We have often valued sports practice to the extreme compared with other leisure activities, whereas a moderate sports practice combined with other cultural activities would undoubtedly be more protective.

In fact, the extent to which sporting activity is a health behavior remains to be seen: we have clearly seen that the problem of doping involved not only elite athletes, but also amateur runners, the “Sunday champions”. Consequently, doping should not be the tree that hides the woods, the scourge that should be eradicated so that sport has only positive effects. When an individual practices intensively, we must also ask ourselves about the existential difficulties that practice may cause or hide. In any case, the practice of sport must integrate a risk reduction dimension.

9.3. The digital child and the issue of screens

> The digital subject – who commands a surface that obeys him with a finger and an eye – enjoys a satisfaction: that of making the will and the doing coincide, immediately and without fail... (M. Desmurget).

If there is one contemporary development, it is the daily interaction of the child with digital technology and artificial intelligence (use of laptops and tablets, game consoles, cellphones etc.). These technologies form part of the child's social environment, a situation that never previously existed in the history of humanity.

It is common to observe that most children handle digital objects with much less difficulty than adults, even though they do not know all the implications. They are born with digital technology.

Psychological research has long studied how children, based on their everyday experience, construct an intuitive understanding of their physical and social world. However, less is known about how children's intuitive knowledge of the technological world in which they live is conceptualized and represented by their mental models, for example, in the interactions between children, computers and consoles.

The time spent by children in front of screens (tablets, video games, smartphones and television) has become extremely important: in cumulative time, 2-year-olds spend 3 hours per day; between 8 and 12 years old, this time increases to 4 hours 45 minutes; between 13 and 18 years old, it reaches 6 hours 45 minutes (Desmurget 2019). Annually, screen time is now twice that of time spent in school.

Some thinkers, such as Michel Serres, have been able to rejoice in this evolution, seeing in this new "digital", "numerical", "millennial" generation a new intelligence, a new way of understanding the world and adapting to it.

However, increasing numbers of studies are denouncing the risks of these uses of screens. There are various types of distinct risks: risks related to socioemotional and cognitive development, health risks (obesity and cardiovascular) and risks related to the toxicity of the blue light which makes our screens bright. These risks are more important in children and require the vigilance of the parents[1] and professionals in a position to alert them.

This situation is even more serious when the child is younger. For a child under the age of 2, it is impossible to talk about "adapted" programs. The only thing that counts is the number of hours spent in front of the screen, which is always at the expense of essential activities at this age. Every hour spent by a young child in front of a screen is stolen from these legitimate acquisitions and the consequences are felt well beyond the first years.

1 The example of Steve Jobs, the inventor of Apple, who forbade the use of computers to his own children, is often quoted!

9.3.1. *The determinants of early exposure to screens*

To better understand the temporality of the increase in screen time over the 0–3-years-old period, studies have identified factors associated with exposure trajectories (Prieur 2020).

In Finland, the STEPS study, with two years of follow-up, focused on identifying factors associated with a change in screen time during the first two years of children's lives. For the 634 children for whom screen time was measured at 13 and 36 months, the daily average was 55 minutes per day. When fathers were more involved with their children, the increase in screen time between 13 and 36 months was less. When maternal education was higher, the mother was younger, her personal screen time was lower, the child was cared for during the day and the child's body mass index (BMI) was lower, the increase in screen time between 13 and 36 months was lower.

Trajectories of physical activity and screen time were studied in an Australian longitudinal study, using a daily diary. The authors found that half of children maintained low levels of both physical activity and screen time, a quarter of children had increased physical activity and low screen time and a quarter of the children had low physical activity and increased screen time. Most at risk for the first and last clusters were children of mothers from non-English speaking backgrounds, children who did not live with both biological parents, children from the most affluent homes and neighborhoods, only children and children whose parents had poor mental health.

Predictors of screen time were also identified in a study using data from Growing Up in Singapore Towards Healthy Outcomes (GUSTO), incorporating television and other screen time. Malay or Indian ethnicity, compared with Chinese ethnicity, younger maternal age, lower maternal education and longer parental TV time were associated with increased total child screen time.

Analysis of survey data from the ELFE cohort in France, in which the prevalence of daily television exposure at age 2 was 68%, confirmed that parental education, parental income, maternal employment status and maternal age were negatively associated with exposure. Gender did not affect screen exposure, with screen use essentially the same for boys and girls at age 2.

While the presence and number of siblings seemed to be associated with varying use of certain media, it was observed that, from the age of 2, only children use a computer or tablet and play with a smartphone more frequently. In families with more than two children, children play console video games more frequently.

Certain child characteristics, such as low emotional regulation at nine months, appear to be associated with increased television use at age 2. The associations are slightly stronger in lower socioeconomic backgrounds. However, it is not known whether this low emotional regulation is responsible for the later appetite for television use, or whether it is already the consequence of screen use before nine months, which only continues at two years.

Similarly, is attachment a cause or a consequence? We know that social interactions are becoming increasingly virtual, through the Internet, even replacing social interactions for some. We can ask ourselves if the type of attachment plays a role in the involvement of the subject on the Internet.

For subjects with insecure attachment (especially the preoccupied), social networks offer a kind of good solution, as they fear close contact with others.

Young children are increasingly using the virtual world, for example in their relationships with their grandparents. How do they perceive these exchanges? What is the impact on their social skills? So much research work to be done.

9.3.2. *Mobile digital screens*

The exposure of children aged 0–6 years to mobile digital screens (smartphones and tablets) is increasing and is causing concern. A review of international literature has analyzed this use and its effects on the child's psycho-affective development, including certain aspects of psychomotor and cognitive development (Clément 2020).

It shows that this use remains low compared to that of television, except in the most underprivileged environments; however, that it is in addition to, and not a substitute for, previous screen use. Four aspects appear to be significant in this regard: (1) the use of mobile digital screens by the children themselves; (2) whether or not they use them interactively; (3) the existence or otherwise of parental guidance; (4) the interposition of the digital screen in the parent–child relationship when parents use them in the presence of their young children.

On the final point, "parental technoference" is defined as an interruption in parent–child interaction due to parents' use of technological communication devices during times when they are caring for their children (Clément 2020).

9.3.3. *The consequences of screen use for children*

9.3.3.1. *Intellectual skills*

In order to identify the specific role of screens on development, other factors that might influence development must be controlled for in multivariate analyses.

Within the GUSTO cohort, the average time spent watching television was two hours per day at age 1. After adjustment for available maternal and child variables, composite and verbal IQs at age 4.5 were decreased as time spent watching television increased. In contrast, bedtime reading was associated with an increase in IQ.

Even controlling for parental cognitive stimulation during childhood, maternal education and cultural level, an additional hour of television per day before age 3 had a significantly negative effect on children's reading, comprehension and memory skills at age 6.

9.3.3.2. *Language acquisition*

Not only do screens not increase the linguistic capacity of the children who look at them, but they also slow down their learning.

9.3.3.3. *Attention and concentration skills*

Television interferes with the development of a child's attention span and concentration if they are playing in a room where it is on, even though they are not watching it. This is because the more play time is reduced by a distracting environment, the more likely it is that the child will experience difficulty concentrating and paying attention later on. Children who have grown up with screens are generally less self-reliant, less perseverant and less socially adept.

9.3.3.4. *Academic performance*

In view of the three preceding consequences, it is not surprising to observe a correlation between time spent in front of screens and academic failure, regardless of the type of screen (TV, smartphone, game console and computer) and whether they are individual or family.

9.3.3.5. *The relationship with time*

When a child scribbles, stacks blocks or moves a toy, they discover at the same time their capacity to change the world and the fact that this modification is irreversible. But when the child watches television or a DVD, each moment is sufficient in itself, filled with colors, movements and emotions, hence the difficulty in conceiving the irreversibility of actions.

9.3.3.6. *Social risks*

The more time children spend in front of screens, the less time they have for creative play, interactive activities and other fundamental cognitive and social experiences. Skills such as sharing, appreciation and respect for others, which are ingrained in early childhood, are at risk.

9.3.3.7. *Harassment*

Each additional hour of daily television between the ages of 2 and 3 increases the risk of being considered a victim or scapegoat by classmates at age 10 by 10%. This is probably because television makes us passive and a child who perceives themselves as a spectator of the world, rather than an actor capable of influencing situations, is less inclined to respond to the aggressions they experience.

9.3.3.8. *The construction of empathy*

The first years of life constitute a particularly critical period in the development of the areas of the brain involved in the self-regulation of emotional intelligence. It is at this age that the child learns to constitute the faces of others as a support for shared emotional construction. However, every hour spent in front of a screen is an hour lost for a face-to-face exchange with an adult or another child.

9.3.3.9. *Hyperactivity*

Results of analysis of data from the Japan Childrens' Study cohort indicated a positive association between television exposure at 18 and 30 months and the occurrence of hyperactivity problems, adjusting for relevant maternal and family variables.

9.3.3.10. *Health risks*

The light from screens, in particular the blue LED component, presents two risks. The first is the damage to the retina, the epithelium of which, according to current research, seems not to regenerate. This threat is particularly important for young children for which the crystalline is not yet opacified. Therefore, in the same way that we put sunglasses on young children when they are in the sun, so we should adopt the same vigilance in avoiding putting them in front of screens.

The second problem posed by the blue light from LEDs concerns their power to inhibit the secretion of melatonin, the key hormone for falling asleep. These blue lights, to an extent, deceive the brain into believing that it is daylight, so that vigilance is exacerbated. This causes the subject who is in front of a screen at night not to feel the need for sleep, which results in a restriction of sleep time, but also in a disruption of nycthemeral rhythms that can lead to fatigue, attention disorders and affect school performance and social life. These problems are mainly related to the consequences of the use of screens in the evening and at night; the role of parents is therefore crucial, especially since, although the strictly medical negative effects of the misuse of screens concern all age groups, they are clearly more deleterious for children and adolescents.

Screens present multiple other health risks due to the resulting sedentary lifestyle and lack of physical exercise, such as obesity, cardiovascular diseases and psychopathology.

9.3.4. *To conclude on screens*

Determinants of high exposure time included low socioeconomic conditions, family conditions (single-parent families and only children), maternal symptoms of stress or depression and high parental exposure to television.

Whether the exposure is involuntary or voluntary (the child is in the same room as the television or the child is sitting in front of the television, tablet or phone), the consequences are harmful: the baby's attention is no longer focused on play, their body or interactions with the environment.

The vast majority of studies have reported an impact on development from early exposure to screens.

The effect size of screens on IQ and on the occurrence of externalized symptoms seems to be of the same order as that relating to intoxication from certain environmental pollutants.

Exposure time under age 3 appears to equate to less time for the development of psychosocial skills, such as self-regulation, self-confidence and comprehension, which later translates into less engagement in school and more academic difficulties.

It also means less time for movement, which results in different activity patterns, dietary habits and body mass index than is the case in children who have not been over-exposed to screens in early childhood.

So, is exposure to screens simply the complement of a lack of attention to play, to the body and to interactions?

Observing whether alternatives to screens are available seems essential: the lack of access to toys, leisure activities and outdoor equipment, or the lack of people available for interaction, which may be associated with disadvantaged socioeconomic conditions, would all encourage early exposure to screens in toddlers, which could aggravate health inequalities from the earliest age.

In the future, could this harmful trend be corrected by parents? It is difficult to say; either they would have to resist the invasion of life by the visual, which would be impossible, or alternative strategies are needed, as with seat belts in cars, or smoking in public places, which would have been "impossible" goals a few decades ago.

All these harmful consequences apply to all home screens, whatever their type, because play very quickly prevails over the educational; as for the screens used in schools, ICTEs (Information and Communication Technologies for Education) will be dealt with in the second volume of this book on practices, but we can already say that the educational benefits of digital technology are also being questioned (Desmurget 2019).

9.3.5. *Recommendations regarding screens*

Based on these alarming findings, seven main recommendations have been formulated (Desmurget 2019):

1) No screens before age 6! No negative impacts are expected from this absence and replacing screens with reading, puzzles, Lego, physical exercise, music, conversation and boredom will be much more beneficial to the child.

2) After age 6, no more than 30 minutes (before age 12) to one hour (after age 12) per day.

3) No screens in the bedroom (for sleep and content control).

4) No inappropriate content (violence, pornography and addiction, for instance, all have very negative influences).

5) No screens in the morning before school (excitement will translate into fatigue at school).

6) No screens at night before going to sleep (for the duration and quality of sleep).

7) One thing at a time (there should be no screens during meals, homework or family discussions, as multitasking creates distraction).

We should remember, in view of the chapter on parenting styles and finding the right balance, that these seven recommendations, in order to be properly applied and understood by the child, must be the result of a "negotiated authority", in other words, they must not to be applied without explaining to the child their rationale and the risks of screens.

9.4. Video games

With an estimated global market value of more than $135 billion, video games are ubiquitous and more in demand than ever, by children and adults[2] alike.

YouTube has been the gateway for children to digital and video games: initially dedicated to streaming and free music, YouTube has gradually opened up to video games and has become the main vector of digital practices, especially among 6–10 year olds. This began in 2017 with the development of a game, Fortnite, which now has 250 million users worldwide.

Fortnite has moved children from individual practice to group practice, or "digital socialization": they download Fortnite from YouTube onto their Switch, tablet or smartphone; a hundred players can compete and play at the same time; then, when the game is over, kids return to YouTube to read comments or tutorials about the game. The child may well be playing with other participants from the same neighborhood or even the same school. Exchanges, even romantic friendships with avatars in the 10–11 age group can occur. We are well in a perspective of genetic psychology; Fortnite prepares the child for the use of social networks, such as Facebook, in adolescence.

Parents would probably be appalled to learn that 8–10 year olds can spend four hours a day playing video games, or even 10 hours during school vacations.

The majority of parents believe that these games have a positive influence on their children's lives, that they promote development in several areas, including cognition, positive mood, physical well-being and prosocial behavior.

In addition to the minimal risks of convulsions or eye damage, it is the consequence of what is called "stolen time" (due to screen use) which induces a delay in acquisition (language, interactions, fine motor skills), especially in children under 3 years old, for which the correlative consequences of stolen time are the most deleterious. We also note there is an emotional overreaction from the child when the screen is turned off and a risk of a lack of construction of their sociability.

In children over the age of 3, video games play a more negative role, the more violent they are; this fact contradicts the "cathartic thesis of video games", which is contradicted by numerous studies.

2 Among American adults, 49% play video games.

These games lead to an attenuation of the physiological reactions of players when confronted with scenes of violence in real life, as well as an increase in their aggressive behavior immediately after the game, the more their "avatar" looks like them. This leads to aggressive behavior, aggressive cognition, aggressive affect, physiological arousal and desensitization to real violence.

9.5. The use of telephones

One-third of children have a cellphone and four times as many older children have one and send text messages as younger ones. For these children, the transition to middle school, with the acquisition of this phone, could constitute a sort of "rite of passage" that would allow them to access the world of the "big kids", by seeking to extract themselves from the world of the "little kids" through the search for autonomy and the quest for peer group affiliation (Berdot-Talmier *et al.* 2020).

Children from higher socioeconomic backgrounds are less likely than those from lower socioeconomic backgrounds to own a phone. Given that the telephone can be a status symbol, we can hypothesize that more children from poorer backgrounds will own a telephone in order to feel more in line with current social (and even consumer) norms.

Girls prefer to use it for hyper-coordination, that is, in a search for social communication, whereas boys are more in search of micro-coordination, a more functional use based on the coordination of time and space.

Moreover, more girls text their friends, while more boys text family; this difference is due to gendered social skills, with girls favoring dyadic relationships with greater intimacy, while boys will be more willing to meet up with their peers outside (Berdot-Talmier *et al.* 2020).

Three factors can improve understanding of the relationship between parents, adolescents and cellphones:

– First, the telephone can be understood in terms of parents' attempts to maintain constant contact with young people, but it will also give young people the opportunity to control their environment and activities by "cutting the cord".

– Second, it can be seen as a safety device, which can be used by both parents and children.

– Finally, the cellphone is a symbol of adolescent and group culture that allows for the creation or maintenance of social ties. Also, young people may be "hanging out" on the phone while other activities are taking place at home, such as household chores, in which they are expected to participate, which could lead to conflict within the family, with a negative evaluation of social behaviors (Berdot-Talmier *et al.* 2020).

9.5.1. *The telephone and the mother–infant relationship: "Hello, Mommy's texting... Hello, Mommy, it hurts..."*

One risk for the mother–child relationship and attachment lies in the mother's "distractibility" when fixed on her cellphone. What could be the long-term consequences of this relationship parasitized by screens and this momentary absence of parental availability (or parental technoference)?

This is reminiscent of the disruption of the dyad caused by the "still face" experience, discussed in the chapter on attachment, which causes distress.

9.5.2. *Telephone addiction*

With the popularity of smartphones among adolescents, phone addiction is increasingly attracting the attention of researchers. For example, approximately 20% of Chinese adolescents reported suffering from smartphone use disorders. Phone addiction has adverse consequences on the psychological and physical health of individuals: it is associated with negative emotions, interpersonal problems, low educational attainment and suicidal thoughts.

There is a close relationship between addiction to phones and the Internet, with telephone addiction being considered a new manifestation of Internet addiction. Many studies have confirmed the association between parent–child relationships and Internet addiction; however, a few studies have been conducted on the association with telephone addiction.

These two disorders have similarities and differences: both involve vulnerable personalities, but, unlike the Internet, phone addiction is more associated with social anxiety.

The quality of life and educational level of the parents play mediating roles:

– Quality of life partially mediates parent–child relationships and telephone addiction.

– The association between parent–child relationships and telephone addiction decreases as educational level increases.

9.6. Social networks (TikTok, Snapchat, Facebook, Instagram, etc.)

Currently, the gateway to social networks is the Chinese application TikTok because it is very easy to use. Its principle is to put videos online, filming yourself with your smartphone or using videos of celebrities, and all sorts of special effects are easily created with the application. Long before the access to Facebook, the child's narcissism can be exercised from their digital identity.

Second, almost all adolescents (94%) in developed countries use social media platforms, such as Snapchat or Facebook.

Snapchat is currently the most popular application, as adolescents are now well aware that parents are on Facebook and watching them. The principle of Snapchat is to send photos or videos to each other that can disappear or be quickly deleted; these visuals are embellished with emojis and, when peers react, smileys in the form of flames testify to others' interest in their digital expression. Thus, popularity within groups can depend on the number of flames, which can increase or decrease.

A 2011 survey of a sample of 1,200 French children and adolescents (aged 8–17) found that 48% of children in this age range have an account on the social network Facebook and 18% of those under 13 are also registered (Berdot-Talmier *et al.* 2018). Legally, access to Facebook is prohibited for children under 13, but a number of them are registered anyway and, more interestingly, for the 18% identified in the survey, 97% of the parents are aware of their child's registration.

However, as mentioned above, adolescents do not put the same content on Facebook, which is monitored by adults, as on Snapchat, which is not. They work like advertising or event professionals: they adapt their communication ("top of the class" or "rebel") to the audience and the tool. Thus, they work more on the visual on Instagram, because the photos stay there, than on Snapchat where they just pass by.

37% of children aged 13 and under with a social network profile log in using their personal computer and 10% using their cellphone. Girls outnumber boys, at 59% and 49%, respectively.

Internet use and time spent on the Internet can have a negative impact on adolescents. Indeed, during the first year, Internet use was positively correlated with a decrease in communication between family members.

In contrast, the positive role of computer-mediated communication on feelings of belonging and well-being could also be observed among adolescents, but only among adolescents using online communication to maintain existing friendships and not to form new relationships (Berdot-Talmier *et al.* 2018). Thus, the concept of "extimacy" has been proposed for this very recent trend of communicating publicly about one's intimacy, reflecting a shift in the relationship to others.

Online communication can serve as a social compensation for some adolescents: those who have relationship difficulties with their parents and/or who experience difficulties in their daily lives are more likely to develop online friendships than adolescents who do not.

It would appear that these young people develop intimate online relationships in order to gain support and companionship that they cannot obtain in the offline context. The Internet and online social networks do provide an opportunity for young people who are stigmatized or face multiple challenges in their daily lives to find peers in similar situations with whom they can communicate and form friendships.

Thus, in the perspective of socialization, which is so important at this age, adolescents no longer differentiate between ordinary and digital social norms; the virtual world has become as much a place for social exchange and identity construction as the real world and as much, if not more so, for integration and the fight against the sidelining of the reference group. The eternal questions, such as "Who am I?" or "Do I identify with my biological sex?" now find their answers on computer screens. The equally eternal mirror game between personal identity ("What do I think of myself?") and social identity ("What do I think others think of me?") is now played out on the virtual stage. To quote a psychoanalytical metaphor, the Internet has become the other stage of life, the one where we experiment and search for approval, conformity to norms or, on the contrary, our transgressions, but especially away from the parents' gaze.

Furthermore, the Internet can help adolescents to experiment with actions that they can later apply in real-life social situations, which will ultimately support their social integration. Thus, children can spend a lot of time on the Internet as they feel more comfortable communicating in this context, compared with face-to-face communication.

However, the increased ease of communicating anonymously online increases the risk of being solicited by malicious strangers and/or receiving abusive or bullying messages from "friends" or casual online acquaintances. These messages, also known as "cyberbullying", can be numerous and can have deleterious consequences for the adolescent who is the victim (see the section below on cyberbullying).

Thus, communication with strangers and a friendship with "celebrities" could be risk factors, while communication with friends would be a protective factor.

For children (who should not normally have a profile on Facebook…), Facebook use does not seem to affect the socioemotional adjustment of children aged 9–12 years, except for boys who present more adjustment disorders compared with girls (Berdot-Talmier *et al.* 2018).

9.6.1. *The importance of the visual: selfies/selfie ecstasy*

Children and adolescents' use of social media is dominated by visual communication, including posting and commenting on photos and videos of themselves or others. Research over the past few decades has suggested that perceived physical appearance is one of the subdomains of self that contributes most to adolescents' overall self-esteem – particularly among girls.

As adolescents increasingly use social media photographs and videos as key ways to present themselves, the importance of physical appearance to the individual may be even greater. In addition, the appearance of others on social media is often idealized or selectively presented to maximize the attractiveness of their own presentations.

Over time, this social media environment can create appearance standards that are difficult to achieve and that most children and adolescents will not be able to live up to, thereby creating a gap between the perceived and ideal physical self. Self-regulation theory suggests that such a gap between the perceived and ideal self can lead to negative emotions (such as sadness and disappointment) and lower self-esteem. This effect is particularly strong in girls (Steinbekk and Wichstrom 2021).

Thus, there is a potential threat to self-esteem in young people, but the negative impact may depend on the types of social media engagement. Young people who actively post updates (i.e. they use social media autonomously) may position themselves to receive positive comments and confirmation of their appearance and thus exhibit higher self-esteem, whereas young people who primarily view and respond to the posts of others (in other words, who use social media in a manner directed by others) are exposed to these idealized presentations without receiving positive comments on their own appearance, resulting in decreased self-esteem (Steinbekk and Wichstrom 2021).

We understand that we need to study social media use in a more nuanced way with respect to self-esteem, since, rather than overall frequency of use, specific social media behaviors may affect well-being differently. Social media users, parents, professionals and policymakers need to be aware that different types of social media use, and not social media use *per se*, can detract from or improve children's and adolescents' self-esteem.

9.7. Music

For this section, our bibliographic source is Isabelle Peretz's French book, *Apprendre la musique. Nouvelles des neurosciences*, published in 2018. We note that there are very few studies in developmental psychology on children and music.

The child's relationship with music is genetically programmed, or "pre-wired". Research on the brains of newborns from one to three days old shows that the cerebral connections of the auditory cortex in the right hemisphere are already in place to perceive the pitch and duration of sounds. As soon as the child is introduced to harmonic or melodic dissonance, it activates the right auditory cortex more than the left.

The hierarchical organization of a melody, a cadence with a dominant note, the tone and the movement towards a tone that gives stability to the melody, is already perceived at the beginning of life. In the same way, the other dimension of music is rhythm: the brain of the newborn reacts to the omission of a strong beat in a rhythmic sequence, even when the tempo is not very marked, the brain reacts like an oscillator.

These dispositions of the newborn are not only genetically programmed, but are also *in utero* experiences. During the last trimester of gestation, the fetus perceives and registers sounds, the mother's voice, of course, and also the surrounding music.

As with language, children do not learn to react to music (its universal dimensions, the pitch and duration of notes, their hierarchy, the repetition of patterns, etc.); it is innate, but they learn to react to classical, jazz or Indian music according to their environment. Thus, an American baby will be more comfortable with a four beat rhythm, a Turkish baby with a five eighth note rhythm, but a Turkish baby will prefer a regular five eighth note rhythm to an irregular rhythm.

By the end of this learning process, at about age 6, children understand as well as adults do if a note is wrong or out of tune. As with many aspects of development, perception far precedes expression. Music education can obviously reinforce and accelerate these innate skills.

Each country supports this musical education to a greater or lesser extent, with France generally being the poor student.

The importance of music education is best understood when we realize the extent to which making music stimulates and enhances intellectual and social skills in individuals as young as six months of age.

Six-year-olds who receive piano lessons for a year gain a few IQ points more than those who receive drama lessons or no lessons at all, a phenomenon observed in Canada and Europe.

Adolescent students participating in a music ensemble were found to have higher average academic achievement rates in math, biology and English. This benefit was not observed for graphic arts. Before concluding that learning music favors academic learning in adolescence, it is necessary to verify that the sociocultural background of the parents, which is known to be closely linked to academic success, is not a confounding factor.

In contrast, the intellectual benefit is no longer observed when professional musicians are compared with other professions. Music students at university do not have a higher IQ than students in other disciplines. There is a cognitive benefit to making music as well as everything else, but not instead of everything else.

There is certainly a mathematical aspect in music theory (intervals of tone and duration), but music and math seem to be two distinct brain activities: mathematicians (at a doctoral level) are no more musicians than linguists. These two types of intelligence would thus be distinct: musical intelligence and logical-mathematical intelligence.

Regarding the relationship between music and reading, we can obviously ask ourselves whether reading notes and reading words are related; it has been observed that teaching music at the age of 8 improves reading results, but it is mainly through rhythm training that this correlation is observed. Thus, dyslexia therapy is based on this training, by treating the rhythmic difficulties of the dyslexic child in both music and reading.

A simple explanation at the neurobiological level stems from the fact that making music encourages school learning and that this activity improves executive functions; these functions, said to be transversal and managed by the prefrontal cortex, are diverse (memory, attention, inhibition, flexibility, planning) but all contribute to our adaptation, whether in school or in life in general.

We also know that musical activity will shape and "sculpt" the brain: playing the violin or the piano does not leave the same traces in the motor and auditory cortexes and in the prefrontal areas; this is what is called neuroplasticity.

Since learning music is not mandatory like school education, this enables researchers to compare subjects with different onset ages and, as might be expected, the earlier the subject begins learning, the greater the neuroplasticity.

This neuroplasticity role conferred by musical activity can obviously be used in other contexts (such as rehabilitation of lesions and degenerative diseases).

The question of neuroplasticity obviously raises the question of the critical period, as for language learning. Neuronal phenomena, such as myelination and pruning, continue later for the auditory cortex (up to 18 years) than for the visual cortex. As far as learning music is concerned, it can be said that individuals who start before the age of 7 will have more facility.

Various studies on this subject show that children who start playing music early, around the age of 6, show enlargements of the auditory and motor cortex. However, cortical changes are observed at all ages of life (provided that we play, not just listen).

A question that has always been posed in the psychology of music is the respective roles of talent and effort. While effort is considered indispensable (reaching a professional level requires at least 10,000 hours of practice), the existence of talent is an undeniable requirement. In a Gaussian curve, between the 2.5% of prodigies and the 2.5% who are totally resistant to music, 95% of us could reach a professional level if we were to put in enough time.

The case of perfect pitch: only 10% of western musicians have perfect pitch; there is certainly a genetic origin: in the United States, 47.5% of musicians of Asian origin have perfect pitch, as against 9% of Caucasians. It is also common in autistic people. Musicians with perfect pitch have particular cortical morphologies. This may result from the use of connections between adjacent neural networks that are normally inhibited, but is not related to musical talent. There may be a critical period around the age of 6 years, when the child may acquire perfect pitch, but this is still controversial.

Not liking music (or musical anhedonia) would be linked to a depleted connection between the nucleus accumbens and the auditory cortex (and not to a hysterical symptom linked to an unconscious trauma as Freud thought who was himself a musical anhedonic).

The social nature of musical learning: while some children and adolescents learn in schools and academies, many others learn by imitating "model" musicians or by transmission in a private setting. Learning by imitation is probably one of the most effective strategies, as imitation is an innate process that occurs early in life.

Music is linked to the interaction between human beings, and this very early in life: babies prefer the same tune or rhythm played by a human being to the same tunes or rhythms played by machines.

Massed or distributed learning: distributed learning seems to be more efficient; rather than repeating the same piece 10 times a day, it would be better to repeat it once a day for 10 days, notably because of the influence of sleep and dreaming on the hippocampus and other brain structures in charge of memorization.

10

Emerging Issues

10.1. Children living in same-sex parent families

If there is one subject in developmental psychology that receives a lot of media attention, it is that of children living in homoparental families, the number of which has considerably increased recently. Moreover, and it must be said, it is mainly activists and journalists who express themselves on this subject, based on religious or ideological convictions, but without any competence in scientific psychology. Some people even see an anthropological rupture, the end of civilization, the family being one of its pillars.

There are also positions held by psychologists, sociologists or lawyers, but these are generally based on theoretical presuppositions (the psychoanalysis of the parenting process, the rights of the child, the rights of parents, and so on), but not on research findings on the development of these children.

So, what is it really? First of all, we don't know exactly how many of them there are: in the United States, it is estimated that there are between 3 and 14 million children, so we can see that there is a lot of imprecision. In the Netherlands, the number is estimated to be around 20,000, in Germany 650,000 and in France several tens or even hundreds of thousands. Despite this lack of knowledge, it is clear that we are no longer talking about just a few marginal cases.

The term "homoparentality" was introduced in France in 1997 by the Association for Gay and Lesbian Parents and Future Parents (*Association des Parents et futurs parents Gay et Lesbiens*, APGL) and has been used ever since.

With the provision of PACS in 1999, and then the right to marry for homosexual couples, homoparental families became one of the types of "new families" and began in the early 2000s to constitute a chapter of scientific manuals on the family.

Of course, PACS only deals with the question of the couple and not with that of filiation, but it is part of a more general movement of upheavals in maternity and paternity (such as: legislative changes, progress in medicine and medically assisted reproduction techniques, techniques and practices that bypass sexuality and redefinition of couple relationships and parental responsibilities) and raises the question of the right to a child and the legitimacy of self-realization through the parenting process (Vecho *et al.* 2017). The question of rights is the most socially tense issue, with a number of court decisions where homosexual parents have had their parental rights taken away in divorce situations.

We can also recall that respective attitudes towards marriage and filiation are influenced by cultural factors. For example, in the United States, marriage is considered more "sacred", whereas filiation poses less problems, but in France, it is the opposite (Vecho *et al.* 2017).

Since it is biologically impossible for two people of the same sex to be parents of the same child, homosexual parents develop various strategies in order to achieve their parenthood:

– medically assisted procreation is, for the moment, prohibited in France and lesbian couples go to Belgium to have access to AID (Artificial Insemination by Donor);

– the practice of surrogacy is also prohibited in France, but not in the UK or the US, where the high cost of this practice makes it marginal for French men;

– adoptions by homosexual couples or by single homosexuals are not prohibited under French law, but are often refused by the General Councils, based on the argument that these family structures would be harmful to the child's development. However, in many other European countries, this reticence does not exist;

– a co-parenting approach can be undertaken based on private initiatives: a gay couple and a lesbian couple agree to give life to a child; the couples agree on who will be the biological parents and even on the status and roles of each of the four actors with the child (Vecho *et al.* 2017);

– finally, the most frequent solution (but unfortunately, no longer the solution most frequently studied by researchers) is where the homosexual couple is formed after the birth of the child, after a previous heterosexual union, and is therefore a special case of a blended family.

A meta-analysis of research on the development of children living in same-sex parent families was conducted by Vecho *et al.* (2017). She was able to identify 35 cases having an experimental device. Of these, 57% were conducted in the United States and 43% in Europe, with Belgium and the United Kingdom leading the way in this area and only one case being French. The low number of studies was due to the problem of access to the population, which, in spite of everything, is still not very visible and not very inclined to the idea of exposing children.

We notice that studies are still oriented by two variables:

– the vast majority has been focused on female homoparental situations, with very little research on male homosexual couples;

– marital status has not been taken into account, and its influence is therefore not known; living with two parents or with a single parent is not at all the same situation for the child.

Similarly, studies have progressively focused more on children than on adolescents or young adults.

While children from a previous heterosexual union were previously the only ones studied, it is now mainly children born by AID that are studied.

Sampling biases may exist because recruitment of same-sex parent families is primarily through advertisements in publications targeting the gay and lesbian population, word-of-mouth, homosexual parent associations and the use of families from other research samples.

Aspects of the development of this population of children that have been studied are:

– Sexual orientation, gender identity and behaviors: one of the first questions raised is whether homosexual parents transmit their sexual orientation to their children, although this type of mechanical transmission has not been demonstrated. Beyond the common sense notion that almost all homosexual people have heterosexual parents, we see that up to 10% of children self-identify as homosexual, which is consistent with the various estimates of the proportion of homosexuals in a given population (Vecho *et al.* 2017). Regarding gendered behaviors, daughters of lesbian mothers prefer more activities deemed masculine and masculine clothing than daughters of divorced heterosexual mothers.

– Psychological and behavioral problems: no significant difference was observed between children from homoparental families and children from heteroparental families on these aspects (such as anxiety, hyperactivity and externalized disorders). Both are essentially positioned outside the pathological zone.

– Social skills and relationships: the results of research are, for the moment, very discordant with regard to the differences between children of lesbian mothers and children of heterosexual couples concerning the perception of acceptance by peers.

– Family dynamics and parent–child adjustment: these aspects do not seem to pose any particular problems.

– Self-esteem and self-perception: these aspects do not seem to pose any particular problems.

– Intelligence: no difference was observed with the usual IQ tests.

– Contact with grandparents and other adults: these aspects do not seem to pose any particular problems.

– Secrecy of origin (for children born by AID): 54% of children do not want to know the identity of the donor (with no significant difference according to the sex of the children), 27% want to know the donor's identity and 19% only want non-identifying information.

The general conclusion that can be drawn from studies carried out in the United States and northern Europe is that there is no major impact on the well-being and psychological development of children from homoparenting, nor is there any inducement to homosexuality for the children concerned. There are still very few French studies, which may raise the question of the transferability of American results.

However, it now seems well established that when children of homosexual parents have adjustment problems, factors other than the parents' simple sexual orientation are responsible for these difficulties. Moreover, attachment theorists will not be surprised by these results: it is the quality of the bond that is much more important for a child's future than family structure.

In fact, it is the researchers' viewpoint that has changed, as has that of the general population: in the past, children of homosexual parents were only studied from the point of view of verifying deviance; today, they are considered to be a general population whose psychosocial functioning is studied. Finally, children living in homoparental families suffer the same stigmas as children of divorced parents did a few decades ago and we have seen how these attitudes have little scientific validity.

Another indication of the change in attitudes towards homosexuality is that many homosexuals used to choose to enter into heterosexual relationships, get married and have children; proportionally fewer do so today.

Finally, one aspect clearly shows that, from the child's point of view and from their social relationships, same-sex parent families are not as "new", "unprecedented" or "broken" as we might think. If we look at the nature and modalities of the ties maintained with grandparents, we see, as in blended families, the maintenance, in part, of traditional relational patterns and the asymmetry classically observed in heteroparental families in grandparental investment: grandmothers more than grandfathers and biological more than non-biological grandmothers are involved with their grandchildren (Vecho *et al.* 2017). So, nothing new under the intergenerational sun, then.

10.2. Homeless children

The homeless population in Île-de-France has increased by nearly 300% in the last 10 years (about 2,000 families in 1999 compared to 6,000 families in 2009), according to a report by the municipal social care service *115 de Paris*. There has also been a change in the profiles of homeless people: for example, in 1999, there were mostly single men between the ages of 20 and 50, whereas since 2011, there has been a very clear increase in the proportion of women and children.

The few studies carried out on this population show that a large proportion of homeless families are foreigners, in precarious administrative situations, and single parents. Accommodation facilities are overcrowded, far from city centers and unsuitable for these families.

It is important to study the mental health of the mothers and children in these families because they combine several risk factors: precariousness, homelessness and immigration.

The Homeless Children and Families (*Enfants et Familles sans logement*, ENFAMS) survey was conducted by the Paris SAMU Social Observatory in 2013 among families housed in social hotels, emergency shelters (*Centre d'Hébergement d'Urgence*, CHU) or social reintegration centers (*Centre d'Hébergement de Réinsertion Sociale*, CHRS), as well as asylum seekers (*Centre d'Accueil de Demandeurs d'Asile*, CADA). The ENFAMS questionnaires were translated into eight written languages and the interviews were conducted face-to-face by interviewer-psychologist pairs in 17 languages.

Depression in mothers is a common disorder with a high risk of chronicity (20%), suicide and post-traumatic stress disorder (PTSD), as mothers in these families have a high exposure to traumatic events due to their migratory journey and difficult living conditions.

Children from homeless families have higher levels of psychological disorders than children in the general population. These studies have identified associated factors such as maternal mental health, housing conditions and housing instability.

Mothers have a high prevalence of major depression (29%) and post-traumatic stress disorder (19%) and their children had high levels of emotional and behavioral difficulties (21%).

Factors associated with mothers' depression were: not knowing how to speak French, suicidal risk, post-traumatic stress and foregoing medical care; factors associated with mothers' post-traumatic stress were: leaving the home country because of a violent situation, depression and residential instability.

Emotional and behavioral difficulties in children were associated with parents' region of birth, family residential mobility, children's health and overweight, children's sleep patterns, mothers' suicidal risk, children's dislike of their homes and being teased at school.

The healthcare system and primary care professionals must take advantage of every contact with these families to screen for mental health disorders and refer them to existing services to facilitate their access to care.

10.3. Migrants

Migrants are a particular population that experiences adversity before, during and after forced displacement. As a result, many of them experience symptoms of post-traumatic stress disorder (PTSD).

PTSD can be transmitted from mother to child and is associated with altered cortisol responses. On the other hand, positive parenting practices, such as maternal affection, counteract psychopathology in early childhood.

Children's cortisol is indeed associated with mothers' cortisol after forced displacement and this association depends on maternal condition.

Unaccompanied minors are a new patient group resulting from migration that poses new problems for institutions and identity issues.

10.4. Children of military personnel

Military families face unique stress factors linked to a military lifestyle. These include frequent relocations, geographic separations from extended family and friends and recurring separations due to the military member's training obligations. One of the most significant sources of stress affecting these families appears to be the military member's missions.

Major world events in recent decades have produced more frequent and longer deployments to active combat zones. Although military families tend to be resilient to the challenges associated with deployment, it appears to affect the functioning of spouses and their children. Deployment may be associated with increased depressive symptoms in military spouses and emotional problems in children (Tupper and Bureau 2018).

One cause of these correlations lies in attachment: deployment of the father significantly predicts children's attachment. Indeed, the proportion of children's insecure attachment is correlated with home absence conditions and is significantly higher compared to the general population (Tupper and Bureau 2018).

On the other hand, spouses of deployed partners report that their children exhibit some form of anxiety (worry, crying, sleep disorders and fear of being left behind by the military parent). It is reasonable to assume that children who experience the loss, in most cases temporary, of a parent through deployment are likely to experience increased anxiety related to the availability of the remaining parent. As a result, these children are more likely to develop an insecure attachment to aforementioned remaining parent.

Another possible explanation is that even if parents are able to handle the stress of deployment well, they may still experience high anxiety about their partner's security, as well as the impact of deployment on their children's emotional functioning. Such anxiety experienced by the non-deployed parent could negatively affect the child's openness and security of attachment. Furthermore, spouses with a deployed partner must manage several tasks associated with running a household; taking on the responsibility of these additional tasks would likely affect the mother's openness and responsiveness (Tupper and Bureau 2018).

In the current climate of global instability, it is unlikely that the number of military deployments will decrease. With more deployed service members having children than in previous conflicts (such as World Wars I and II and Vietnam), it is critical that parents, educators and other professionals understand the impact of deployment on children of military parents, particularly in the area of parent–child attachment, as we have seen that children with insecure attachment are at an increased risk for emotional and social difficulties throughout life.

10.5. Disaster psychology (wars, bombings, tsunamis, earthquakes)

Disaster psychology refers to the old debate on causality in psychopathology and the role of trauma in the etiology of psychological disorders.

According to a recent UNICEF report, one in five children, or around 530 million children worldwide, is growing up in the context of ethnic, religious, national or tribal conflict.

Raising children in a region of chronic and unpredictable stress has deleterious consequences for the mother's brain, in addition to the well-documented effects on her parenting behavior. There is an intergenerational brain-behavior link between maternal social brain activations and prosocial behaviors in children, tracing a trajectory from maternal brain to child social behavior during the transition to adolescence from impairments in the neural basis of empathy in mothers living in a war zone and raising children under chronic stress conditions (Levy 2019); such disruptions are shaped by educational models given over time and have implications for children's prosocial and empathic capacities in early adolescence.

This highlights the need to develop targeted interventions for mothers who are raising their children in the shadow of war and conflict.

10.5.1. *Attacks*

Children have recently been at scenes of attacks: Stade de France, Bataclan and nearby terraces (November 13, 2015), Promenade des Anglais (July 14, 2016) and Barcelona (October 2017).

The objective of the contradictory examination of the child is therefore to respond to the Dinthilac mandate; clinicians look for clinical elements constituting the post-traumatic syndrome by trying to differentiate the child's symptomatology at various moments of development and evolution.

The questions posed by the various traumas that can affect a child include:

– Is a child victimized in the same way depending on the nature of the external event that affects them?

– Are children's feelings linked to their developmental age, to what they perceive from the reactions of the adults around them?

Faced with a terrorist attack, a situational framework is added, which concerns both the victim and the professional who may be with him (the medical consultant).

These questions include:

– Is the child a physically and/or psychologically injured direct or indirect victim, a spectator of a family disaster with several victims, some of them deceased, from the same family?

– What will happen to their feelings, experience and self-image as a result of the comments and attitude of the adults around them, including school and healthcare providers?

The symptoms most frequently cited by professionals are: floating anxiety, language delay, sleep disorders, disabling nightmares, night waking, daytime fatigue, elements of fear in the presence of intense noises, hypervigilance, loss of autonomy, somatization, enuresis, rumination, revivification and aggressiveness.

10.5.2. *The children of Aceh (the tsunami)*

In the aftermath of the tsunami, the children of Aceh felt that there was a lack of people to talk to and with whom to discuss their feelings. They still felt the sadness, horror and trauma of the tsunami, but they often kept their feelings to themselves. Finally, they all accepted the tragedy as a divine fate. The different responses show differences in the way they see their futures. Some are very optimistic and still believe they have a role to play in society, while others are confused, unemployed and lost, to the point of feeling uncertainty about where their next meal will come from. Survivors have also spoken about the different types of support they received immediately after the disaster, including continuation, long-term and immediate support. How young survivors coped with the immediate aftermath of the tsunami depended on the support they received from their communities and the extent of their own inner strength and will to survive. The combination of these internal and external resources has enabled them to develop personal resilience to survive the tsunami, both in the short- and long-term.

10.6. Political influences

There are few studies on the influences of public policies on child development. Yet, they have a strong impact on the social determinants of children's health and the social norms that influence families.

If we take the example of the penultimate presidential election in the United States, it was noticeable that Trump's cartoonish policy positions (such as cuts in health and environmental programs, support for the gun lobby and sexism) have already had negative psychological and physiological consequences on the life expectancy of American children. We saw in the chapter on mortality that this explains why the richest country in the world has a very high infant mortality rate.

Beyond Trump, Republican administrations are generally associated with higher rates of suicide, homicide, unemployment and social inequality; military spending and tax cuts are reducing social protection and healthcare coverage.

Thus, the political party and ideology of the president have predicted overall and race-specific infant mortality in the United States since 1965, up to the present day. Republican presidencies and the socially conservative ideology of US presidents are strongly associated with slower declines in infant mortality rates, overall and for Caucasian and African American infants, compared with Democratic and social liberal presidents.

About half (46%) of the infant mortality gap between Caucasian and African American populations, about 20,000 additional infant deaths, and most if not all of the infant mortality rate gap between the United States and the rest of the developed world, can be attributed to the 28 years of Republican administration.

10.6.1. *Children, citizenship and politics*

The International Convention on the Rights of the Child adopted by the UN in 1989 states that the child has "a right to express freely express their views in all matters concerning their life [...]. Views of children [...] must be given due weight in accordance with the age and maturity of the child"; however, we have seen, with the activism of teenager Greta Thunberg, how this wishful thinking on the part of the UN has difficulty overcoming adult skepticism.

In France, "children's municipal councils" were created in the 1970s, and there are about 2,000 of them today; class councils are often children's first "political" experience: one out of every four pupils will have been a class delegate at some point. However, children can be skeptical that their opinions are being taken into account: half of the children think that these structures are cosmetic or "for show".

One debate still persists: is the child still a "blank page" or a fully-fledged citizen?

In fact, from early childhood, the child is an actor in the internalization of social norms; the child "does things with what we make of him".

10.7. The environment (neighborhood, nature, city)

"It takes a whole village to raise a child" (African proverb).

10.7.1. *The neighborhood*

Children who grow up in affluent or less affluent neighborhoods exhibit different levels of physical, psychological and cognitive development. Neighborhood socioeconomic level is the most commonly measured and consistent predictor, even after controlling for family influences. Research has focused on the influence of negative features of children's built and social environments, including physical deterioration, neighborhood disorder and crime and social cohesion.

10.7.2. *Contact with nature*

Intriguing new findings are emerging regarding the potential role of positive features of children's built environment on cognition and health. A number of recent studies have reported positive associations between neighborhood vegetation, or the quantity of leaves and green space growing in a neighborhood, and children's cognitive and academic test scores in urban and suburban settings (Reuben 2019).

These results raise the exciting possibility that children may derive cognitive benefits from spending time in or near green spaces and that the "greening" of urban neighborhoods deprived of vegetation may result in improved cognitive outcomes for children. However, before investing in neighborhood-level interventions based on these findings, we need to ensure that these associations are indeed due specifically to vegetation and not to confounding factors (such as other neighborhood characteristics and sample selection bias).

For example, there is a social gradient from exposure to greenery when children have a higher socioeconomic status. They live more in green neighborhoods and the magnitude of the association between economic status and exposure to greenery increases in adolescence as children age.

A number of mechanisms have been proposed to explain the links between children's exposure to neighborhood greenery and their performance in cognitive and academic tests (Reuben 2019):

– strictly biophysical theories argue that ambient vegetation enhances children's cognitive development by reducing environmental stress factors, such as noise, heat and air pollution, that impair cognitive performance and learning, particularly in high load urban spaces;

– according to biocognitive theories, green spaces and vegetated areas naturally produce lower emotional arousal through evolutionarily determined pathways;

– finally, biosocial theories argue that the "greenness" of neighborhoods simply reflects the presence of parks and open spaces, which appear to provide children with unique environments for physical activity, risk taking, control, self-regulation and social interaction, each of which can promote cognitive development and learning.

While several studies have linked higher levels of greenery in nearby schools to better test scores and classroom behavior for elementary and secondary students, few studies have examined cognitive outcomes of individual children in relation to greenery in residential neighborhoods.

Two Spanish studies have reported positive associations between greenery in residential neighborhoods (measured using satellite imagery) and children's performance in attention and working memory tests, assessed cross-sectionally at ages four to five and seven. A recent study in the United Kingdom reported positive associations between greenery in residential neighborhoods (as measured by land use data) and children's performance on a single spatial work task, assessed at age 11 (Reuben 2019).

The E-Risk Longitudinal Study, a nationally representative 1994–1995 birth cohort of children in Great Britain (1,658 participants living in urban and suburban areas), was used to determine whether children's cognitive development during childhood and adolescence was predicted by greenery in residential neighborhoods, using at-home cognitive tests and satellite imagery data.

The association between green measures and cognitive measures does not hold after controlling for family or neighborhood socioeconomic status: children raised in "green" neighborhoods show better overall cognitive ability, but association is likely due to family and neighborhood socioeconomic characteristics (Reuben 2019).

Although family and neighborhood socioeconomic status fully explain the links between neighborhood greenery and children's overall cognitive development, the possibility that targeted "greening" interventions can affect other important health and developmental outcomes for children cannot be ruled out.

For example, a neighborhood greening intervention trial in Philadelphia recently reported that greening vacant lots significantly improved the mental health of residents in surrounding neighborhoods, with the most significant improvements reported for neighborhoods with participants living below the poverty line (Reuben 2019).

The effects of greenery have also been studied in relation to externalized disorders (Weeland forthcoming). The results of the study showed that neighborhood greenery was neither a promoting nor a protective factor. However, adolescents who reported more stressful life events showed more externalizing disorders, with this effect being stronger among adolescents growing up in disadvantaged neighborhoods (rather than in less green neighborhoods).

While the impact of air pollution on respiratory and asthmatic problems in children is now well known, less well known is the association between air pollution exposure and behavioral problems in children. Data on 13,182 children from eight European birthing centers was analyzed (Ainhoa 2019): overall, 8% of children were classified as having symptoms of depression and anxiety and 7% had symptoms of aggression. Prenatal and postnatal exposure to air pollution is associated with depressive and anxiety symptoms or aggressive symptoms in children aged 7–11 years.

10.7.3. *Urban planning*

Will we ever have child-friendly cities? In the chapter on children's road safety, we saw how, because of the motorization of countries, city traffic poses safety issues for children, as well as health issues (including lack of physical exercise, play areas and obesity).

It is clear that we are no longer dealing only with a road safety problem, but more generally with urban planning: how do we think about children in cities? How do we take into account their needs and uses? Generally, the designers of urban spaces only think of children as "vulnerable", "inattentive" and "turbulent", in short, as a source of constraints.

Few urban planners are like Louis Kahn, who, as early as the 1940s in Philadelphia, has been integrating this problem and its issues into his thinking and raising the question of the attribution of certain uses to urban spaces. Kahn places great importance on parking lots, which he sees as a type of protective enclosure around a downtown area, largely reserved for pedestrians, and providing cars with their rightful place, without eliminating them completely.

He seeks to encourage the reclamation of street spaces by and for urban life that necessarily includes children. In the new residential neighborhoods on the outskirts of Philadelphia, he proposes dead-end alleys for cars and a system of paths and plazas behind the houses, away from traffic, intended primarily for the youngest children.

What is at stake is a refusal to see public spaces transformed into simple traffic lanes, to risk seeing the street disappear as a place of community life and to marginalize, or even exclude, children, this final refusal serving as the yardstick for the phenomenon.

Moreover, segregation of automobile and pedestrian traffic is a fantasy that keeps returning. Le Corbusier, himself, wanted to raze the city center of Paris and to install silo-buildings along straight streets prohibited to pedestrians. In his opinion, this would have ensured the safety of both types of users. In Chandigarh, he had developed his famous "theory of the seven Vs", with a very assertive hierarchy and functional differentiation.

Unlike Le Corbusier, Kahn wants to reintroduce pedestrian spaces everywhere, as well as layouts that favor co-presence, cohabitation and sharing, in short, what he calls "availabilities".

10.8. Cyberbullying

Since the end of the 1990s, a new form of peer-to-peer harassment has emerged with the arrival of the Internet and social networks: cyberbullying.

Cyberbullying was initially considered an extension of so-called traditional bullying, taking place face-to-face and often at school, but is now considered to have potentially more serious consequences than face-to-face bullying (Arsène and Raynaud 2014).

In terms of both victimizations and assaults, the prevalence of cyberbullying is still lower than that of traditional bullying, but is currently increasing sharply. It is more relevant to adolescents (between 13 and 16 years of age), whereas traditional bullying peaks at age 12 (Arsène and Raynaud 2014). There are no gender differences.

85% of cyber-aggression and cyber-victimization takes place in the family home. Cyberbullying that uses visual media, such as photos or videos, as well as cellphone calls, is perceived as more hurtful and more negative than texting and Internet messages. The psychopathological consequences are more pronounced, the victims are more affected and the risk of psychological distress is greater. Overall, the consequences are more negative for the subject than traditional bullying (Arsène and Raynaud 2014).

Thus, nearly 40% of young cyber-victims present psychological distress; this rate rises to 50% if the young people are both cyber and traditional victims of the same aggressor and drops to 20% if the aggressor is unknown or different.

There is a co-occurrence between the two forms of bullying, cyber and traditional, between 30% and 95% of cross-victimization or cross-aggression. When the frequency of victimization increases, the co-occurrence between the two forms of bullying also significantly increases; being an actor or victim of bullying in one area predisposes us to become either a victim or an aggressor; being a cyber-aggressor strongly exposes us to the risk of becoming a cyber-victim.

There is also a significant association between high Internet and computer use and involvement in cyberbullying: using the Internet for more than three hours per day increases the risk of being a cyber-victim by a factor of 4, compared with those who use it for one hour per day (Arsène and Raynaud 2014).

The majority of adolescents are reluctant to tell an authority figure that they are victims of cyberbullying and are more likely to disclose to their parents that they are victims of traditional bullying. The threat of confiscation of the material is primarily put forward to explain this reluctance, as victims prefer to be victimized than isolated from their peers (Arsène and Raynaud 2014).

Depressive syndromes are two to three times more common among cyberbullying victims than among non-victimized children and adolescents, as well as there being significantly higher rates of suicidal ideation, suicide attempts and suicide. There are also significantly more behavioral disorders and antisocial behaviors than among young people who are not involved.

Frequency and repetition of acts proportionately increase behavioral problems, as well as the onset and severity of thymic disorders and self-aggressive acting out (Arsène and Raynaud 2014).

Both cyber-aggressors and victims are characterized by poor relationships with their caregivers and receive less parental care and attention than the control group, especially for the cyber-aggressors–cyber-victims group.

Cyber-victims are also characterized by high consumptions of psychoactive products, generally between two and three times more than the control group. Various psychosomatic manifestations, although not specific, have also been noted, especially headaches, abdominal pain and sleep disorders.

Given all of these factors, it should come as no surprise that cyber-victims are significantly more likely to fail at school and exhibit more absenteeism. Both cyber-aggressors and cyber-victims report having a poor image of school, as well as a feeling of insecurity in school (Arsène and Raynaud 2014).

The risk factors are cumulative; being a cyber-victim is associated with being a teenager; having a major depressive disorder; being a cyber-aggressor or a victim of traditional bullying; and having psychosocial difficulties and borderline personality traits.

Psychological distress is associated with being a preadolescent (age 10–12); being harassed via photos and videos; having contact in real life with their cyber-aggressor; being abused by an adult, being followed by a stranger or a group of abusers; and being abused both online and in real life by the same person.

The more factors involved, the higher the risk. Young people who are both cyber-offenders and victims are particularly at risk and should be monitored.

10.9. Covid-19

Children have only comprised a small proportion (about 2%) of Covid-19 infections worldwide and usually develop only very minor forms of the disease. In France, pediatric cases (0–14 years) represent 1% of all symptomatic hospitalized cases.

Various factors explain this difference in the effect on children compared to seasonal influenza: less exposure to travel, especially international; lower severity of viral infections in children; better immune responses in children frequently exposed to various respiratory viruses; and different distribution or maturation of receptors to different Covid-19 variants. Finally, it also seems that children are mini-transmitters of the virus in the propagation of the epidemic, at least in nurseries, kindergartens and elementary schools, the potential for contamination increasing from junior high school. This final point is very important because it must be taken into account when considering the reduction of school dropout rates in children, the harmful effects of which are known (see below).

Lockdown, on the other hand, has changed the lives of children and adolescents. The consequences of the pandemic and the health crisis are still far from being fully known since the pandemic is still ongoing. Nevertheless, we know from the literature on quarantines and lockdowns that they can have serious psychological consequences for children, such as sleep and anxiety disorders, reduced physical activity time, reduced social interaction, desynchronization of circadian rhythms, prolonged boredom and intra-family violence (Bobo and Lin 2020). Covid-19 has virtually impacted every aspect of the psyche.

First of all, the relationship with death: we have witnessed a "return of death" through the macabre and daily count from the Director General of Health. Numerous analyses of human behavior before the epidemic pointed to a psychological disappearance of death, a fantasy of immortality (fueled by the tech industry, children have multiple "lives" in their video games) and a sequestration of the experience of death (hidden in places made for it).

Death no longer has a place in our society and is no longer "visible" to children; all of a sudden, now we have daily counts of the dead. A fundamental and metaphysical question arises: are our societies learning to die again?

Still on this theme, there is now the fear of disturbances of mourning, with many "pathological mournings", in children and adolescents who have lost a loved one; in fact, the impact of death is being tamed using ceremonies, and ways of forming a community around the victim, both during and after death. The funeral ritual is there to anchor the mourning process, to install it in the life of the living.

The management of negative emotions (fear, anxiety, depression, post-traumatic stress) has also been an important psychological consequence for children and adolescents. For the moment, the observations of clinicians during the first lockdown have been an increase in existing symptoms but no development of major pathologies. The first observations of clinicians on the effects of the second lockdown have, at the time of publication of this book, been more alarming: there is talk of a doubling of suicide attempts in children under 15. Obviously, there are inequalities in the effects of lockdown (from factors including social class, housing conditions and psychological fragility).

The relationship with time has also been greatly impacted and put on pause for two months. With a lockdown, life can cease to unfold in the automatic mode of acceleration and the dread of delay, which we often content ourselves with, and forgetting the importance of living in the moment. Lockdown has compelled us to "occupy", "spend" and "kill" time; we fear boredom. What seems to be dreaded in these lockdown times, as much as death, is boredom; however, boredom is a hatred of time.

Lockdown has put a stop to school, dance, guitar lessons, soccer and anything else that turns children's schedules into ministerial agendas. There is a big difference between structuring time and filling it. Structuring our time has been very useful during our current period of confinement. Punctuating time does not mean filling it up, but, on the contrary, insinuating blank intervals during which the child can find themselves.

As with the issue of domestic violence, the issue of abuse during lockdowns must also be addressed. We know that social isolation is a risk factor for child abuse: all types of child abuse become more frequent during school vacations, summer vacations and natural disasters (epidemics, hurricanes, and so on). Women in abusive relationships and their children are more likely to be exposed to domestic violence and abuse when family members spend more time in close contact with each other and when families face additional stress, financial problems and/or unemployment.

The risk of abuse is also increased because a lockdown weakens child welfare services and disrupts prevention measures: the lack of social follow-up during lockdowns means that domestic violence and child abuse may go unreported. For example, consultations in maternity wards and child protection services have been limited to emergency cases. Parent–child meetings with social workers have been suspended and day care centers for children with disabilities have been closed.

Government instructions to stay home and fear of catching Covid-19 have led to a sharp decline in emergency room visits and hospital appointments (by 45% for adults and 70% in pediatric services since mid-March 2020), resulting in fewer opportunities for child abuse screening (Caron and Plancq 2020).

For example, the national child abuse hotline received 14,531 calls between April 13 and 19, 2020, compared with 7,674 over the same period in 2019, an 89% increase. Between March 16 and April 12, 2020, law enforcement home visits increased by 48% compared with the previous year (Caron and Plancq 2020).

Domestic accidents have also been influenced by lockdowns: emergency services and fire departments report an increase in these accidents because confined living increases the risk of domestic accidents for children. Indeed, children have to be supervised continuously 24 hours a day (no nursery, no school), single-parent families are more at risk and teleworking at home diverts parents' attention.

Confinement encourages the child to explore the home, which will be all the more dangerous if the parents' vigilance is lacking. In addition to the common risks of burns, drowning and electrocution, there are also dangers from antiseptic solutions, disinfectants and medicines left within the reach of small children.

With respect to children with physical disabilities, the ECHO (*Enfant Confinement Handicap besOins*) child lockdown disability needs survey was specifically created to report on the experiences, challenges and needs of physically disabled children and their parents during Covid-19 lockdowns (Cacciopo and Bouvier 2020). It was intended for parents or legal guardians of children aged 0–18 years, with physical disabilities (such as cerebral palsy, neuromuscular disease and orthopedic disease), with or without other associated impairments.

Lockdowns have negatively affected morale (44% of children), behavior (55% of children) and social interaction (55% had no contact with other children). Overall, 44% of children stopped their physical activities; 76% were home schooled; 22% maintained medical follow-ups; and 48% and 27% continued physiotherapy and ergotherapy, respectively. For more than 60% of children, parents followed through with therapy. Parents' main concern was rehabilitation (72%) and their main difficulty was the mental burden (50%); parents complained about lack of help and support (60%).

This study has thus shown substantial effects on the health of physically disabled children and the loss of opportunity, with massive interruption in medical follow-up and rehabilitation, during lockdown. Regular assessments of health benefits/risks are therefore essential to support families and ensure continuity of care during a pandemic.

Finally, the mental health conditions of children and adolescents with attention deficit hyperactivity disorder (ADHD) were studied during lockdown (Bobo and Lin 2020). Paradoxically, according to their parents, the majority of the children and adolescents studied experienced either improved well-being or a stable overall psychological condition. A decrease in anxiety is linked to a decrease in school constraints, through the interruption of face-to-face schooling and a "tailored" pace.

Similar observations were made at the Maison de Solenn, a psychiatric consultation center for adolescents in Paris: phobic adolescents reported having lived well during this period and finding lockdown "comfortable".

Thus, children and adolescents with ADHD do not systematically experience a worsening of their symptoms during periods of lockdown. These results are contrary to the initial fears of specialists and families concerned by ADHD. For these children, for whom "outside" is a source of conflict and stress, the return to school must be carefully prepared and accompanied.

Moreover, the apparent good short-term tolerance of lockdown does not prejudge its longer-term tolerance. For example, a study of the H1N1 pandemic found that children who experienced physical isolation had a fourfold increased relative risk of developing post-traumatic stress disorder (Bobo and Lin 2020).

It is therefore time to limit the negative psychosocial effects of lockdown (dropping out of school, educational conflicts with parents, abuse, lack of vaccination protection and breaks in follow-up for chronic illnesses). Children must find the socioeducational environments essential to their development and the preventive medical follow-ups essential to their health.

The challenge for children returning to school will be learning to live together without excessive fear of each other and rediscovering the world through play and learning.

The question of the compulsory wearing of face masks from the beginning of the 2020–2021 school year has raised many questions: relating to teachers' difficulties in exercising their profession, particularly regarding spoken language, and the cognitive slowing down of the brain, for instance in insecure, anxious or depressive children[1]. However, no difficulties or opposition have yet been observed among children. Finally, as family gatherings are one of the dangerous vectors of transmission of the virus, the wearing of face masks by children becomes an act of civic-mindedness to protect their grandparents and constitutes, in a way, a first introduction to care.

Coming out of lockdown, one area of concern in the deconfinement process has been the compliance of adolescents and young adults with preventive measures (barrier signs, social distancing, and so on), as they have often been identified as a group that is potentially non-compliant with public health measures designed to curb the spread of the epidemic. They often have only mild symptoms or are asymptomatic while being infected, so their potential to spread the virus is high, as they also tend to have extensive social networks and active social lives.

We are beginning to see the first studies on the precursor traits of non-compliance with measures to curb the spread of the virus, which logically fall within the psychic space of antisociality: impulsivity, selfishness and psychopathy have been associated with non-compliance (Nivette and Ribeau 2021).

One Swiss study (Nivette and Ribeau 2021) is particularly interesting because it used a longitudinal study conducted in Zurich since 2004: subjects were followed up from 7 to 20 years of age, the age at which they are asked about Covid-19.

Results showed that compliance rates for Covid-related measures were relatively high and slightly better for social distancing than for hygiene measures. Non-compliance was higher among men, those with higher education, higher socioeconomic status and those from non-migrant backgrounds. These associations were primarily due to associations with non-compliance with hygiene measures.

Analyses of antecedent and concurrent risk factors suggested that non-compliance was associated with the following characteristics: low acceptance of moral rules, legal cynicism, low shame or guilt, low self-control, high engagement in delinquent behaviors and association with peers exhibiting social deviance.

Although it is unlikely that public health campaigns can effectively alter characteristics related to an individual's antisocial potential in emergency situations such as a pandemic, it is possible to manage the effects of some antisocial risk

1 Were they going to have a *still face* experience? As a face mask comes off as quickly as it is put on, babies love these games of hide and seek. Freud had thus observed in 1920 in his grandson this *cotton reel game*, known as the *fort-da* experience, based on the disappearance and return of an object.

factors in the short-term through techniques such as "nudges"[2] (Nivette and Ribeau 2021).

Hygiene and social distancing behaviors are in part determined by different mechanisms. For example, negative attitudes towards authorities (low perceived legitimacy of the police and low trust in government) were associated with social distancing non-compliance but not with hygiene non-compliance. Compliance with social distancing measures implies greater or more restrictive behavior change, with direct consequences for psychological, social and economic well-being.

---

2 A *nudge* is a technique to induce individuals or a whole human group to change a behavior or to make certain choices without being under constraint or obligation and which does not involve any sanction. This method of influence is qualified as "libertarian paternalism", because it allows people to make their choices without coercion.

Conclusion

So what have we learned in the last 40 years, since we graduated from university?

C.1. Awareness of the early influences (positive and negative) of the prenatal and postnatal (fetal, microbiota) environments

Is birth a second birth? The fetus, with its immensity of already available, programmed neurons and recording events over a period of nine months, already has a life that orients the future and is in constant interaction with the maternal organism, the genetic, prenatal, psychological and social problems of the mother being solicited in this co-construction.

For example, after birth, the melody of crying has similarities with the mother tongue (due to the impregnation of language into the fetus).

Updating these early influences also impacts on risks from the very start of life. We have seen, for example, that medically assisted reproduction is a risk factor for prematurity and morbidity, that genetic screening poses difficult problems from the point of view of ethics and eugenics and that it enables knowledge of the child's sex, one of the first elements in the construction of parental adherence to gender stereotypes.

Still on the subject of early risks, we know more today about prenatal exposures, whether these are due to maternal behaviors (alcohol, tobacco) or environmental pollution (chemical pollutants, endocrine disruptors), as regards behaviors and diseases, or to antibiotics as regards microbiota and allergies. As Beck taught us in *Risk Society*, it is no longer nature but developments in science and technology that are producing risk in contemporary societies.

In the postnatal environment, we have noticed how modern sedentary lifestyles, the lack of physical exercise in women and postpartum depression can have important consequences for the child.

C.2. Early development of certain perceptual and cognitive skills

Still on the subject of precocity, we have discovered that certain perceptual and cognitive skills develop earlier than first thought.

In the fetus, it is mainly the sensory aspects that have been studied (taste, smell, hearing). Studies on infants have raised an important epistemological issue: recent research on the perception and cognition of infants questions Piaget's theory of assimilation (the child understands the world through actions; the infant acts very little, but perceives). New methods of observation and experimentation, such as the "transgression of expectations" or "impossible situations", have brought to light a more important precociousness than was assumed from the dating of traditional concepts, Piagetian or otherwise. The infant possesses intuition before cognition: "does this situation correspond or resonate with my brain or not?"

Speaking of the child's brain, the application of brain imaging technology has changed our understanding of cognitive development through many new observations about information processing in the brain. For example, brain areas that were known to be associated with functions such as language, facial recognition, arithmetic skills and mentalization, from neurology and neuropsychology in adults, appear to be already associated with these functions in childhood. They can therefore be thought of as "starter kits": the future of the cognitive functions is already "mapped out", even though these functions do not yet exist. The child's brain prefigures the adult brain.

Finally, cognitive precocity also refers to a certain bypassing of the theoretical model of "stages" with a "waves" model: from birth, the newborn possesses multiple cognitive strategies which are all in competition to understand the world; the child therefore launches them like waves which overlap, to arrive on the shore of understanding. With experience and depending on the situation, the child will use one strategy or another.

C.3. New concepts in the field of cognition

Still on the subject of cognition, the field has been strongly renewed by new concepts: the theory of mind, metacognition, mirror neurons and embodied cognition.

C.3.1. *The theory of mind*

Theory of mind refers to the ability to attribute mental states (intentions, perceptions, knowledge and beliefs) to others and to ourselves and to understand that they are different from our own. Again, estimates of the ages of onset of these skills may depend on the techniques employed: with implicit tasks, it is observed that children may understand a false belief earlier than previously found.

C.3.2. *Metacognition*

Metacognition, or the ability to monitor our own mental states and processes (such as memory, attention and errors), is a cognitive function of the prefrontal areas that develops during infancy.

C.3.3. *Mirror neurons*

Mirror neurons (neurons that are activated, not when we perform a behavior, but when we observe others performing that behavior) exist from birth, but in limited numbers, and their number will then develop through learning, socialization and observation of others.

C.3.4. *Embodied cognition*

Embodied cognition is a new approach, which can be positioned in the filiation of the Wallon school, which considers that cognition is at all times influenced by our body's morphology and by its sensorimotor systems. Cognition is no longer differentiated from perception and action. This new theoretical approach could also have important consequences for the education of children: unlike Piaget who believed that the child's thought started from the concrete to become abstract, this embodiment approach shows that the concrete always remains present through development and that this could help to overcome the difficulties that many subjects encounter with abstraction.

C.4. The need to develop an integrative approach

Based on the discoveries about the neuroplasticity of child and adolescent brains, one epistemological conclusion is that we need to break out from "research silos" in order to develop an integrative approach.

Within this approach, we have seen how developmental psychology, clinical psychology, medicine, educational sciences, neuroscience, sociology, biology, anthropology, and so on, can be brought together. The aim is to create a "developmental science", a transdisciplinary developmental psychology and to rewrite the old story of nature and nurture, as epigenetics has revolutionized the way we understand the interactions between genetics and environment.

The integrative approach does not oppose the traditional clinical approach to stressful childhood life events; it explains how these childhood and adolescence experiences "sculpt" neural systems during periods of plasticity, which are periods of both vulnerability and opportunity for prevention and intervention. Understanding child and adolescent trajectories, which is the core of developmental psychopathology, will require breaking out of "knowledge silos" and working together, cooperating across disciplines.

C.5. A spiral causality produced by interactions

To approach causalities in development, we have seen how the aspects of mediation, moderation and spiral causality are fundamental: a cause produces an effect that becomes the cause of something else; a characteristic of the child or of his/her environment only plays a role in relation to the interaction with another characteristic.

We have found these interactions in almost every chapter: we saw, for example, how, for the mother's job, the mode of custody or divorce, these factors only interact with other factors. A single environmental aspect is no longer the same and the effect becomes very different.

Beyond the family, ecological approaches to development, in the wake of Bronfenbrenner, highlight the interactions between the various facets of the child's environment: their family characteristics, their neighborhood, the built environment and nature, municipal policies and the governance orientations of the country.

C.6. At the heart of self-endangerment: the lack of sensitivity to loss

Through the various themes of self-endangerment (risk taking, addiction, transgression), a transversal mechanism has been highlighted: the lack of sensitivity to loss.

The risk taken is often, in fact, inversely proportional to the level of perceived fear. An important mechanism here could be a *lack of sensitivity to loss*, produced by *the epigenetic effects of early emotional stresses*, such as anxious attachments or various forms of abuse.

These epigenetic effects are located at the intersection of biological and emotional histories. If we consider, for example, the genes that control responses to fear and stress, the emotional environment will gradually shape the child's HPA axis. Emotional stress early in life causes a weakening or destruction of neurons in the hippocampus, the area of the brain that encodes emotional memories, which will produce a lack of sensitivity to loss. A byproduct of childhood emotional history and anxious attachments, alexithymia, may also be related to this lack of feelings.

This neural damage caused by emotional stress will be associated in adolescence with risk taking, impulsivity and addiction. The hazards of life will lead to excessive risk taking in extreme sports, addiction to opiates or alcohol or alternatively to delinquency, but the same psychobiological mechanism will be common to these three futures.

C.7. Gender differences, gender and stereotypes

Some differences related to biological sex, or those related to gender and psychological identity, were obviously already observed 40 years ago, such as the verbal advantages of girls and the spatial advantages of boys.

What is perhaps clearer today is the extent to which the weaker sex is the male sex. There are so many aspects of fragility and vulnerability in boys, and in all the biological, psychological and social domains, that they produce multiple consequences for schooling, mortality, socialization, and so on. On the psychological level, masculinity is an essential element of the relationships to risk, to rules and to others, three dimensions which form the basis for self-endangerment throughout life.

Also new have been the insights generated about " stereotype threat", the fear of underachieving because of a negative, endorsed stereotype ("girls suck at math", "women can't drive", and so on).

We have seen that it is the beliefs of parents and the adherence of parenting practices to gender stereotypes that will progressively influence the behavioral associations of masculinity, and it is this that must be changed in the future if we are to improve men's lives in any way.

C.8. The family environment, again and always

Many interesting knowledge works have been produced on parenthood; let us recall that it is at the heart of four objectives: the transmission of cultural, social and symbolic capital; the acquisition of autonomy by the young person[1], with the characteristics of their generation (e.g. their use of digital and virtual technology); the development of citizenship and otherness (how to live with others); finally, probably the most important, emotional and affective exchanges. In this field of parent–child relations, there is both continuity and extension.

C.8.1. *Extending the attachment domain*

If we take the example of the first, so fundamental bond between the infant and his mother, there is not much to add today to the attachment model proposed by Bowlby; however, subsequent work has extended the attachment domain: first to the father, then to siblings, to peers and finally to objects.

C.8.2. *The family, a gatekeeper and a kite*

The family environment acts as both a "gatekeeper" and a "kite", and both functions are indispensable: the gatekeeper is the negotiated authority, the setting of limits with affection and the maintenance of dialog and trust; it also has a supporting function, even if it is not always perceived as such by the child. The kite is the attachment and, as everyone knows about kites, it needs a thread; otherwise, it will fly off, but not too short; otherwise, it will not fly at all. The child, like the kite, rises all the higher into space as it is less constrained by the thread of the link. If this thread is too short, it pushes the individual to take risks. The link will enable the child, within this "blind spot" that is the family, with all its internal scars, sufferings and ruptures, to become the sculptor of their spirit, the magician of their own life.

C.8.3. *Transmission between reproduction and resilience*

The question of intergenerational transmission of behaviors is always central to the interplay between reproduction and resilience; we have seen that this transmission virtually affects every aspect of the child's life, that confounding factors, mediation and moderation are frequent and that the view of these questions profoundly changes if we study the transmission retrospectively or longitudinally. Aspects of multifinality (or "transdiagnostics") are also observed: to take just one

---

1 We recall the Latin root of the word education: *educere* (to bring out), to bring the child out of the family cocoon.

example, the type of parental drinking predicts the child's later drinking as an adult, but it also predicts the child's future obesity.

C.8.4. *The trade-off between risk and protection*

Trade-offs between risk and protective factors are necessary, for example, between biological and sociological factors: breastfeeding seems to be much better for the child, but the mother's employment is also more desirable for other reasons.

C.8.5. *Major structural changes*

Finally, it is the very structure of the family that has changed significantly over the last 40 years: homoparental families, blended families, single-parent households, and so on. We have seen that in the comparison between blended families and single-parent households, the question of managing ties and conflicts remains fundamental, as it was before in "traditional" families.

C.9. Historical developments

One question runs through each chapter of this book: whether the frequencies of children's behaviors and situations tend to decrease, increase or remain stable.

This immediately raises the question of the validity of the measurement of the phenomenon: is it really increasing, or is it just because we notice it more? Is it really decreasing, or is it just because we don't pay attention to it anymore?

C.9.1. *On the increase*

Certain phenomena are undoubtedly on the increase: twin births, prenatal exposure to pollutants, sedentary lifestyle and lack of physical exercise, obesity, children's mobility by car to the detriment of pedestrian mobility, the earlier onset of behavioral problems, the lengthening of adolescence, the instability of youth and maternal employment.

C.9.2. *In decline*

Some behaviors decline over time, such as adolescent smoking[2] and cannabis use and child abuse[3] and neglect; measures or campaigns can influence these prevalences.

---

2 On the other hand, vaping is on the increase.

C.9.3. *Remaining stable*

Some phenomena unfortunately remain static through the years: the impact of social belonging on school performance[4] and the impact of an insecure attachment on self-endangerment, to name just two examples.

C.10. New research themes generated by societal developments

New themes have been introduced, not by research in developmental psychology, but by society and its evolutions, including children living in homoparental families, homeless children, migrants, disaster psychology (tsunamis, earthquakes, attacks, wars), the environment, the question of screens, cyberbullying and Covid-19.

These themes will generate a multiplication of and diversification in the fields of research, interventions and practices of psychologists, which will form the basis of the second volume of this book. We have seen, particularly with regard to children living in homoparental families, how little research has been done, as well as how it contradicts ideological prejudices.

It has been noted that new threats to child development, generated by technological developments, such as cyberbullying, are more harmful than traditional bullying and that cyberbullies and cybervictims have similar characteristics.

Finally, the Covid-19 pandemic, still ongoing at the time of writing, has disrupted the lives of every child on the planet; while it predictably reveals social inequalities in developmental consequences, it is too early to draw general psychological conclusions about its impact on the child and adolescent psyche.

To conclude, the psychological study of the child always shows us that he is "the father of the man", and this shows in this endless and exciting renewal of knowledge.

3 Overall, however, some types of abuse (physical abuse) may be decreasing more than others (neglect) in the modern period.

4 Also, with 20% of young French people living below the poverty line, this phenomenon is unlikely to improve.

Appendix

Definitions of Some Concepts Used in this Book

A.1. Phylogenesis/ontogenesis

Phylogenesis refers to the animal origins of human behavior, the inheritance of evolution; thus, we have passed from Lamarck's model of the heredity of acquired characters to Darwin's model of natural selection through adaptation and finally to De Vries' model of random genetic mutations.

Ontogenesis refers to the development of the individual, which is the subject of this book: how does a baby become a person, how does he/she build his/her personality, his/her thinking, and so on?

A.2. Factor/marker

A *risk factor* increases the likelihood of an event occurring in subjects exposed to the risk, compared with subjects not exposed to the risk, and we can explain the causal mechanism (e.g. smoking and lung cancer).

A *risk marker* is not directly causal, but its association with the occurrence of an event reveals the existence of underlying risk factors which are themselves the causes of the phenomenon (e.g. early drinking behavior in adolescence predicts alcohol misuse in adulthood, but this early onset reveals risk factors such as family conflict and social exclusion).

A.3. Epigenetic factors

Epigenetics is the study of changes in gene expression that do not involve changes in the DNA sequence and that can be transmitted during cell division. We keep the same genes throughout our lives, but it is their expression and their influence on our behavior that can greatly vary over time, depending on various factors or events. This concept has rendered obsolete all the radical oppositions during the 1970s between the hereditarists (gray-haired child psychiatrists with bow ties, who advocated that everything during development was innate) and the environmentalists (young psychiatrists or hairy psychoanalysts and leftists who advocated that everything was acquired).

A.4. Externalized and internalized behavioral disorders

In the case of externalized problems, negative emotions are directed against others, manifested by lack of control, anger, aggression and frustration; delinquent acts, accidents, suicides, runaways and destruction fall into this category. We differentiate, among the externalized disorders, between aggressive and delinquent behaviors which do not necessarily refer to the same causes.

In the case of internalized behavioral problems, negative emotions are self-directed, manifested by inhibition, fear and anxiety; psychopathology, addictions, eating disorders, shyness, withdrawal, fatigue and headaches fall into this category.

When distinguishing between these two types of problems, we should not forget about interactions and temporal sequences, or "developmental cascades". For example, externalized disorders in children (such as hyperactivity/attention deficit syndrome) disrupt their adjustment to school, and this disruption in adolescence will lead to internalized disorders in young adults.

References

Ainhoa, J. (2019). Prenatal and postnatal exposure to air pollution and emotional and aggressive symptoms in children from 8 European birth cohorts. *Environment International*, 131, 104927.

Ainsworth, M.D. and Blehar, M.C. (1978). *Patterns of Attachment: A Psychological Study of the Strange Situation*. Erlbaum, Hillsdale.

Albinhac, A.M.H. and Bouvard, J.M.P. (2019). Étude du lien parental dans l'enfance chez les enfants et adolescents avec anorexie mentale. *L'Encéphale*, 45, 121–126.

Almodovar, J.-P. (1981). Les expériences fraternelles dans le développement de l'enfant. In *Frères et Sœurs*, Soulé, M. (ed.). ESF, Paris.

Amat, F. and Houdouin, V. (2020). Microbiote et développement de l'asthme. *Revue française d'allergologie*, 60(6/7).

Amir, D. and McAuliffe, K. (2020). Cross-cultural, developmental psychology: Integrating approaches and key insights. *Evolution and Human Behavior*, 41(5).

Andler, R. and Richard, J.B. (2019). Baisse de la prévalence du tabagisme quotidien parmi les adultes : résultats du Baromètre de Santé publique France 2018. *BEH – Bulletin épidémiologique hebdomadaire*, 15, 271–277.

Ariès, P. (1973). *L'enfant et la vie familiale sous l'Ancien régime*. Le Seuil, Paris.

Arsène, J. and Raynaud, J.-P. (2014). Cyberbullying (ou cyberharcèlement) et psychopathologie de l'enfant et de l'adolescent : état actuel des connaissances. *Neuropsychiatrie de l'enfance et de l'adolescence*, 62(4), 249–256.

Assailly, J.-P. (1988). Des "peurs enfantines" aux "angoisses de l'adolescence" : une étude des filiations. *Enfance*, 41(1), 61–73.

Assailly, J.-P. (2007). *Jeunes en danger. Les familles face aux conduites à risques*. Imago, Paris.

Assailly, J.-P. (2014). *Why Do Young People Drink?* PAU, Barcelona.

Assailly, J.-P. (2017). *Why Do Young People Drink*. PAU Éducation, Barcelona.

Assailly, J.-P. (2019). *La mortalité des jeunes*. Codes Rousseau, Sables-d'Olonne.

Assailly, J.-P., Corbillon, M., Duyme, M. (1989). Transmission intergénérationnelle et comportement parental : étude longitudinale d'enfants placés. *Neuropsychiatrie de l'enfance et de l'adolescence*, 37, 7.

Bandura, A. (1977). *Social Learning Theory*. Prentice Hall, Englewood Cliffs.

Bathelta, J. and Scerif, G. (2019). Whole-brain white matter organization, intelligence, and educational attainment. *Trends in Neuroscience and Education*, 15, 38–47.

Baumrind, D. (1985). Familial antecedents of adolescent drug use: A developmental perspective. In *Etiology of Drug Abuse: Implications for Prevention*, Jones, C.L. and Battjes, R.J. (eds). NIDA/Government Printing Office, Washington.

Beck, U. (2001). *La société du risque. Sur la voie d'une autre modernité*. Aubier, Paris.

Belsky, J. and Pensky, E. (1988). Developmental history, personality and family relationships: Toward an emergent family system. In *Relationships within Families*, Hinde, R. and Stevenson-Hinde, J. (eds). Clarendon Press, Oxford, England.

Belsky, J., Youngblade, L., Pensky, L. (1990). Childrearing history, marital quality and maternal affect: Intergenerational transmission in a low-risk sample. *Development and Psychopathology*, I, 294–304.

Berdot-Talmier, L. and Koliouli, F. (2020). Impact de la téléphonie mobile et de l'adaptation intériorisée sur la satisfaction de vie des enfants âgés de 9 à 12 ans. *Psychologie française*, 65, 121–139.

Berdot-Talmier, L. and Zaouche Gaudron, C. (2018). Impact de l'utilisation de Facebook sur l'adaptation socio-affective des enfants de 9–12 ans. *Neuropsychiatrie de l'enfance et de l'adolescence*, 66(3), 154–164.

Bergmeier, H. and Paxton, S.J. (2020). Early mother-child dyadic pathways to childhood obesity risk: A conceptual model. *Appetite*, 1 January, 104459.

Bernard, J.Y. (2017). Breastfeeding, polyunsaturated fatty acid levels in colostrum and child intelligence quotient at age 5–6 years. *The Journal of Pediatrics*, 183, 43–50.

Bernard, J.Y. and De Agostini, M. (2013). Breastfeeding duration and cognitive development at 2 and 3 years of age in the EDEN mother-child cohort. *The Journal of Pediatrics*, 163(1), 36–42.

Bernard, J.Y. and van der Waerden, J. (2016). Prenatal caffeine exposure and child IQ at age 5.5 years: The EDEN mother-child cohort. *Biological Psychiatry*, 80(9), 650–651.

Bobo, E. and Lin, L. (2020). Comment les enfants et adolescents avec le trouble déficit d'attention/hyperactivité (TDAH) vivent-ils le confinement durant la pandémie Covid-19 ? *L'Encéphale*, 46, S85–S92.

Bornstein, M.H. (2020). Maternal sensitivity and language in infancy each promotes child core language skill in preschool. *Early Childhood Research Quarterly*, 51, 483–489.

Bowlby, J. (1978). *L'Attachement*. PUF, Paris.

Branger, B. and Picherot, G. (2019). La mortalité infantile en France ne baisse plus depuis dix ans. *Perfectionnement en pédiatrie*, 2, 270–279.

Bronfenbrenner, U. (1977). Towards an experimental ecology of human development. *American Psychologist*, July.

Cacciopo, M. and Bouvier, S. (2020). Emerging health challenges for children with physical disabilities and their parents during the Covid-19 pandemic: The ECHO French survey. *Annals of Physical and Rehabilitation Medicine*, August 18, 101429.

Caron, F. and Plancq, M.C. (2020). Was child abuse underdetected during the Covid-19 lockdown? *Archives de pédiatrie*, 27(7), 399–400.

Casey, B.J. (2015). Beyond simple models of self-control to circuit-based accounts of adolescent behavior. *Annual Review of Psychology*, 66, 295–319.

Changeux, J.-P. (1983). *L'homme neuronal*. Fayard, Paris.

Choquet, M. and Com-Ruelle, L. (2003). *Les adolescents français face à l'alcool*. Focus alcoologie, IREB, Karlsruhe.

Choquet, M. and Moreau, C. (2019). *Les jeunes face à l'alcool*. Eres, Toulouse.

Clément, M.-N. (2020). Les 0–6 ans et les écrans digitaux nomades. Évaluation de l'exposition et de ses effets à travers la littérature internationale. *Neuropsychiatrie de l'enfance et de l'adolescence*, 68(4), 190–195.

Clément, C. and Hamelin, C. (2019). En rabattre à l'arrivée du deuxième enfant : enquête sur les normes et les pratiques éducatives de parents diplômés. *Revue française des affaires sociales*, 4, 27–48.

Collin, S.M. (2018). Childhood sleep and adolescent chronic fatigue syndrome (CFS/ME): Evidence of associations in a UK birth cohort. *Sleep Medicine*, 46, 26–36.

Connelly, R. and Platt, L. (2014). Cohort Profile: UK Millennium Cohort Study (MCS). *International Journal of Epidemiology*, 43(6), 1719–1725.

Cornet, J. (1977). *Faut-il battre les enfants ? Relations entre les accidents et la violence éducative*. Hommes et Perspectives, Paris.

Cui, B. and Nguyen, T. (2020). The effects of interaction quality on neural synchrony during mother-child problem solving. *Cortex*, 124, 235–249.

Dąbrowski, K. (1972). *Introduction générale a la théorie de la désintegration positive*. Editions Saint-Yves, Quebec.

Damasio, A.R. (1994). *Descartes' Error: Emotion, Reason, and the Human Brain*. Grosset/Putnam, New York.

Degli Espostia, M. (2019). Long-term trends in child maltreatment in England and Wales, 1858–2016: An observational, time-series analysis. 4, March [Online]. Available at: https://www.thelancet.com/journals/lanpub/article/PIIS2468-2667(19)30002–7/fulltext.

Degli Espostia, M. (2020). Child maltreatment and the risk of antisocial behaviour: A population-based cohort study spanning 50 years. *Child Abuse & Neglect*, 99, 104281.

Delbarre, M. (2020). Comportements d'attachement d'enfants d'âge préscolaire consultant en pédopsychiatrie : lien avec des caractéristiques psychologiques maternelles. *Neuropsychiatrie de l'enfance et de l'adolescence*, 68, 100–105.

Demedardi, M.C., Brechet, C., Gentaz, E., Monnier, C. (2021). Prosocial lying in children between 4 and 11 years of age: The role of emotional understanding and empathy. *Journal of Experimental Child Psychology*, 203, 105045.

DEPP (2019a). Note d'information : l'évolution des performances en calcul des élèves de CM2 à trente ans d'intervalle (1987–2017) [Online]. Available at: https://www.education.gouv.fr/l-evolution-des-performances-en-calcul-des-eleves-de-cm2-trente-ans-d-intervalle-1987-2017-11978.

DEPP (2019b). Note d'information : les performances en orthographe des élèves à la fin de l'école primaire (1987–2007–2015) [Online]. Available at: https://www.education.gouv.fr/les-performances-en-orthographe-des-eleves-en-fin-d-ecole-primaire-1987-2007-2015-1991.

Desmurget, M. (2019). *La fabrique du crétin digital, les dangers des écrans pour nos enfants*. Le Seuil, Paris.

Dugas, A. (2019). *Le rêve chez l'enfant*. Bibliothèque nationale du Québec, Montreal.

Elias, N. (1973). *La civilisation des mœurs*. Calmann-Lévy, Paris.

Even, M. and Sutter-Dallay, A.-L. (2019). La santé mentale des enfants placés. Une revue de la littérature. *L'Encéphale*, 45(3411), 340–344.

Freud, S. (1926). *Inhibition, symptôme et angoisse*. PUF, Paris.

Gardner, H. (1983). *Frames of Mind: The Theory of Multiple Intelligences*. Basic Books, New York.

van Gennep, A. (1909). *Les rites de passage : étude systématique*. E. Nourry, Paris.

Gire, C. (2020). Qualité de vie des enfants nés extrêmement prématurés à l'âge scolaire : étude QPQoL. *Perfectionnement en pédiatrie*, 3(1), 102–103.

Goldschmidt, L. and Richardson, G. (2019). Brief communication. Prenatal alcohol exposure and offspring alcohol use and misuse at 22 years of age: A prospective longitudinal study. *Neurotoxicology and Teratology*, 71, 1–5.

Goleman, J. (1997). *L'intelligence émotionnelle*. Robert Laffont, Paris.

Gomajee, R., El-Khoury, J., EDEN mother-child cohort study group (2017). Early life childcare and later behavioral difficulties: A causal relationship? Data from the French EDEN study. *Journal of Economic Behavior & Organization*, 181.

Gordona, R.A. (2020). Child care arrangements and gender: A national portrait of preschool-aged children. *Early Childhood Research Quarterly*, 53, 40–49.

Granié, M.-A. (2007). Gender differences in preschool children's declared and behavioral compliance with pedestrian rules. *Transportation Research Part F: Traffic Psychology and Behaviour*, 10(5), 371–382.

Granié, M.-A. (2010). Gender stereotype conformity and age as determinants of preschoolers' injury-risk behaviors. *Accident Analysis and Prevention*, 42, 726–733.

Granié, M.-A. (2011). Différences de sexe et rôle de l'internalisation des règles sur la propension des enfants à prendre des risques à vélo. *Recherche – Transports – Sécurité*, (1/2), 67–81.

Granié, M.-A. (2013). Genre et rapport au risque dans l'espace routier : de la compréhension au levier pour l'action. *Questions vives recherches en éducation*, 9(19), 65–88.

Harkness, S. and Super, C.M. (1994). The developmental niche: A theoretical framework for analyzing the household production of health. *Social Science & Medicine*, 38(2), 217–226.

Heude, B. and Forhan, A. (2015). Cohort profile: The EDEN mother-child cohort on the prenatal and early postnatal determinants of child health and development. *Int. J. Epidemiology* [Online]. Available at: http://dx.doi.org/10.1093/ije/ dyv151.

Hofstede, G. (1984). *Culture's Consequences: International Differences in Work-related Values*, volume 5. Sage, Thousand Oaks.

House, B.R. and Silk, J.B. (2013). Ontogeny of prosocial behavior across diverse societies. *Proceedings of the National Academy of Sciences*, 110(36), 14586–14591.

Humphreys, K.L. (2020). Child maltreatment and depression: A meta-analysis of studies using the Childhood Trauma Questionnaire. *Child Abuse & Neglect*, 102, 104361.

Huppert, E. and Cowell, J.M. (2018). The development of children's preferences for equality and equity across 13 individualistic and collectivist cultures. *Developmental Science*, e12729.

Im, Y. (2018). Role of first-year maternal employment and paternal involvement in behavioral and cognitive development of young children. *Infant Mental Health Journal*, 39(4), 449–465.

Jeammet, P. and Bochereau, D. (2007). *La souffrance des adolescents*. La Découverte, Paris.

Jeffrey, D. (2008). *Jeunesse à risque : rite et passage*. Presses de l'Université Laval, Quebec.

Jouvet, M. (2000). *Le sommeil et le rêve*. Odile Jacob, Paris.

Keller, H. (2013). *Cultures of Infancy*. Routledge, Abingdon-on-Thames.

Kohlberg, L. (1973). Continuities in childhood and adult moral development revisited. In *Life-Span Developmental Psychology: Personality and Socialization*, Baltes, P.B. and Schaie, K.W. (eds). Academic Press Inc, Orlando.

Konner, M. (2010). *The Evolution of Childhood: Relationships, Emotion, Mind*. Belknap Press, Cambridge.

Kristjansson, A.L. (2018). Maternal smoking during pregnancy and academic achievement of offspring over time: A registry data-based cohort study. *Preventive Medicine*, 113, 74–79.

Lamb, M. (1996). *The Role of the Father in Child Development*. Wiley, New York.

Lee, A. and Hood, B. (2021). The origins and development of attachment object behaviour. *Current Opinion in Psychology*, 39, 72–75.

Léger, M. (2020). Étude des altérations des habiletés sociales chez des enfants ayant un trouble déficit de l'attention/hyperactivité : comparatif avec des sujets contrôles et des sujets présentant un trouble du spectre de l'autisme. *L'Encéphale*, 46(5), 326–333.

LeVine, R.A. (2008). *Anthropology and Child Development: A Cross-Cultural Reader*. Wiley, New York.

Levy, J. (2019). Chronic trauma impairs the neural basis of empathy in mothers: Relations to parenting and children's empathic abilities. *Developmental Cognitive Neuroscience Journal*, 38, 100658.

Lubart, T.I. (2006). *Enfants exceptionnels : précocité intellectuelle, haut potentiel et talent*. Bréal, Paris.

Main, M. (1998). De l'attachement à la psychopathologie. *Enfance*, 3.

Main, M. and Cassidy, J. (1988). Categories of response to reunion with the parent at age 6: Predictable from infant attachment classifications and stable over a 1 month period. *Developmental Psychology*, 24, 3.

Main, M. and Kaplan, N. (1985). Security in infancy, childhood and adulthood: A move to the level of representation. In *Growing Points of Attachment Theory and Research, Monographs for the Society for Research in Child Development*, Bertherton, I. and Waters, E. (eds). Wiley, New York.

Malinowski, B. (1929). *The Sexual Life of Savages in North-Western Melanesia: An Ethnographic Account of Courtship, Marriage, and Family Life Among the Natives of the Trobriand Islands, British New Guinea*. Martino Fine Books, Eastford.

Mallet, P. (2015). *L'amitié entre enfants ou adolescents. Une force pour grandir*. Armand Colin, Paris.

Mead, M. (1928). *Coming of Age in Samoa. A Study of Sex in Primitive Societies*. Mentor-New American Library, New York.

Melchior, M. and Hersi, R. (2015). Maternal tobacco smoking in pregnancy and children's socio-emotional development at age 5: The EDEN mother-child birth cohort study. *European Psychiatry*, 30, 562–568.

Meyer, E. (2020). Étude des comportements parentaux dans les liens entre symptomatologie du TDAH et comportements agressifs chez les enfants entre 3 et 6 ans. *Annales médico-psychologiques, revue psychiatrique*, 178(3), 303–309.

Miljkovitch, R. (2006). *L'attachement au cours de la vie*. PUF, Paris.

Moé, A. (2018). Mental rotation and mathematics: Gender-stereotyped beliefs and relationships in primary school children. *Learning and Individual Differences*, 61, 172–180.

Molenaar, N.M. (2019). Prenatal maternal psychopathology and stress and offspring HPA axis function at 6 years. *Psychoneuroendocrinology*, 99, 120–127.

Moreau, C. and Sauvage, A. (2007). *La fête et les jeunes. Espaces publics incertains*. Apogée, Rennes.

Morel, V. (2020). Mort et handicap chez le nouveau-né et l'enfant : représentation et enjeux dans la société française. *Médecine palliative – Soins de support – Accompagnement – Éthique*, 19(3).

Morrongiello, B.A. and Rennie, H. (1998). Why do boys engage in more risk taking than girls? The role of attributions, beliefs, and risk appraisals. *Journal of Pediatric Psychology*, 23(1), 33–43.

Morrongiello, B.A., Midgett, C., Stanton, K.L. (2000). Gender biases in children's appraisals of injury risk and other children's risk-taking behaviors. *Journal of Experimental Child Psychology*, 77(4), 317–336.

Morrongiello, B.A., Ondejko, L., Littlejohn, A. (2004). Understanding toddlers' in home injuries I: Context, correlates, and determinants. *Journal of Pediatric Psychology*, 29(6), 415–431.

Muthukrishna, M. and Henrich, J. (2019). A problem in theory. *Nature Human Behaviour*, 3(3), 221–229.

Narea, M. (2020). Maternal and non-maternal care in infancy and later child cognitive, language and motor development in Chile: Does type of care matter? *Early Childhood Research Quarterly*, 51(2nd quarter), 204–214.

Nivette, A. and Ribeau, D. (2021). Non-compliance with Covid-19-related public health measures among young adults in Switzerland: Insights from a longitudinal cohort study. *Social Science & Medicine*, 268, 11337.

Obradovic, I. (2017). Représentations, motivations et trajectoires d'usage de drogues à l'adolescence. *Tendances*, OFDT, 122, 8.

OFDT (2019). Usages d'alcool, de tabac et de cannabis chez les adolescents du secondaire en 2018. *Tendances*, 132.

Okechukwu, C. and Chen, J. (2018). Children whose mothers use marijuana may try it at a younger age. *American Journal of Preventive Medicine*, 24 September.

Ouimet, M.C. and Brown, T.G. (2007). Neurocognitive characteristics of DUI recidivists. *Accident Analysis & Prevention*, 39(4), 743–750.

Parker, J.S. and Benson, M.J. (2004). Parent-adolescent relations and adolescent functioning: Self-esteem, substance abuse and delinquency. *Adolescence*, 39, 155.

Parrat-Dayan, S. (1997). La place du jeune enfant dans la société à travers l'évolution des pratiques de maternage. *Journal de pédiatrie et de puériculture*, 10, 121–125.

Pereira Da Costa, M. (2019). Théories de l'intelligence : concepts et évaluations du haut potentiel. *Neuropsychiatrie de l'enfance et de l'adolescence*, 67(3), 152–157.

Peretz, I. (2018). *Apprendre la musique. Nouvelles des neurosciences*. Odile Jacob, Paris.

Peyre, H. (2017). Les étapes du développement à 4, 8, 12 et 24 mois prédisent-elles le QI à 5-6 ans ? Résultats de la cohorte mère-enfant EDEN. *European Journal of Paediatric Neurology*, 21(2), 272–279.

Peyre, H. (2019). Sex differences in psychomotor development during the preschool period: A longitudinal study of the effects of environmental factors and of emotional, behavioral, and social functioning. *Journal of Experimental Child Psychology*, 178, 369–384.

Piaget, J. (1928). *Judgment and Reasoning in the Child*. Routledge & Kegan, London.

Pierrehumbert, B. (2003). *Le premier lien. Théorie de l'attachement*. Odile Jacob, Paris.

Prieur, C. (2020). Exposition des enfants de 0 à 3 ans aux écrans : résultats des cohortes de naissances sur les déterminants et les conséquences en termes de développement. *Neuropsychiatrie de l'enfance et de l'adolescence*, DOI: 10.1016/j.neurenf.2019.12.003.

Renzulli, J.S. (2003). The three-ring conception of giftedness: Its implications for understanding the nature of innovation. *The International Handbook on Innovation*, 79–96.

Reuben, A. (2019). Residential neighborhood greenery and children's cognitive development. *Social Science & Medicine*, 30, 271–279.

Rigal, N. and Rubio, B. (2016). Is harsh caregiving effective in toddlers with low inhibitory control? An experimental study in the food domain. *Infant Behavior & Development*, 43, 5–12.

Rodera, E. (2020). Maternal separation and contact to a stranger more than reunion affect the autonomic nervous system in the mother-child dyad ANS measurements during Strange Situation Procedure in mother-child dyad. *International Journal of Psychophysiology*, 147, 26–34.

Rodriguez-Tomé, H. and Zlotowicz, M. (1972). Peurs et angoisse dans l'enfance et l'adolescence. *Enfance*, 3–4.

Rogoff, B. (2003). *The Cultural Nature of Human Development*. Oxford University Press, Oxford.

Rollet, C. and Morel, M.F. (2000). *Des bébés et des hommes*. Albin Michel, Paris.

Rubio, B. and Rigal, N. (2008). Measuring willingness to try new foods: A self-report questionnaire for French-speaking children. *Appetite*, 50(2/3), 408–414.

Rubio, B. and Rigal, N. (2017). Parental concerns and attributions of food pickiness and its consequences for the parent-child relationship: A qualitative analysis. *Journal of Child Health Care*, 1–11.

Safra, L. and Tecu, T. (2016). Neighborhood deprivation negatively impacts children's prosocial behavior. *Frontiers in Psychology*, 7.

Savard, N. (2014). Violence conjugale, stress maternel et développement de l'enfant. *Canadian Journal of Behavioural Science/Revue canadienne des sciences du comportement*, 46(2), 216–225.

Schuckit, M.A. (1998). Biological, physiological and environmental predictors of the alcoholism risk: A longitudinal study. *Journal of Studies on Alcohol*, 59.

Schuckit, M.A. and Smith, T.L. (2006). The relationship of behavioural undercontrol to alcoholism in higher-functioning adults. *Drug and Alcohol Review*, 25.

Setoha, P. and Zhoa, S. (2020). Parenting by lying in childhood is associated with negative developmental outcomes in adulthood. Brief report. *Journal of Experimental Child Psychology*, 189, January.

Sheehy-Skeffington, J. and Thomsen, L. (2020). Egalitarianism: Psychological and socio-ecological foundations. *Current Opinion in Psychology*, 32, 146–152.

Steinbekk, S. and Wichstrom, L. (2021). The impact of social media use on appearance self-esteem from childhood to adolescence – A 3-wave community study. *Computers in Human Behavior*, 114, 106528.

Steinberg, L. (2010). A dual systems model of adolescent risk-taking. *Developmental Psychobiology*, 52(3), 216–224.

Sternberg, R.J. (1985). *Beyond IQ: A Triarchic Theory of Human Intelligence*. Cambridge University Press, Cambridge.

Streri, A. (2018). *Ce que connaît le nourrisson. Méthodes et faits*. In Press, Paris.

Thomsen, L. (2019). The developmental origins of social hierarchy: How infants and young children mentally represent and respond to power and status. *Current Opinion in Psychology*, 33, 201–208.

Todd, E. (2020). *Les luttes de classes en France au XXI*[e] *siècle*. Le Seuil, Paris.

Tordjman, S. and Kermarrec, S. (2019). Mythes et réalités sur les enfants à haut potentiel intellectuel en difficulté : les apports de la recherche. *Neuropsychiatrie de l'enfance et de l'adolescence*, 67(3), 130–139.

Torres Pacheco, M. (2019). Low weight, socioeconomics and behavioral issues: Examining a population in the Northeast of Brazil. *Heliyon*, 5, e0239.

Traoré, T., Forhan, A., Sirot, V., Kadawathagedara, M., Heude, B., Hulin, M., de Lauzon-Guillain, B., Botton, J., Charles, M.A., Crépet, A. (2018). To which mixtures are French pregnant women mainly exposed? A combination of the second French total diet study with the EDEN and Elfe cohort studies. *Food and Chemical Toxicology*, 111, 310–328.

Troupel-Cremel, O. and Zaouche-Gaudron, C. (2006). De l'attachement mère-enfant à l'attachement fraternel : évolution des paradigmes de recherche. *Psychologie française*, 51, 205–215.

Tupper, R. and Bureau, J.-F. (2018). Deployment status: A direct or indirect effect on mother-child attachment within a Canadian military context? *Infant Mental Health Journal*, 39(4), 466–477.

Turiel, E. (2015). Moral reasoning in psychology. *International Encyclopedia of the Social & Behavioral Sciences (2nd Edition)*, 803–805.

Turner, S. (2020). Child maltreatment and sleep problems among adolescents in Ontario: A cross sectional study. *Child Abuse & Neglect*, 99, 104309.

Tursz, A. (2000). La santé de l'enfant. In *Les inégalités sociales de santé*, Fassin, D., Grandjean, H., Kaminski, M., Lang, T., Leclerc, A. (eds). INSERM/La Découverte, Paris.

Tursz, A. (2014a). Prévenir la maltraitance des enfants par le renforcement du rôle des médecins et de la coordination entre secteurs professionnels. Report, Comité de suivi du colloque national sur les violences faites aux enfants/Sénat, Paris.

Tursz, A. (2014b). Les infanticides en France : peut-on les repérer, les compter, les prévenir ? *Archives de pédiatrie*, 21.

Tursz, A., Crost, M., Gerbouin-Rerolle, P., Beauté, J., Romaro, H. (2005). Quelles données recueillir pour améliorer les pratiques professionnelles face aux morts suspectes de nourrissons de moins de 1 an ? Étude auprès des parquets. Report, Ministère de la Justice, Paris.

Vaivre-Douret, L. (2019). Caractéristiques développementales de l'enfant à "hautes potentialités" et compréhension de trajectoires vers la dépression à l'âge scolaire en primaire et au collège. *Neuropsychiatrie de l'enfance et de l'adolescence*, 67(3), 140–151.

Vandentorren, S. and Pirus, C. (2006). Mise en place d'une cohorte nationale de 20 000 enfants : approche pluridisciplinaire du projet Elfe (Étude longitudinale française depuis l'enfance). *Revue d'épidémiologie et de santé publique*, 54(2), 90.

Vecho, O., Schneider, B., Zaouche-Gaudron, C. (2017). Revue de la littérature. Homoparentalité et assistance médicale à la procréation : que sait-on du développement des enfants de mères lesbiennes ? *Neuropsychiatrie de l'enfance et de l'adolescence*, 66(6), 382–395.

Vygotsky, L.S. (1980). *Mind in Society: The Development of Higher Psychological Processes*. Harvard University Press, Cambridge.

van der Waerde, J. (2019). Domain-specific physical activity and sedentary behavior during pregnancy and postpartum depression risk in the French EDEN and Elfe cohorts. *Preventive Medicine*, 33–39.

Weeland, J. (forthcoming). The greener the better? Does neighborhood greenness buffer the effects of stressful life events on externalizing behavior in late adolescence? *Health & Place Journal.*

Weisner, T.S. (2002). Ecocultural understanding of children's developmental pathways. *Human Development*, 45(4), 275–281.

Whiting, J. (1977). A model for psychocultural research. *Culture and Infancy: Variations in The Human Experience*, 29–48.

Winnicott, D.". (2005). *Playing and Reality*. Routledge Classics, London.

Worthman, C.M. (2010). The ecology of human development: Evolving models for cultural psychology. *Journal of Cross-Cultural Psychology*, 41(4), 546–562.

Zazzo, R. (1960). *Les jumeaux, le couple et la personne*. PUF, Paris.

Zlotowicz, M. (1974). *Les peurs enfantines*. PUF, Paris.

Index

G, H

I, J

L, M

O, P

R, S

T, Z

Other titles from

iSTE

in

Health Engineering and Society

2021

BÉRANGER Jérôme
Societal Responsibility of Artificial Intelligence: Towards an Ethical and Eco-responsible AI
(Technological Prospects and Social Applications Set Volume 4)

NADOT Michel
Discipline of Nursing: Three-time Knowledge

2020

BARBET Jacques, FOUCQUIER Adrien, THOMAS Yves
Therapeutic Progress in Oncology: Towards a Revolution in Cancer Therapy?
(Health and Patients Set – Volume 2)

MORILLON Laurent, CLAVIER Viviane
Health Research Practices in a Digital Context
(Health Information Set – Volume 4)

PAILLIART Isabelle
New Territories in Health
(Health Information Set – Volume 3)

2019

CLAVIER Viviane, DE OLIVEIRA Jean-Philippe
Food and Health: Actor Strategies in Information and Communication
(Health Information Set – Volume 2)

PIZON Frank
Health Education and Prevention
(Health and Patients Set – Volume 1)

2018

HUARD Pierre
The Management of Chronic Diseases: Organizational Innovation and Efficiency

PAGANELLI Céline
Confidence and Legitimacy in Health Information and Communication
(Health Information Set – Volume 1)

2017

PICARD Robert
Co-design in Living Labs for Healthcare and Independent Living: Concepts, Methods and Tools

2015

BÉRANGER Jérôme
Medical Information Systems Ethics

Printed and bound by CPI Group (UK) Ltd, Croydon, CR0 4YY

15/09/2026

14962351-0006